DATE DUE			
GAYLORD			PRINTED IN U.S.A.

SCIENCE AND THE MEDIA

In the days of global warming and BSE, science is increasingly a public issue. But what should scientists communicate to the general public? To what extent can the public understand and be involved in scientific debate? How does this involvement affect the shaping and organization of scientific activity? Why do scientists sometimes turn to the media and publicize their findings rather than communicating their findings only with their peers?

Science and the Media provides a theoretical framework which conclusively answers all these questions and allows us to understand why and how scientists address the general public. In the first part of his work, Massimiano Bucchi reviews the existing literature in this field and highlights the pitfalls of current approaches. He then develops his core argument that turning to the public is not simply a response to inaccurate reporting by journalists or to public curiosity, nor a wish to gain recognition and additional funding. Rather, it is a tactic to which the scientific community is pushed by certain 'internal' crisis situations. The third part of this work examines three cases of scientists turning to the public: the cold fusion case, the COBE/Big Bang issue and Louis Pasteur's public demonstration of the anthrax vaccine, a historical case of 'public science'. Finally, Bucchi presents his unique model of communications between science and the public, carried out through the media.

This is a thoughtful and wide-ranging treatment of complex contemporary issues, touching upon the history and sociology of science, communication and media studies. Bucchi's theories on scientific communication in the media are a valuable contribution to the current debate on this subject.

Massimiano Bucchi is a research fellow in the Department of Sociology at the University of Trento, Italy.

ROUTLEDGE STUDIES IN SCIENCE, TECHNOLOGY AND SOCIETY

1 SCIENCE AND THE MEDIA
Alternative routes in scientific communication
Massimiano Bucchi

SCIENCE AND THE MEDIA

Alternative routes in scientific communication

Massimiano Bucchi

London and New York

First published 1998
by Routledge
11 New Fetter Lane, London EC4P 4EE

Simultaneously published in the USA and Canada
by Routledge
29 West 35th Street, New York, NY 10001

© 1998 Massimiano Bucchi

Typeset in Garamond by
Florencetype Ltd, Stoodleigh, Devon
Printed and bound in Great Britain by
TJ International Ltd, Padstow, Cornwall

British Library Cataloguing in Publication Data
A catalogue record for this book is available
from the British Library

Library of Congress Cataloging in Publication Data
Bucchi, Massimiano 1970–
Science and the Media: alternative routes in
scientific communication / Massimiano Bucchi.
p. cm. – (Routledge studies in science, technology and society; 1)
Includes bibliographical references and index.
1. Communication in science.
2. Communication of technical information.
3. Communication in science–Case studies.
4. Communication of technical information–Case studies.
I. Title. II. Series.
Q225.B83 1998
501′ .4–dc21   98–9973
CIP

ISBN 0–415–18952–7

'Können Sie di Relativitätstheorie nicht mit einfachen Worten erklären?' fragte einmal eine Dame den Physiker Einstein. 'Meine Dame,' begann er, 'ich ging einmal mit einem blinden Freund spazieren. Es war heiß, und ich wollte ein Glas Milch trinken.
'Milch,' sagte mein freund, 'trinken verstehe ich aber was ist Milch?'
'Eine weiße Flüssigkeit, antwortete ich.'
'Flüssigkeit verstehe ich,
aber was ist weiß?'
'Die farbe einer Schwanenfeder.'
'Feder verstehe ich, aber was ist Schwan?'
'Ein vogel mit einem gebogenen Hals.'
'Hals verstehe ich, aber was ist gebogen?'
'Da verlor ich die Geduld, nahm seinem Arm und streckte ihn: Das is gebogen,' sagte ich.
'Danke, antwortete der Blinde – Jetzt weiß ich, was Sie mit Milch meinen.'

Axel Görlitz

'A certain selection and discretion must be used in producing a realistic effect', remarked Holmes. 'This is wanting in the police report, where more stress is laid, perhaps, upon the platitudes of the magistrate than upon the details, which to an observer contain the vital essence of the whole matter. Depend upon it, there is nothing so unnatural as the commonplace.'

Sir Arthur Conan Doyle

CONTENTS

CONTENTS

FIGURES

PREFACE

In Woody Allen's *Bullets over Broadway*, a jealous gangster sends a body-guard to look after his lover, an actress who is rehearsing a theatre play with other actors. Despite objections by the director, the bodyguard is allowed to sit in the theatre while the rehearsals take place. Gradually, he begins to offer comments and suggestions which contribute to shaping the structure of the play and ultimately its success. This work is about similar situations that arise within the process of scientific communication; i.e. when the public, which is institutionally excluded from such processes, is 'invited', or at least allowed, to actively participate in them.

Consider for instance the following events:

> Two scientists call a press conference to present their discovery to the public prior to the official publication of their paper in a scientific journal.

> A scientist organizes a public experiment to prove the effectiveness of a vaccine and therefore the correctness of his theory, which is strongly opposed by many of his colleagues.

> A researcher invites journalists to witness the injection of blood taken from an infected patient into his own finger to prove that a virus is harmless.

In the following pages I will argue that such events[1] not only challenge what is known as the 'canonical account' of public communication of science, but also more sophisticated models designed to understand this very problem.

Chapter 1 places the main object of analysis – the phenomenon of scientists 'turning to the public' – within the state of the art of public communication of science studies. It traces the major accomplishments and shortcomings of existing theories and models, and argues further exploration of the issue is needed in order to throw light on the communicative interactions between science and the public.

Chapter 2 sets out the main theoretical guidelines of analysis and interpretation. An excursus on the role of metaphors and paradoxes in public communication of science is added.

Chapter 3 presents the three case studies carried out to illustrate the main features and variants of the turn to the public.

Chapter 4 returns to the central arguments of the work bearing the material from the case studies in mind.

Beside the 'primary case studies' explicitly conducted for this work, several other cases of scientists turning to the public drawn from the literature are mentioned in the following pages, usually with a footnote which recounts the story related to the case.

ACKNOWLEDGEMENTS

I am in the first place grateful to Klaus Eder and Renato G. Mazzolini, who have supervised the research leading to this book. I should thank Bruce Lewenstein of Cornell University for his comments on an earlier draft and for guiding me through the rich collection on cold fusion at Cornell. Antonio Zecca has helped me to understand the main technical issues at stake in the cold fusion story. Other comments and suggestions have come from Rima Apple, Thomas Broman, Pierpaolo Giglioli, Bruno Latour, Federico Neresini, Ronald Numbers, Hans M.A. Schadee and Roger Silverstone. I also wish to thank the Publications Committee of the European University Institute, the Department of Sociology of Trento University and all the scholars and students at these institutions and at the University of Wisconsin, who during the last four years have commented on partial presentations of this work.

1

INTRODUCTION

The 'canonical account' of public communication of science

It is maintained that one of the most salient features of modern science is its greater autonomy from the general public compared with the past. This autonomy rests primarily on the widening 'knowledge gap' between researchers and the generally educated that has marked the last three centuries of the history of science and which has resulted in the stable codification and institutionalization of the scientist's professional role.[1] Today, researchers place considerable importance on their autonomy and distance from the general public and to the existence of a general agreement, within society, concerning who can be deemed a specialist and what really counts as scientific knowledge. This process of professionalization, autonomization and disentanglement from both the public and from general culture has been accompanied by the creation of new channels of communication between specialists and non-specialists. The diffuse relationship which used to link scientists with the public has been replaced on the one hand by formal education (which is also the traditional and most widespread means of recruitment of new members to the scientific community) and on the other by a series of media spaces where scientific knowledge can be presented to wider audiences. According to Shapin, 'The differentiation and specialization of science meant that scientific knowledge no longer enjoyed a matter-of-course place in general culture. Yet that same differentiation created an opportunity for the explicit "popularization" of science, and thus, for literary forms designed to convey otherwise inaccessible or impenetrable scientific knowledge to sectors of the public'.[2]

This presentation of science to the public has taken several different forms (books, magazines, educational films, radio and television programmes), although often labelled with the same term 'popularization'.

Already in 1686, in his *Entretiens sur la pluralité des mondes*, Fontenelle recognized the need to satisfy both 'la gens du monde' and 'les savants'. During the following decades, this double narrative tended to split more and more into two different orders of discourse: one for the scientist's colleagues, the other one for the educated public. By the end of the following century, this second language had already focused on specific and paradigmatic audiences: women (as 'symbols of ignorance, goodwill, curiosity')[3] for instance, through periodicals like *The Ladies' Diary* and books like *Il Newtonianesimo per le dame* by Francesco Algarotti (1752) or *L'Astronomie des dames* by Joseph Jérome Lefrançois de Lalande (1785).

It is only since the second half of the nineteenth century, however, that one can really talk of 'large scale' communication of science, explicitly addressed by its authors not just to specific audiences but to the general public ('grand public'). According to Raichvarg and Jacques, scientific and technological stories were increasingly 'given' to the public without the public overtly looking for them. The authors provide in particular three examples:

1   The daily press, which created a real 'feuilleton scientifique' (along with the traditional 'feuilletons littèraires') by documenting salient events in science and technology (ranging from announcements of new discoveries, to earthquakes, to explosions in laboratories).
2   General interest magazines devoting considerable space to scientific information.
3   Fairs and exhibitions where the major advances in science were presented (photography, models of the body, later x-rays).

This addition to a model of communication of science 'à la carte', i.e. one addressed to a select, motivated audience, of a model of 'science du chef' with its fixed menu whose delights the general public was urged to sample,[4] was a crucial step in securing a conception of public communication of science as benevolent alms-giving by scientists to a large and poorly informed audience.

As the written communication of science to the public consolidated itself as a specific media genre (with its appropriate rules of access and formats[5]), the nature of its performers also became clear. The existence of a category of writers responsible for the 'dissemination' of scientific knowledge was soon acknowledged, and indeed deemed essential, given the sensational advancement and specialization of the natural sciences. Journalists and journalism became increasingly prominent within this category: even those writers with different backgrounds (mostly teachers of sciences and researchers) regularly published either articles or previews of their forthcoming books in newspapers.

This briefly and imperfectly sketched account of the historical transformations shaping public communication of science has been greatly overemphasized and absolutized over time by researchers and, consequently, by the other actors involved in the process, such as journalists or research managers. This progressive shedding over and disciplining of the public has been in fact presented as essential for the consolidation of the scientific enterprise as we know it today and depicted as an 'inevitable' process, necessary for the effective pursuit of scientific truth. Recent works in the history of science have instead shown the extent to which the present relations between scientists and non-scientists are the result of 'massive historical achievements' by the scientific profession and have therefore questioned teleological explanations such as the one mentioned above.[6]

Nevertheless, general opinions on such themes as 'science and the media' or 'communication of science to the public' revolve around those same truisms that are part of the so-called 'canonical account' of the communicative relationships between science and society.[7] The basic arguments of this account can be summarized as follows:

1   The scientific enterprise has become too much specialized and complicated to be understood by the general public. For example, in December 1919, when two solar eclipses had finally confirmed Einstein's general theory of relativity, *The New York Times* gave great emphasis to a comment allegedly made by Einstein himself: 'In the world there are no more than a dozen of persons who could understand my theory.'[8]
2   Therefore, a form of mediation is needed in order to make scientific achievements more suitable and accessible for the public. This mediation requires the intervention of a new professional figure: a 'third person' (in general, the science journalist) who can manage to bridge the gap between scientists and the non-scientific audience, by understanding the former and communicating their ideas to the latter.[9] The introduction of this 'third person' is essential for researchers as they can claim to be completely indifferent and extraneous to the process. It is the journalist, after all, who takes their theories and sentences and rearranges them for the public where 'rearranging', according to the scientists, usually means 'distorting'. For example, 'Natural knowledge . . . is perceived as watered down and then trickled down for popular consumption, along the way losing theoretical content.'[10]
3   This mediation is most often described through the metaphor of linguistic translation. As a sort of interpreter, the 'third person' should simply accomplish the task of reformulating scientific discourse in more simple words. From this point of view, the problem of communicating science to the public, then, is reduced to a mere matter of linguistic competence.

This series of arguments involves some deeper assumptions about the nature of scientific discourse and about the nature of scientific work at large. According to such views, in fact, the public discourse of science starts where scientific discourse ends. Once the task of producing 'pure', reliable knowledge has been accomplished, knowledge can be offered in a simplified form to non-experts. The use of terms like 'popularization' or 'dissemination' is itself symptomatic of this idealized and largely unproblematic vision of public communication of science. Such a vision has its roots in the professional ideologies of scientists and journalists.[11] Through the canonical account, scientists dismiss any involvement in the process and are thus free to deprecate its faults and excesses, namely inaccuracy and spectacularization. Journalists, on the other hand, need it in order to justify their role and to give sharper focus to the nature of their task.

What is more striking, however, is that the canonical account of public communication of science is not to be found solely in the opinions and judgements of scientists and journalists. In fact, a 'positivist' and diffusionist model of science communication has by-and-large dominated literature in this area. Until the 1970s, contributions were almost exclusively of a prescriptive tenor: books were written by scientists and leading scientific writers which documented the inaccurate coverage of science by the media and offered advice to journalists to help them improve their writing and understanding.[12]

The position of scientists in the definition of the issue 'communicating science to the public' has also been powerful enough to influence research work. Not surprisingly, therefore, of the three main groups of actors involved in the process (scientists, journalists, and the public), research has focused pre-eminently on the latter two. Media studies have analysed the rules and constraints of scientific journalism and identified the 'structural difficulties in reconciling the demands of science with the exigencies of newswork'.[13] A 'blame the messenger' perspective has therefore emerged, in which limits inherent to journalistic practice (limits of time, education, etc.) have been indicated as responsible for misrepresentations of scientific ideas to the public and, consequently, for the insufficient appreciation of scientific achievement by the public itself.[14] A typical contribution to this perspective draws a comparison between scientific 'original' ideas and their media representation; or a group of scientists is asked to judge the accuracy of journalistic coverage about a specific issue in their field.[15]

Very similar reflections are inspired by studies focusing on the side of the public. Until very recently, the 'public understanding of science' approach was to be easily identified with measurements of the degree of awareness and understanding about scientific issues reported by the media in a given sample of the population.[16] Again, these measurements have been ostensibly science-centred, with scientists as the only observers authorized to assess accuracy and reception levels. In the next section, however, I will try to show that it is exactly in this area that the canonical account was first called into question.

It is clear that such a 'science-centred, paternalistic and pedagogic' orientation[17] entails not only an idealized vision of scientific activity, but also a normative approach to the processes of communicating science to the public. Terms like distortion, sensationalization and inaccurate translation only make sense by reference to the most outdated models of communication. As a unidirectional, linear communication transfer from one sender (the scientific community) to a completely passive receiver (the broad, uninformed public), the process should in no way affect the nature and content of original information. Therefore, efforts should be devoted to the minimizing of all those 'noises' which impede proper reception and understanding (and are, it goes without saying, nothing but a byproduct of journalistic mediation).[18] A graphic representation of the canonical account is given in Figure 1.1.

The social representation of scientific theories

As we have seen, one of the key assumptions of the canonical account is that lay audiences simply absorb, in an impoverished and lessened form, ideas which stem from scientific activity. Given the proper transmission of information, people will be led along the 'royal avenue' to scientific awareness.

Studies in cognitive and social psychology, together with important advances in fields such as risk-communication have instead shown the extent to which scientific knowledge is elaborated and manipulated at the popular level. Scientific knowledge has therefore been recognized to be an essential component in the formation of 'social representations', i.e. 'sets of values, notions and practices regarding social objects that constitute a mean of orientation and perception of responses'.[19] According to Moscovici, the diffusion of scientific theories among non-specialists creates a 'second-hand common sense' derived from science. 'Science was before based on common sense and has made common sense less common; now common sense is science become common.'[20]

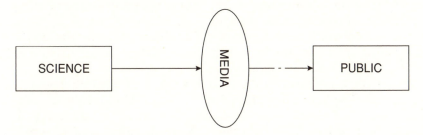

Figure 1.1 The canonical account

Note: Keywords are 'mediation'; 'distortion'; 'sensationalization'; 'science as "too difficult" for the lay public' ('specialization'); the media as a 'dirty messenger' for science; 'blame the messenger'

Thus, studying the social representation of a scientific theory means analysing the transformations which this theory encounters when it is 'transferred to a consensual universe, circumscribed and represented'.[21]

These transformations may occur in the construction of the representation (external transformative processes) or within the representation itself, as it becomes more and more consolidated (internal transformative processes). In the former case, there are two main mechanisms at work: 1) objectification; and 2) anchoring.[22]

1 By means of objectification selection is made among items and at the same time the selected items are given greater concreteness and relevance. Different and even contradictory elements embedded in the theory are coagulated in a schematic and coherent unit. For example, a 'personification' of theories takes place: Einstein becomes the image of relativity and all psychoanalysts have (for Moscovici's interviewees) the face of Freud. At this stage, concepts are visualized in metaphorical images like 'wave' or 'corpuscle' and purely logical/formal relations are given ontological status. What eventually remains of psychoanalysis is merely the dualism between conscious/unconscious that leads to the complex through repression. The neurological theory which posits a functional specialization between the two hemispheres of the brain becomes a clear-cut contraposition between 'right brain' and 'left brain', art and mathematics, 'right persons' and 'left persons'.[23] Similarly, to take a more recent example, popular images of AIDS tend to collapse the disease into the HIV virus.[24]

2 It is at this point that the mechanism of anchoring comes into operation: the previously selected elements of the theory become relatively autonomous from the overall picture and can therefore be inserted into pre-existing (cognitive and social) relations. 'Scientific theory gets incarnated in the texture of everyday life, thus enlarging, narrow-focusing and rendering instrumental a number of common sense theories.'[25] Analogies play in this sense a fundamental role as instruments of identification and classification, as they integrate new information into a familiar universe. Some elements of the theory are decontextualized and then recontextualized in other areas.

None of these processes can occur without an accompanying linguistic arrangement. The keywords of a theory are decontextualized, get 'automatized' and then become stereotypes able to explain a wide range of phenomena (theoretical meanings are enriched with 'common sense' ones). The outcome of the process is a 'thematic language', a linguistic space which surrounds the social representation, its centre is a 'zero degree symbol' (complex for psychoanalysis, HIV for AIDS) which constitutes at once a synthesis and a mode of identification.

Internal processes complete the formation of the social representation, fashioning it into a real instrument for the mapping of reality. What in theory is simple description, becomes explanation: people behave in a certain way because they have complexes or because they are 'left' people.

The role of scientific imagination

I have briefly presented the contribution made by the social representation approach to the topic 'science and the public' because it marks an important step beyond the canonical account without essentially departing from it. The important advance is achieved by questioning the idea that science is simply 'disseminated' and transferred from scientific communities to the public context. Popular knowledge about science is not just a 'diminished simulacrum, simpler, weaker or distorted in proportion to the distance between the learned and the lay communities'.[26] Rather, it is a complicated tangle of processes and transformations through which science is appropriated, used or simply neglected by different audiences. 'Popular science may diverge from learned science not because the latter is poorly understood but because it is elaborated by its recipients for different purposes'.[27]

There are, however, at least two senses in which the social representation approach keeps itself within the confines of the canonical account.

In the first place, it retains a unidirectional vision of the communication process: scientific formulation remains the sole original point of departure. Second, it locates transformation processes only in stages subsequent to scientific construction. Yet one should bear in mind that most of the transformation processes identified by such an approach are to be found in the works of scientists themselves. Metaphors, visual images and 'prototheories'[28] are not just embellishments with which to dress up a theory when presenting it to the public (in place of esoteric calculations and formal expressions).[29] Instead, they are constitutive elements of the theory itself.[30] This is not to imply that a scientific theory cannot be enriched or transformed by its subsequent public presentations. However, these possible 'enrichments' or transformations often stem from those same representation processes employed by scientists. 'It is the researchers themselves who propose reinterpretations susceptible of constituting representations.'[31] Therefore, the problem is not just one of describing what happens to scientific theories as soon as they cross the borders of the scientific enclave. It is also that of understanding 'how scientists, after elaborating theories, or simply concepts characteristic of their discipline, do transform them in order to make them suitable for propagation within differentiated publics'.[32]

In Chapter 2, I shall exemplify the foregoing discussions by examining two elements – metaphors and paradoxes – which play a key role both in core scientific activity and in public communication of science.

A communication *continuum*

It should by now be clear that the contributions of the history and sociology of science to our topic have for long been of little relevance compared with those of other disciplines (like social psychology, cognitive sciences, linguistics). This lack of interest in the public side of science may be explained by the fact that the historical tradition has in the past been largely committed to a rationalist and elitist reconstruction of scientific work.[33] It may be more surprising, though, to note that sociologists of science, even those accustomed to the most radical of theoretical frameworks, have paid even less attention than historians to the relationships between scientists and their audiences in society.

An interpretation of this is offered by Cooter and Pumfrey:

> if all science was to be regarded as socially permeable there was no particular need to study the popularization of science to access this sociability ... Thus, from a sociology of science perspective, the best that could be said for the popularization of science was that it served to maintain the authority of science by legitimating the fiction of its autonomy and the asocial production of its 'truths'.[34]

It is also not unlikely that sociologists of science have been merely more sophisticated victims of the 'canonical account': public communication of science, as a practice completely detached from science and entrusted to other social actors, bore little interest for those concerned only with the influence of social factors on core scientific activity.[35]

More recently, however, contributions from both fields have increased in number and significance. They address the canonical account critically and plausibly, by recasting the public communication of science within the general context of the 'scientific field'.[36] Since it is strictly linked to other stages of scientific practice, and since it often involves scientists themselves either as sources or as authors,[37] communication of science to the public cannot be the sole province of media or journalism studies, which regard it just as another genre of media communication. Instead, recent accomplishments in the study of scientific discourse (for example, concerning scientific rhetoric or the role of metaphors and visual images) can be fruitfully applied to science communication studies.[38]

In place of the clear-cut distinction between science and its dissemination, a 'continuity' model of communicating science has therefore been suggested.[39] A *continuum* in the exposition of scientific ideas can be mapped in which differences inevitably occur due to different contexts and styles of communication/reception, but only as a matter of degree. Barriers between genuine knowledge/audiences and popular discourse cannot be sharply drawn, even if they are often used by scientists to define and preserve their authority over knowledge.[40]

One of the most detailed models of this *continuum* has been described by Cloître and Shinn,[41] who identify four main stages within the process of scientific communication:

1 *Intraspecialist* This is the more distinctly esoteric stage, the prototype for which is an article in a scientific journal. Empirical data, references to experimental activities and graphs prevail.

2 *Interspecialist* To this stage belong several kinds of text, from the truly interdisciplinary articles published in 'bridge journals' like *Nature* and *Science*[42] to the papers presented at meetings among researchers in the same discipline, but working on different topics. Compared to the previous stage, texts here are more likely to represent theoretical concepts in concrete form.[43]

3 *Pedagogical* What Fleck calls 'textbook science'[44] is the stage where the theoretical body is already developed and consolidated and where the current paradigm is most completely presented.[45] The emphasis here is on the historical perspective and on the cumulative nature of the scientific enterprise.

4 *Popular* Cloître and Shinn unite under this label both articles about science in the daily press and the 'amateur science' of TV science documentaries and magazines like *Scientific American* or the French *Science et Vie*. They identify in such texts a greater quantity of metaphorical images and marked attention to issues relating to health, technology and the economy.[46]

Cognitive trajectories and their obstacles

A typology of this kind invites us to imagine a sort of 'cognitive trajectory' for scientific ideas which carries them from the intraspecialist expository context to the popular one, passing through intermediate stages. This conceptualization can be usefully employed provided one introduces the following specifications:

1 A synchronous approach should accompany this sequential perspective. The same researchers can simultaneously communicate their work at different levels, by publishing specialist and popular articles.

2 The trajectory is by no means immune to 'obstacles'. It may happen that some ideas fail to find an adequate exposition at one of the levels. Cloître and Shinn use the term '*crystallization*' to describe the process which prevents some concepts from passing from an expository style to another. It is not difficult to accept, for instance, that not every

scientific theory or discovery is well suited to the general media, or that they may suit one medium but not another (e.g. magazines rather than TV). This is less a matter of complexity of some theories, however, than of the specific constraints of each format. Announcements of scientific discoveries or advances may fit more or less well with media practices (e.g. newsmaking) or into general thematic areas that already attract public attention.[47]

One should not think of crystallization as being limited to the step towards popular exposition. A specialist contribution may be of no interest to the contiguous fields and therefore will fail to reach the interspecialist stage. Balmer provides an interesting example of 'temporary crystallization' at the pedagogical level.[48]

Sickle-cell anaemia is caused by a genetic deficiency of haemoglobin which causes the affected cells to assume an irregular shape. It affects only black people (in the United States one black child out of fifty suffers from it) and is transmitted hereditarily. The disease was first diagnosed by the physician James Herrick in Chicago. In 1949 Pauling proved that sickle haemoglobin has a different molecular structure from the normal one; in 1957 the differences between the two molecules were defined and in 1966 Marayama was able to draw a complete model of the disease. In textbooks and university books, however, no reference was made to this anaemia until the mid-1970s, when it gradually gained public attention. After some TV documentaries on the disease, subscriptions were organized for the people affected and the disease was even mentioned by President Nixon in a speech on health problems (February 1971). In 1972 research funds to study this kind of anaemia grew from one million to ten million dollars and the black population was massively screened.

According to Balmer, it is because of this public resonance of the disease that since the late 1970s textbooks have begun to devote increasing space to it. The case is also interesting because it illustrates (at least partially) another variant of the trajectory depicted above, which Cloître and Shinn call 'deviation'. An idea does not necessarily have to pass through all the four stages in sequence: it can simply skip some of them by jumping to those that follow.

> In deviation, cognition is intentionally shifted from one expository genre to another with the idea in mind that the expository standards and criteria of the alternative category are more felicitous for the growth of the idea at hand.[49]

This process, which Cloître and Shinn do not elaborate, is the main focus of this work. In comparison to their general formulation, the present analysis is limited to those cases where the target expository genre (i.e. that to which

10

knowledge is intentionally shifted) is located at the popular level,[50] and the source expository genre is at the intraspecialist or interspecialist level. I would also argue that the shift is not always made in order to improve theory elaboration. This can be one of the consequences (furthermore, mostly one not clearly intended by those who actually foster the shift), but different aims and effects can be pursued. I refer not only to the search for political and material support from the public. For example, the importance of public appeal in particular cases of controversy or paradigm shift has been variously hypothesized and studied.[51] It seems that there may be conflicts (crisis situations) which cannot be resolved within the scientific community, and which therefore require the intervention of the public to determine the success of one party over another.

The popular stage and its implications

As I have already pointed out, studies of science have, under the influence of the canonical account, paid little attention to public communication of science as an integral part of scientific discourse. They have instead assumed the existence, at a certain moment, of a 'completed' and 'definite' scientific fact which can be taken and brought to external audiences. The role of the public has at best been that of providing a passive environment ('climate of opinion') in which knowledge can be spread. However, here I consider the activity of communicating knowledge at any level to constitute a fundamental element of that complex mosaic which is a scientific fact.[52] The concepts of syphilis and AIDS that pathologists share today are not untouched by the transformations they have undergone in passing from the esoteric to the exoteric sphere.[53] Scientists themselves can make use of the information and of the images which circulate at this level. Cloître and Shinn document the appropriation by specialists of a metaphor ('the ant in the labyrinth') originally designed to explain the brownian motion of particles in popularization texts.[54] A research study conducted by Phillips shows that articles appearing in *The New England Journal of Medicine* are cited twice as much by specialists if they are also mentioned in a daily paper like the *New York Times*.[55] Approximately one-third of the scholars involved in the debate on the mass extinction of dinosaurs as resulting from the collision of the earth with a meteor reported that they had first heard about the Alvarez hypothesis from the general media.[56]

One of the cases of 'deviation' thoroughly explored in Chapter 3 – the cold fusion case – illustrates this point quite well: especially in the first phase of the controversy, scientists had to rely heavily on journalistic sources in order to obtain information, and they used the general media to exchange experimental results and comments.[57] A similar pattern can also be observed in the days immediately after the announcement of the COBE satellite

11

discovery of ripples in cosmic background radiation, when 'astronomers had to respond to journalists off the cuff, without knowing the details of the COBE announcement'.[58]

In such cases one could even argue that, just as it happens for a certain form of political discourse, scientific discourse at the public level is only apparently 'public': communication at this level is not actually meant to address the general public, but to reach a vast number of colleagues rapidly by sending them 'coded messages' without having to conform to the times and constraints of specialist communication.[59] Pons and Fleischmann's initial press conference is a clear example of this, since it was designed mainly to secure them priority in the discovery.

These active influences of the popular discourse of science cannot be reduced to feedback mechanisms of public support and legitimation as even some innovative studies seem to envisage.[60] By often emphasizing a unilateral interpretation of Fleck's theory, they regard the popular stage as the final (and often, decisive) stage in that process of stylization, 'distancing from the research front', and production of factuality and apodicticity which is the construction of scientific evidence.[61] According to Whitley:

> The more removed the context of research is from the context of reception in terms of language, intellectual prestige and skill levels, the easier it is for scientists to present their work as certain, decontextualised from the conditions of its production, and authoritative.[62]

In this view, it is not difficult to devise a 'social itinerary of recognition' for a scientific fact, flowing parallel to the cognitive trajectory. The intraspecialist level is the minimum threshold for knowledge to be presented; by reaching the interspecialist level the sectorial recognition is transformed into a more general one which involves the wider scientific community (this does not necessarily mean 'every physicist' but possibly, for example in the cold fusion case, 'every nuclear physicist'). Through citations by other researchers and its mention in textbooks a theory becomes part of a certain knowledge heritage and through the mass media it gains public recognition.[63]

This model, which is sketched in Figure 1.2 as funnel-shaped, to indicate its emphasis on the growing solidity and simplification that a scientific fact acquires stage by stage, should probably not be questioned as such. It can undoubtedly be a useful reference tool since it describes a sort of ideal communication flow in routine conditions. Especially in the aforementioned 'deviation cases', however, the picture of the process should be slightly more complicated. In such cases, public discourse of science does not simply receive what filters through preceding stages: it may be at the very core of the dynamics of scientific production. That there might be more than one type of communicative practice hidden under the general

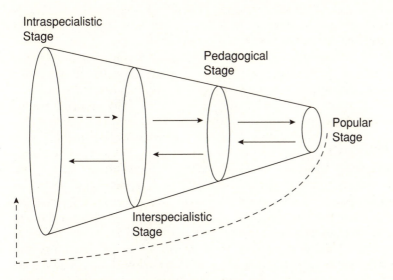

Figure 1.2 A continuity model

Source: After Shinn and Whitley (1985) and Hilgartner (1990)
Note: Keywords are 'expository continuum'; 'distancing from the research front'; 'consolidation'; 'production of certainty'

label of 'public communication of science' is also suggested by Peters, who introduces a similar distinction between 'routine' ('scientific-oriented') and 'problem-oriented' communication of science in the media, to be in turn subdivided into 'consensus-oriented' and 'conflict-oriented' communication of science (framed in the media as 'scandal' or as 'controversy'). For my purposes here, it is sufficient to distinguish between two main modalities of the public communication of science:

1 A 'routine', consensual, unproblematic trajectory that is adequately described by the continuity model. In spite of its ideological connotations, popularization is on the whole not an inappropriate term for this process.[64]
2 An alternative trajectory, i.e. the one represented by deviation processes, which could reasonably be made to coincide with what Peters means by 'problem-oriented' public communication of science.

Some relevant formal and substantial differences seem to be respectively associated with these two modalities. At a formal level, when the popularization modality is activated, scientific issues are likely to be framed in spaces explicitly devoted to the communication of science: e.g. amateur scientific magazines (*Scientific American*, *Science et Vie*), the science sections of newspapers. On the other hand, in deviation processes, scientific issues more frequently appear in general media contexts as well: e.g. the general interest sections of newspapers, television news broadcasts.

At a more substantial level, with popularization, the outcome of communication at the public level is relatively straightforward: as a chiefly 'celebratory', discourse[65] it further strengthens the certainty and solidity of theories and results. This is what the 'funnel', continuity model is about. On the other hand, when deviation processes take place it is not possible to determine a priori what the outcome of communicating at the public level will be or which interests will be best served. For example, scientists make increasingly frequent use of press conferences and articles in the daily press to announce their discoveries. It takes a fair amount of time for an article to be published in a scientific journal (and therefore the chances of being anticipated increase) and the risk of plagiarism arises from the anonymous examination of manuscripts by colleagues before publication. In such cases, 'deviation' to the public stage can actually enhance the peer-review process, but it is also likely to be sanctioned as an attempt to bypass this process and to gain 'improper recognition' outside the scientific community.[66]

Possible effects in terms of legitimation (or, in some cases, even delegitimation)[67] are not separable from those concerning the definition of cognitive boundaries and of roles related to the processes of knowledge production. At this level, scientific facts (together with their networks of professional figures and institutions) can be consolidated as the routine model predicts, but they can also be dissolved, deconstructed (by the scrutiny to which they are subjected, and by the recontextualizing of some of their elements), or simply black-boxed for different uses.[68] Given that the approach adopted here means that it is not only important to study how science enters the public domain but also how the public enters the scientific arena, it is worth noting that the same perspective can be applied to the use of common sense by scientists.[69]

The study of public discourse of science in cases of deviation should be seen, therefore, as an opportunity to recapture 'the plurality of sites for the making and reproduction of scientific knowledge'.[70]

2

WHEN SCIENTISTS TURN
TO THE PUBLIC

So far, I have tried to outline two main points:

1   That certain communicative situations ('deviations' in Cloître and Shinn terminology) can be accounted for neither within the canonical model nor within the continuity model of public communication of science.
2   That it is in these situations that the contribution of the public discourse to scientific communication can become most evident and therefore amenable to investigation.

I shall now try to build an explanatory hypothesis on this rather descriptive dimension by addressing the problem of the conditions under which scientists might be stimulated and/or allowed to *deviate* their normal expository practice towards the public level.

Deviation to the public seems related to peculiar crisis situations which cannot be managed within the scientific community. These situations may often involve the definition and negotiation of scientific boundaries. The concept of 'boundary work'[1] is applied here in a very general sense to encompass three broad types of demarcation strategies. It refers in the first place to the boundaries between science and non-science. Boundaries can be restricted to exclude competing professional practices (as in the case of the Scottish anatomists against the phrenologists described by Gieryn),[2] or in turn they can be made more flexible in order to incorporate such practices within the dominant framework (as in the case of acupuncture which has been studied by Webster).[3] Such boundary definitions are not only defensive. For instance, public speeches and popular writings by Tyndall in late nineteenth-century England can be easily interpreted as efforts to extend the boundaries of science to the detriment of religious tradition and engineering practice.[4]

However, public support is particularly necessary when what is at stake is not just the negotiation (however massive) of the boundaries but rather their very constitution. As long as a discipline has not yet been recognized as such (and therefore until it is granted authority and prestige), it is essential for researchers to prove the relevance of their work for society at large. In the mid-nineteenth century, in a period of great importance for the institutionalization of science in Germany (and particularly rich in terms of popular scientific publications), scientists like Helmholtz, Virchow or Schleiden attributed great importance to addressing the public and arousing its interest in their work.

The following quotation is taken from a series of popular lectures (*Die Pflanze und ihr Leben*) published by Matthias J. Schleiden in 1848. The definition and organization of biology that followed the birth of evolution theory had not yet taken place, and botany was developing from a mere activity of collection and systematization of data into new perspectives in areas such as embryology and morphogenesis.[5]

> In the lectures collected here I have tried to make clear to the layman the more important questions dealt with in botany, and to show how this science is intimately connected with almost all the most profound disciplines of philosophy and science. I've tried to depict how every fact, or larger group of facts, in botany as in every other field of human endeavour, is capable of inspiring the most serious and important questions and of leading man from what is given him through his senses to a surmised supersensible realm.[6]

One could easily argue that this form of 'constitutive boundary work' is less important today than it was during the second half of the eighteenth century and the first half of the nineteenth, when the profession of science and most of its standard disciplinary areas were being consolidated.[7] However, this form of boundary work is still quite visible with regard to new sectors and fields of inquiry, such as the environmental and information sciences.

Once a discipline has been established and recognized as such, the public no longer plays a constitutive and fundamental role. The public legitimation of science begins then to rest precisely on its autonomy from and indifference to public questions and curiosity.[8]

In his study of the iconography of chemistry in the middle of the nineteenth century, Knight has shown how the role of images changes along with the stabilization and institutionalization of a field. Images become more stylized and linear, losing aesthetic appeal and accessibility. They are no longer used to describe laboratories or machinery but rather to record spectra and emissions in a form only accessible to specialists.[9] Another example, this time with regard to a specific institution, is the case of the Royal Observatory as documented by Chapman.[10] A key role in the process of transforming the Observatory from 'a place where watches were regulated' into a well recognized institution for scientific expertise was in fact played by public visits (organized by the Observatory) as well as by newspaper articles written by invited journalists. It is interesting to observe the similarity between this case and that of the Hubble telescope. When this technological artefact was still being constructed, several years before its launch the director Riccardo Giacconi announced that he would allocate a portion of Hubble's time to the observations of amateur astronomers. As the Hubble project proceeded, such a 'public access' programme was increasingly criticized by professional astronomers and by NASA until it was eventually abandoned.[11]

The appeal to the public level seems important also for defining and questioning of boundaries within science, i.e. boundaries between disciplines: both the cold fusion case (which witnessed bitter public conflict between physicists and chemists)[12] and the late-nineteenth century controversy about 'the end of physics'[13] are interesting examples of this negotiation of internal boundaries. Related to this type of negotiation is the use of the popular stage (as virtually accessible to almost everyone) when ideas need to be communicated simultaneously to different categories of researchers and practitioners.[14]

At an even more internal level, within a discipline, appeal to the public can assist the establishing of a new theoretical tradition (a shift of paradigm) in cases of strong controversies and tensions (e.g. in terms of competition) which cannot be resolved without appealing to external actors.[15] These three levels of conditions are likely to entail a decreasing potential in terms of public mobilization: the thinner the boundary at stake, the less visible it becomes in public terms. One can therefore observe with regard to internal tensions brought to public attention a tendency to transform them into more general matters of demarcation between disciplines, and eventually as matters of demarcation between orthodoxy (science) and deviance (non-science), which can be solved by the public degradation and expulsion of 'heretical scientists' from the scientific arena.[16]

It might be due to processes such as these that some commentators still overlap deviation and deviant science,[17] thereby neglecting the fact that the attribution of a deviant status to a scientific actor or performance is rarely given prior to addressing the public, and is instead achieved also through public negotiation.[18]

I would emphasize with regard to this problem that by the term 'conditions' I do not refer solely to conditions internal to the scientific community. Deviation cases have been described as cases in which scientists are not only stimulated but also actually allowed to deviate. The 'turn to the public' is not only dependent on the will of the researchers and on their convenience. Although my interest here is primarily in those cases where scientists take the initiative, it is clear that the conditions for deviation must be fulfilled not only within the scientific community but also on the public stage and within the general framework of their mutual relations.

The public level can be more or less easily mobilized, depending on the intrinsic public resonance of the issue at stake (and therefore, on the chances of linking it with issues that are already prominent), or on the visibility of the scientific actors and institutions sponsoring it, or again, on the relations (e.g. in terms of autonomy and visibility) between a scientific field and the public at a given historical moment. It is difficult to imagine that Duesberg would be able to organize a public experiment, in his case about AIDS in the same way as Pasteur did, and obtain the same degree and type of attention from the general media as Pasteur received. The recognition and definition of 'crisis' situations, like those to which I have referred, must therefore also take account of the perspective of actors (e.g. media actors) traditionally considered as 'external' to scientific practice.

These reflections could be easily regarded as only indirectly addressing a second aspect: the consequences of deviation to the public. This problem is, however, not only too complex to be thoroughly dealt with on the evidence available here but its treatment in general terms would be misleading and inevitably take us back to the shortcomings of the canonical and continuity perspectives. In fact, in order to overcome such shortcomings one must not impose (as the canonical account and the continuity models sought to do) a general, pre-determined outcome on the process of public discussion of scientific issues. Efforts should instead be devoted to describing it in terms of an open-ended negotiation of ideas and related interests, and one may expect its consequences to go well beyond the scientists' original intentions.

This is most visible when examining the already mentioned cases of scientific controversies in public, which cannot be adequately accounted for within the framework of continuity models. In which sense can a controversial scientific issue be enhanced and given factuality by public presentation? The continuity model seems to imply that this happens in the sense of corroborating the evidence of one side, thereby helping it to strengthen its supremacy over the other. This criterion, however, only applies to those cases of demarcation between science and non-science in which one side embodies official science menaced by a deviant scientific viewpoint.

The same criterion also involves some questionable assumptions. One is the assumption that a controversy enters the popular stage when one party has already been granted predominance at the specialist stages. But this is not always the case. What if the two or multiple sides are both supported by 'respectable' scientists, as in the AIDS controversy or in the whiptail-lizard case?[19] And what if the two sides (as often happens) are by their nature difficult to compare, because they involve different disciplinary and methodological perspectives?

Another related assumption is that the predominance granted to one party at the specialist stages would be automatically amplified and reinforced at the level of public communication. The problem with this assumption is that it underestimates the possibility that the effects of communication at the popular stage may run counter to those of specialist communication.[20] Moreover, it absolutizes the analytical fiction which is introduced by dividing the expository *continuum* into stages, inappropriately identifying it with a temporal sequence.[21] But, as we have seen, there is no privileged stage at which the communication of science must start: cold fusion claims were first presented at the public level; and the label 'Big Bang', which was to become the standard linguistic reference denoting a theoretical approach within astrophysics for both specialist and nonspecialist audiences, was first introduced by Fred Hoyle in 1950 during a 'popular science' radio programme (moreover, the term was originally intended to ridicule the idea).[22]

In most cases, however, communication occurs simultaneously at different levels which continuously exert reciprocal influence on each other.

One last implicit assumption must be considered in explanation of why continuity models are not completely at ease in dealing with controversial science at the public level. It is an assumption that brings us back to that 'functional' concept of public communication of science which I have already criticized on several occasions. Since such models conceive the popular stage as the final, decisive step in the production of scientific certainty and 'facticity', one would expect even controversial situations to find a solution at this stage – most probably a solution consistent with directions stemming from the preceding stages.[23]

This should not simply induce us to address scientific 'success' in public, and scientific 'failure' in public, symmetrically, i.e. without being influenced by the fate that befalls a theory.[24] I would also argue that the study of public negotiations of science may help us to rethink the oversimplified distinction between scientific 'success' and 'failure'. A theory may enjoy differing fortunes at different levels of communication.[25]

It is difficult, even within a single level (including the specialist levels), to portray a controversial process in terms of a clear-cut solution in favour of one of the actors involved. During this process, claims advanced by different actors may gradually merge, or be incorporated into pre-existing theoretical frameworks; or, again, they may play down their original pretensions and retire into bounded communicative niches – as in the cold fusion case.[26] This appears even more difficult in cases (like the ones being discussed here) in which controversies are judged unresolvable at the specialist levels and are then consequently 'deviated' towards the public. At this level, then, issues can become objects of dispute and 'political' part-taking[27] and retain this status for years. A 'final word' is to some extent not needed and not even sought: matters and their competing interpretations may simply drift around ready to be recalled according to future events and needs. Take for instance the controversy provoked by the famous paper in which Alvarez *et al.* related the mass extinction of dinosaurs to extraterrestrial causes (i.e. asteroids colliding with earth).[28] The generality of the Alvarez hypothesis, its relevance to different scientific fields (statistics, geology, palaeontology and astrophysics) and its resonance in terms of images and metaphors (a combination of two mysteries, one from heaven and one from earth; dinosaur extinction as a metaphor for human extinction, as the statistical models used for extinction were drawn from research on nuclear weapons; the word 'extraterrestrial' used in the title of the original article evoking Martians rather than asteroids) has kept the dispute alive for the last fifteen years. Scientists have different *opinions*[29] about it, according to their different perspectives and interests, just as they have on other public issues, and both confirmations and refutations of the hypothesis are presented from time to time.

Another example is the controversy over the genetic roots of homosexuality. This issue first arose in 1991, and since then has been extensively discussed by researchers, in the popular media as well. Along the way empirical data, theoretical frameworks and the need for political correctness[30] have coalesced into such a delicate and complex tangle that it becomes difficult for any researcher to claim a definitive solution.

Deviation to the public should not necessarily induce paralysis at the specialist level. Just as resorting to the scientific arena can serve to exclude from the public debate certain actors who do not have access to scientific expertise,[31] so the appeal to the public can result in the exclusion of actors and hypotheses, not suitable for public presentation, from the scientific arena itself. It is therefore important to note that the direction of the linear *continuum* of communication can be reversed from this perspective as well: the intraspecialist stage may function as a filter for public attention, but the public stage, too, may function as a filter for specialists.

This is evidenced by the AIDS controversy. Once the elements of AIDS as a policy issue and its public communication tracks were set (in 1986 approximately) around the HIV-paradigm, they no longer left room for diverging hypotheses, even at the specialist level.[32] As assessed by orthodox researchers in several interviews, Duesberg's ideas were deemed unacceptable and were ignored from a scientific point of view also – and especially – because they were untenable in public.[33]

To sum up, I am arguing that continuity models, in their effort to overcome the excesses of the canonical account (which had focused almost exclusively on the limits of media presentation of science and, later, on those of public understanding), have gone to the opposite and equally unsatisfactory extreme. Bound to a rigid sociology of science perspective, they have concentrated almost exclusively on scientists' action, by reducing the public to an external, monolithic and taken-for-granted source of support.[34] With regard to scientific communication, the public dimension still largely awaits acknowledgement of its significant degree of articulation and flexibility in relating to specialist networks.[35]

I suggest that communication of science at the popular level may influence core scientific practice in many more different and subtle ways than simple support and reinforcement. As already shown, it can foster the inclusion or the exclusion of actors or theories from specialist discourse; it can make room for new interpretations or confer a different status to existing models by linking them to other public issues and themes. The popular stage can in this sense provide an open space where stimuli, ideas and information are merged and exchanged among different actors and across disciplinary fields, in the absence of the constraints and conventions which bind scientific work and communication at the specialist level.

It should be noted that this brings into new light some dynamics operating at the public level (dynamics crudely labelled as 'distorting filters' in the canonical models), by pointing out their potential for the creation and transformation of scientific ideas. For example, the widely criticized rule of 'journalistic balance', i.e. the tendency to collapse even scientific discussion into two opposite positions,[36] may induce scientists to define their ideas and to take sides. In the case of cold fusion, the initial 'information instability' (i.e. the period when no official specialist publication was available on the matter)[37] did not merely generate 'confusion'; rather, it allowed scientists to float more freely among different positions and theoretical (as well as interest) alliances than formal scientific publications would have permitted.

The continuity model should therefore be supplemented by a multi-level, multivariate perspective that can account for the mutual interactions and the permeable boundaries among different communicative practices.[38]

Metaphors, paradoxes and boundary objects in public communication of science

I have argued that public communication of science can be better understood if we analytically distinguish two modalities within it: popularization and deviation. Only the first modality is sufficiently accounted for by continuity models. By looking at deviation processes I hope to learn something not only about them, but also about popularization and about public communication of science at large, just as by studying revolutions in science one can hope to learn something about 'normal science', i.e. routine scientific practice. To do this, one must try to answer a crucial question: under what conditions is public communication of science performed through the deviation modality instead of being carried out through its standard, popularization modality?

My proposal is to study deviation to the public as associated with 'critical situations' which involve negotiation at different levels of scientific boundaries. This proposal has a twofold implication: on the one hand, deviation to the public cannot be detached from core scientific debate, as the canonical account suggests by giving media actors the entire responsibility for hustling issues into the public arena, because it is related to specific conditions of such debate. On the other hand, deviation to the public level does not simply reinforce the directions taken by the scientific debate at the specialist levels (as the continuity models suggest) but interacts with them in complex ways. The idea that boundary negotiation is what links the core scientific debate to public science, in my view, conciliates both the need to acknowledge the significance of the public level for scientific discourse and at the same time its relative autonomy and specificity. A special continuity is to be thus identified across the levels, which ensures both connection throughout such levels and some features specific to each of them.

I have already identified elements of 'flexible continuity' in the multiple memberships that scientists enjoy, as both sources and audiences of scientific communication, in different levels at the same time. I have only briefly mentioned the key role played by certain linguistic elements such as metaphors. In the next paragraphs I will analyse in more detail these elements.

Metaphors in science

It is not difficult to recognize that public communication of scientific theories displays an extensive use of analogical and metaphorical images,[39] which serve to link an unknown phenomenon or concept to a more familiar one by comparing them. In Schutz's terms, metaphor and analogy operate at the intersection between two provinces of meaning.[40] For Moscovici, they reveal 'a tendency to integrate the object in an existing world, to establish a relationship with it through the mediation of other objects'.[41]

It is essential to distinguish the respective roles of metaphor and analogy. Weinrich[42] inverts Quintilian's ancient definition 'Metaphora brevior est similitudo', by defining analogy as an 'extended metaphor'. Similar, although more articulated, is the definition offered by Vosniadou and Ortony.[43] Among the modes of reasoning 'by similarity', they distinguish between those 'within domain' (i.e. within the same thematic area) and those 'between domain' (i.e. between different thematic areas). The former are of an analogical type, the latter are of metaphorical type. The mathematician who solves a new problem on the basis of a similar problem solved in the past (like Euler when he solved the infinite series sum $[1/n]$ by applying the method for finite series) uses an analogy; the scientist who explains the theory of atoms by comparing them to a flock of sheep makes use of a metaphor.

Scholars have long tended to attribute solely analogical processes to science, considering metaphors as exclusive to literary writing.[44] Black[45] questioned this assumption and criticized the traditional view of metaphor as a substitutive process (a literal expression is replaced by a metaphorical equivalent) and suggested that it should instead be viewed as a more complex form of interaction between a primary topic (what is to be described) and a secondary topic (what serves to describe) which modifies our perception of both. To say, 'society is an organism', selects and emphasizes certain features of the topic 'society' and certain features of the topic 'organism'.[46] Furthermore, there are particularly strong metaphors that create the similarity rather than emphasize it. It is not possible, then, to replace them with non-metaphorical expressions. Boyd[47] elaborates this point by specifying the role played in science by these 'constitutive' metaphors, a role which is primarily linguistic: they come to fill gaps in a theoretical terminology. 'The use of metaphor is just one of many devices available to the scientific community to accomplish the task of *accommodation of the language to the causal structure of the world*.'[48]

Boyd links his discussion to the 'causal theories of reference' by acknowledging the impossibility of defining (as required by logical empiricism) every theoretical term and thereby highlighting the need to identify a 'nondefinitional mode of reference'. His examples are drawn from the use cognitive psychology makes of terms taken from artificial intelligence like 'elaboration' and 'retroaction'. These metaphors do not state once for all the similarities that exist between computers and humans; instead, they stimulate the scientific community to undertake research in order to develop and clarify them (this is what Boyd calls 'inductive open-endedness').[49]

However, Boyd partially distances himself from the theorists of reference by introducing the notion of epistemic access. The use of the label DNA,[50] for instance, allows:

1   'Scientists to report to each other the results of studies of DNA.'
2   'The public articulation, justification, criticism, debate and refinement (in the light of justification, criticism, debate and experimentation) of theories about DNA.'
3   'Verbal reasonings on DNA with respect to questions of data interpretation, theory evaluation, experimental design and so forth. That is, the use of language makes possible not only the formulation of theories and publicity and cooperation in their assessment; it makes it possible for reasoning (whether individual or public) to be verbal reasoning: to take place in words.'[51]

Obviously, there are different degrees of access: the same term allows different access to the biochemical specialist and to the lay person who has only heard it mentioned. According to Boyd, the problem here is not just one of division of linguistic labour. Also involved is a more general problem of division of cognitive labour (inevitably intertwined with the division of social labour). Indeed, there may as well be a passive kind of access. 'Part of one's linguistic competence with respect to an esoteric general term outside one's own field finds expression in one's ability to achieve passive epistemic access to the referent of that term by deferring to the relevant experts.'[52] Epistemic access is differentiated on the basis of the competence of the potential receiver of the metaphor; that is, the heuristic value of a metaphor depends on the abilities (technical, linguistic, intellectual) of the receiver.

It is probably necessary to emphasize that metaphors do not play an exclusively linguistic role. Holton (1986) outlines three reasons why metaphors are employed by scientists.

1   In research practice and theoretical analysis, the scientist meets obstacles that cannot be overcome with the usual instruments of logic and induction.
2   Metaphor allows the creative imagination of scientists to float freely between the scientific world and life-world experience.
3   Finally, metaphors allow scientific language to keep pace with rapidly changing theories. (This latter is the case most thoroughly studied by Boyd.)

Although Holton deems metaphorical images to be of great value, he still seems to consider them just as merely additional devices, less important than those traditionally employed in research. In contrast, according to Mary Hesse, 'the deductive model of scientific explanation should be modified and supplemented by a view of the theoretical explanation as metaphorical redescription of domain of the explanandum'.[53] Edge states in the same vein:

> Metaphorical redescription is often held to be central to theoretical changes in science . . . by radically recasting our perception it [metaphor] creates new problems, observational terms and experimental strategies, and hence largely determines the nature of empirical results.'[54]

Constitutive and popular metaphors

Boyd remains bound to a rigid distinction between metaphors with a constitutive function (those that I have just mentioned) in the process of scientific elaboration and metaphors that have solely the purpose of illustrating certain conceptualizations (purely exegetical, popularization metaphors), such as the presentation of the atom as a miniature solar system. This distinction corresponds in the Aristotelian classification presented by Eco[55] to the difference between proportional metaphor and the other three types of metaphor.[56] A proportional metaphor entails a schema of the type

A:B = C:D. Old age can be defined as 'the sunset of life' because it relates to life just as the sunset relates to the day. Leaving the last element unknown (e.g. when one says 'the neck of the bottle' where man:neck = bottle:X) yields the typical constitutive metaphor that Boyd has in mind. Holton[57] likewise praises the role of certain metaphors in scientific development, but at the same time warns of the risks embedded in the use of metaphors for the purposes of popularization ('metaphor excess'). It should be noted that he uses the term metaphors, but the two main examples he cites are in fact analogies rather than metaphors. The first refers to an article by Einstein in which he describes the intuition that led him to consider the gravitational field as possessing only relative existence, just like the electromagnetic field. The second example is Young's extension to light phenomena of the observations he had made regarding sound.

> Whether by necessity or not, scientists have been reserving a version of metaphor . . . to themselves and to their fellows, while presenting to the public another, baser version.[58]

Yet it is difficult to maintain this distinction between 'noble' (i.e. constitutive, internal to science) and 'poor' (i.e. exegetical, external to science and therefore only suitable for popularization) metaphors outside peculiar analytical perspectives (such as those chosen by Boyd and Holton). As Jacobi[59] has shown, metaphors used in public communication of science (those which Boyd labels pedagogical or exegetical) are most often those same metaphors used for the purpose of theoretical elaboration. An example is again the metaphor of the atom as a 'miniature solar system'. This image has not only been used to introduce Bohr's hypothesis to non-specialists; it has played a central role in the development of modern nuclear theory and still orientates some research sectors.[60] The same applies to the image of the organism as a society (e.g. with the blood cells portrayed as workers), which held generative value for scientists like Virchow and since then has often been used in drawings of the human body for children's books. Other examples are the description of the interaction between antibodies and antigens as a 'war', or of a medicine as a 'bullet' against a virus. This does not imply that there may not be metaphors used exclusively at the constitutive level and metaphors used only at the popularization level; but Boyd's distinction is too simplistic to accept at face value.

A question remains to be answered before I proceed further: what happens when a generative metaphor is used for the purpose of popularization? Is it possible to identify transformations during this process? Boyd does not address such problems, merely stressing that even reiterated use of generative metaphors may not wear out their constitutive potential. In her book on organicistic metaphors, Judith Schlanger[61] has attempted to classify the different levels of metaphor use:

25

1   Intrametaphorical level. At this level we find the metaphors that are most assimilated and made banal through use (e.g. the metaphor in the expression 'genetic code').
2   Metaphorical. Metaphors that are still 'risky' (the author takes as an example the expression 'chemical switch').
3   Suprametaphorical. Boyd's level of constitutive metaphors (e.g. the image of the cell that 'decides').

The same metaphor may shift from one level to the other, moving from 3 to 1.[62] It is clearly possible to overlap this taxonomy with Boyd's notion of epistemic access. The same biological metaphor (such as that of germs as 'invaders of the body') can operate simultaneously at the 1 level for researchers, at the 2 level for medical doctors, at the 3 level for the general public. Holton[63] similarly distinguishes four possible aims of a metaphor. It may:

1   serve an individual;
2   serve the circle of specialists;
3   serve the circle of specialists and the general public; and
4   serve the general public.

Hesse[64] pays closer attention to the possibility that metaphor and literary expression may transform one into the other. The first case, i.e. when a metaphor gradually turns into a literary expression, concerns the same process under discussion here: the reduction to zero of the degree of semantic resonance between the two fields and the complete assimilation of the 'metaphorical scandal' into common sense. An example of this phenomenon is provided by expressions such as 'gravitational field', or 'magnetic field', which have acquired a status of their own.

Metaphors and paradoxes

A paradox lies at the root of every metaphor. The metaphor is in fact built by matching two distant ideas with a resulting effect of surprise. Weinrich[65] describes the distance between the two as a metaphorical arch that must possess sufficient width in order to operate. If the two terms are too close, the effect of the comparison is a strident one ('*contradictio in adiecto*'). It is possible metaphorically to say that 'man is a wolf' but it is not possible to say that 'the male is a female'. This presentation of the metaphor as a 'contradictory predicament'[66] serves to introduce my discussion of paradoxes. Hesse[67] adds similar comments: 'For a conjunction of terms drawn from the primary and secondary systems to constitute a metaphor it is necessary that there should be patent falsehood or even absurdity in taking the conjunction literally.' For Gombrich: 'It is this effort to transcend the limitations of the discursive speech that links the metaphor with the paradox.'[68]

Paradox in science

Like metaphors, paradoxes play a role in the communication of science to the public[69] as well as in scientific enterprise as such. The 'twin paradox'[70] or Russell's paradox[71] have been widely employed by popularizers. Unlike metaphor, which bridges the two dimensions of science and common sense, paradox introduces a discontinuity between the same dimensions, thereby stimulating interest.[72]

The first point to consider is whether it is possible to draw up a classification of paradoxes similar to the one introduced by Schlanger for metaphors. Paradox is traditionally defined as 'a statement that goes against general accepted opinion'.[73] Quine classifies paradoxes into three:

1 Falsidical paradoxes (i.e. surprising results that turn out to be 'false'). Typical examples are Zeno's paradoxes about time, space and movement.
2 Veridical paradoxes (i.e. those that turn out to be 'true', such as the twins' paradox as elaborated by Langevin to make more accessible some aspects of Einstein's theory of relativity).
3 Antinomies. These cannot be solved without modifying part of the current conceptual apparatus (e.g. the paradox of classes introduced by Russell).

It is possible here to apply the same 'genetical' perspective that was used for metaphors. The difference between 1, 2 and especially 3 is not a matter of quality but simply of degree: falsidic paradoxes like Zeno's undoubtedly represented antinomies to the thinkers of his time, and only later advances in mathematical theory have converted them into 1 type paradoxes.[74] Both 1 and 2 may be fruitfully employed at the level of public communication of science. Those belonging to type 3 (antinomies) instead, often need to be given a different formulation if they are to be employed at this level (e.g. Russell's paradox of classes retold as the 'barber's paradox').[75]

Like the 1 level metaphors in Schlanger's typology (i.e. Boyd's constitutive metaphors), antinomies perform a dynamic and generative role in science. Their discovery and the consequent endeavour to resolve them have characterized some of the most important innovations in the history of the sciences.[76] After their solution, this impulse has often been turned – as for metaphors – into a new didactic potential.[77] In the case of paradoxes, too, it is reasonable to talk of a 'differentiated access'. As the definition of Ford and Backoff suggests, a 'surprising result' may represent an antinomy for a group of scientists while leaving the audiences of public communication of science largely indifferent – take for instance the EPR paradox.[78] Conversely, Zenos' paradoxes may be antinomies for a large proportion of the non-scientific audience but merely falsidic paradoxes for the scientific community.[79]

It is not just for the love of symmetry that one can at this stage draw up a synoptic schema like the following:

Level of antinomies	Level of constitutive metaphors
Level of 'ordinary' paradoxes	Level of exegetical metaphors

Here antinomies/'ordinary paradoxes' (i.e. all paradoxes that are not antinomies) on the one hand and constitutive/exegetical metaphors on the other, do not form an exhaustive classification but rather the extremes of a *continuum* of science communication.[80] There might be one intermediate level (as Schlanger and Quine suggest) or several levels between these extremes. The levels, however, do not represent a permanent, stable distinction between more noble and scientific metaphors and paradoxes as opposed to devalued, popular metaphors and paradoxes since the same metaphors and paradoxes can shift from one level to another, or they may be employed at different levels according to the needs of different communicators or audiences.

The role of paradox in scientific communication

While my analysis has so far sought to clarify some features of scientific paradoxes, it remains to explain why such paradoxes prove to be so important at all levels of scientific communication. An essay by Krippendorff[81] offers a useful suggestion. The author defines information as 'a change in the state of uncertainty of an observer which is caused by some event in his world'. Uncertainty (U) is proportional to the number of possible alternatives, i.e.:

$U = \log_2 n$ where n is the number of possible alternatives

Therefore, if $n = 1$ (no alternative available), there is a minimum of uncertainty ($U = 0$). As already defined, information (I) is the difference between uncertainty at a time t_0 and uncertainty at a later time t_1:

$I = Ut_0 - Ut_1 = \log_2 n_0 - \log_2 n_1$

Therefore a message of the simplest type (e.g. a 'yes' or 'no' answer to a question) carries one bit of information because $\log_2 2 - \log_2 1 = 1 - 0 = 1$.

When the message conveyed is a paradoxical one (for instance in the form 'P and non-P' or 'P implies non-P', where P is a proposition) given the impossibility of fulfilling both conditions, the number of alternatives is zero. Thus

$$I = Ut_0 - \log_2 0 = + \text{infinite}$$

The result of a paradoxical message is thus a notable extension to the receiver's knowledge potential. Only his/her potential, however, because what results initially is not increased knowledge but a sort of paralysis. In other words, the subject is faced with a complexity that she/he is unable to handle. When the solution of the paradox is forthcoming, it activates this potential and turns it into a true cognitive capacity. Rowan emphasizes the merits of the kind of scientific writing that, 'stating the lay view that makes a scientific notion seem counterintuitive, acknowledging its apparent plausibility, demonstrates its inadequacy and the greater adequacy of the accepted scientific notion'.[82]

Let us take as an example the usual way in which imaginary numbers are introduced by a teacher of mathematics or by any other 'disseminator' of scientific knowledge. She/he usually starts from an equation like the following:

$$x^2 + 1 = 0$$

This may be solved in the form:

$$x^2 = -1$$

And dividing by x

$$x = -1/x$$

For $x = +1$, we have the contradiction $+1 = +1/-1 = -1$, and for $x = -1$, we have the contradiction $-1 = -1/-1 = +1$

At this stage one can introduce the number $i = \sqrt{-1}$ as the one which makes it possible to resolve the equation.

The use of a paradox in the presentation of scientific theories and results does not merely have the effect of stimulating a person's curiosity. It confronts him/her with a 'cognitive crisis'; by solving the paradox she/he can overcome this crisis and thus reframe his/her understanding of the problem at hand. 'Regardless of the paradox type, dissolution often involves movements to a different level, that is, transcendence by "jumping out of system" ... paradox cannot be understood without leaping those levels tangled in the structure of the paradox to a different level of complexity.'[83]

Boundary objects

In recent years, distinct strands of studies have recognized on the one hand the important role of metaphors in communicating science to non-scientific audiences; on the other hand, they have acknowledged their importance for scientific enterprise as such. In this section I have tried to bring the two strands together to some extent, by arguing that drawing sharp distinctions between the two roles of metaphors (i.e. distinguishing 'constitutive metaphors' from 'popular metaphors') is a somewhat artificial exercise bound to a traditional view of scientific communication. The same metaphors range among different levels of scientific communication and may be used at different levels at different times, as well as to address different audiences simultaneously. I have also sought to extend this perspective to include paradoxes. Like metaphors, paradoxes play an active role in scientific thinking and are extensively employed in the communication of science to non-specialists. Moreover, scholars have identified common dynamics at the core of both instruments, since they are both based on a tension between two elements. This tension, however, works in opposite directions, i.e. metaphor emphasizes similarity while paradox emphasizes contradiction. In the former case, a lay audience may gain understanding of a new element by drawing on a familiar context; in the case of paradox, the old context is reframed according to a 'surprising idea'. The level of antinomies can be considered as the equivalent of the level of constitutive metaphors within paradoxes, i.e. that level at which paradoxical results most effectively drive scientific thought and practice. As in the case of metaphors, however, an antinomy may gradually turn into an ordinary paradox and therefore equally well serve the purpose of addressing larger, non-specialist audiences.

I have shown how metaphors and paradoxes can range among the multiple layers of scientific discourse. The role they play from this point of view can be understood in the light of a more general concept introduced by Star and Griesemer.[84] I refer to the concept of boundary object. A boundary object is an object which is

> both plastic enough to adapt to local needs and the constraints of the several parties employing them, yet robust enough to maintain a common identity across sites. They are weakly structured in common use, and become strongly structured in individual-site use. ... They have different meanings in different social worlds but their structure is common enough to make them recognizable, a means of translation. The creation and management of boundary objects is a key process in developing and maintaining coherence across intersecting social worlds.[85]

In local interaction situations, boundary objects may coincide with the concrete objects used and exchanged by different categories of actors: for instance, in a scientific institution like a museum there may be files, specimens, paper forms or entire libraries which enable cooperation among different practitioners. In the communicative situations that I am about to examine, they may be thought of as the pivotal discursive elements that lie at the core of boundary negotiation in public. They make communication possible without necessarily requiring consensus, for an object may be interpreted and used in quite different ways at different levels of communication and by different groups of actors within a single level: e.g. 'Big Bang' is employed with quite different meanings by specialists and non-specialists, by the supporters and opponents of the Big Bang model.[86] 'Gene' and 'DNA' are familiar examples of boundary objects, labels employed at different levels of scientific communication and thereby providing a common language although they are translated in different ways in a laboratory conversation and in a car advertisement.[87]

When metaphors and paradoxes are active across different audiences (i.e when the same metaphor is both constitutive and exegetical or when a paradox is also an antinomy) they may themselves be boundary objects. When this is not the case, they still play an important role by hooking boundary objects to the different levels of communication, i.e. by placing them in relation to other objects familiar to those attending each level. The role of boundary objects may be played by non-verbal elements such as visual images, which can be similarly employed in different ways at the different levels of communication. A typical example is a photograph taken from a satellite or a fractal image: these can serve as valuable sources of information for the specialist while simply being an aesthetically attractive picture to the general audience.[88]

The concept of boundary object allows us to salvage contributions from the old canonical perspective (e.g. the social representations approach) by setting them in a new framework of 'flexible continuity' between core scientific practice and public discourse of science. For instance, a boundary object such as 'gene' may function as a paradigm at the specialist level and as what Moscovici calls a 'zero-degree' symbol (i.e. the centre of a theory's social representation) at the public level.

The term 'boundary object' itself has important advantages because it emphasizes both the fact that such objects form a bridge between communication at the public level with communication occurring at the other levels (i.e. they cross the boundaries separating one level from another or one audience from another within each level) and the fact that they are employed by different actors in the public negotiation at the internal and external boundaries of science. For instance, the object known as 'cold fusion' was used to displace the borders between the supporters and critics of Pons and Fleischmann's experiment, the borders between chemistry and physics and those between science and non-science. The object 'Big Bang' was similarly used to mark out the borders between believers and opponents of a certain view of the universe's origin, the borders between physics and astronomy, and those between science and religion.

Negotiations in public not only presuppose the existence of boundary objects. They also and obviously concur in shaping the status and contours of such objects: the cold fusion case is an example of how a boundary object can be first brought into being and later dissolved at the level of public communication. This and other aspects of boundary objects, however, will become clearer when I return to the concept in the last part of the work, with examples of boundary objects arising from my case studies analysis.

3

CASE STUDIES

Preliminary remarks

Three case studies of 'scientists turning to the public' are presented here. Given their limited number and the nature of the phenomena at hand, they are obviously not meant to provide statistical evidence or to constitute a representative sample of deviation strategies. By definition, 'deviation' is an alternative – which does not mean infrequent – non-routine modality of public communication of science. It stands in a similar relation to popularization as scientific revolution stands to normal science.[1] Despite the fact (as I will argue more extensively) that elements of deviation are also to be observed on occasions apparently belonging to the routine, popularization modality, it seemed advisable to select cases in which the deviation modality was overwhelmingly predominant so that its nature could be more easily an object of sociological inquiry: 'bold-relief' deviation cases.

These cases, therefore, have been chosen in order to illustrate different features and articulations of the deviation process. They are very different from each another, and the method of analysis has been adapted accordingly. The approach, however, is identical in all three cases, focusing on the shaping of scientific discourse at the popular level and especially on the way in which scientific actors move around this level and interact with other categories of actors.

The first case of deviation to the public that I have studied in depth is the cold fusion affair. This is probably the most striking example of deviation offered by contemporary science. It is a case in which the public level has not just offered an arena for the shaping or unfolding of a scientific controversy; it has been the space in which a scientific 'fact' has been put into being and later dissolved. As I shall try to show, it is likely that without deviation there would have been no scientific fact known as 'cold fusion' just as without deviation it would not have been possible to erase this fact from scientific debate. The salience of the case is well testified by the amount of material available in the popular press.

Although the choice of cold fusion was well-nigh obligatory, when it came to selecting another case for study I was guided by the following criteria:

1   Availability of the material. It should have been a case widely reported in the popular media, and especially in the press, both because I was well aware of the problems involved in using other media sources (e.g. TV, radio) and because I preferred to use the same types of material (e.g. press articles) used for the cold fusion case.

2   If possible, it should have been a case of 'successful' turning to the public (unlike the cold fusion case, which ended in excommunication from the scientific community of both the scientific object and the two scientists involved) because one of the arguments I wished to pursue was that 'deviation' is by no means equal to 'deviant science' although there might be pressures within the science community to have the two overlap. This in no way means that I am concerned here with establishing whether cold fusion is 'true' or not, whether it works or not. A number of physicists, who certainly know much more than I do about neutron and tritium emissions, would be unable to answer such questions. Sociologically, the question is of no relevance to the present analysis, which is not concerned with what happens in the test tubes but with how discourse about test tubes is articulated and developed at the popular level and how this interfaces with specialist practice. In this sense, what matters is that an object known as 'cold fusion' was first pushed into scientific debate and then removed from it by recourse to the level of public communication.

3   I wished also to avoid cases involving health issues, because this would have emphasized the 'public resonance' of an issue and public interest in it. Although these are clearly important conditions for deviation to take place, I was more interested in studying such conditions from the point of view of the actions and reactions of scientists in certain situations. Once again, therefore, I decided to isolate a set of elements in order to render my analysis clearer and more effective.

The COBE-Big Bang case turned out to be an ideal counterpart to the cold fusion case. First, it is a case in which deviation to the public was not eventually framed as deviant science; instead, it was widely appreciated both by the public and the scientific community. It is also a case in which my model of deviation as related to boundary negotiation could be interestingly developed, because the emphasis on the different boundary layers was placed with diverse intensity compared with the cold fusion case.

Finally, the Pasteur-anthrax affair. This is easily the 'most different' case of the three, not least because it occurred more than a century ago. For two main reasons, however, it constitutes a unique opportunity to study the deviation process. First, Pasteur's is a case in which the ultimate private act of scientific practice, the epitome of scientific isolation and specialization, i.e. the laboratory experiment, is performed in public. Note that the experiment in question was not merely replicated before the television cameras, as happened during the cold fusion controversy, or in the presence of public witnesses as on other occasions of the history of science[2] but it was conducted for the very first time in the public domain, its very conditions and meaning being closely negotiated at this level with other actors. In other words, the public was allowed access to that 'backstage' dimension which is usually forbidden to non-scientists.

Second, Pasteur's case also offers the opportunity to see the deviation process and its connection to the more general relationships between science and the public in a historical perspective. The most intense type of boundary negotiation, namely that which helps to establish a new scientific discipline or approach by actually constituting – rather than defending or extending – its boundaries is difficult to observe today, as we can only know *a posteriori* whether the process has really given rise to a new discipline or approach. Ongoing boundary negotiation of this type can only be observed in newly developing scientific sectors such as the information sciences and the environmental sciences. Pasteur's case provides insights into this process of negotiating identities and ownership rights at the public level while a new approach (in this case, the experimental tradition in physiology) is being institutionalized. As in the others, this last case combines different layers of boundaries. A greater degree of fluidity, for instance, is also to be observed with regard to the boundary between science and the public, which was not yet so firmly established in Pasteur's time as it is today.

A detailed account of the materials and methods employed in analysis of each case is given later. For the time being I wish to make an important general point. Scientific discourse at the public level is obviously carried out in a number of different spaces, e.g. magazines, speeches, newspapers and television programmes. However, deviation differs from popularization in that science issues are not merely transferred to more 'institutional', bounded communicative niches likely to be accessed by amateur, science-oriented audiences (e.g. amateur scientific magazines, the science sections in newspapers, television science programmes); they are also to be found in general media news sections, thereby becoming truly 'public issues'. Articles in the daily press have been the principal material analysed in all the three cases, supplemented by other types of document such as taped interviews with the relevant actors involved, television commentaries, other specialist and non-specialist publications, and correspondence (in the form of letters, faxes and e-mail) among scientists concerning a matter of public debate – in general, all those materials that would enable me not only to capture the unfolding of the debate at the public level but also its relation to the other levels of scientific communication.

MAKING AND UNMAKING SCIENCE IN PUBLIC: THE COLD FUSION CASE

> There is a story, I do not remember who wrote it. A man locks himself inside his house, working day and night on the invention of the internal combustion engine. When he finally goes outside, rejoicing, he is run over by a car.
>
> Luca Goldoni, writing on cold fusion,
> *Il Corriere della Sera*, 21 April 1989

Not just 'hyped' science

The cold fusion affair has been portrayed by several observers (including many actors involved in the story) as an example of pathological science, and in particular of a pathological relationship between science and the media.[3] In accordance with the general aims of the work, this chapter concentrates on the second part of this contention and only indirectly addresses the first part of it.[4] That is, I shall challenge those accounts that, in perfect accordance with the premises of the canonical account, have blamed journalists for their alleged amplification of what was otherwise a minor event. According to these accounts, journalistic exploitation of the issue's appeal to the public as promising cheap and clean energy would be the main feature and the sole cause of its substantive presence in the public arena.

I shall try to show that an adequate understanding of the role played by the public level of communication about the cold fusion case concerns more than 'distortion' and 'sensationalization' by the media.[5] Instead, the level of public communication was the crucial discursive space in which the initial definition and, especially, the later deconstruction of the scientific fact known as 'cold fusion'[6] took place. Accordingly, special attention will have to be devoted to show how the scientists became involved in this level, how they moved around it and how they used it to shape the scientific debate itself.

To do so, I shall use materials from the United States, where the story originally developed (and where an impressive collection of documents is kept in the Cornell Cold Fusion Archive at Cornell University, Ithaca)[7] and in particular, materials from Italian daily press coverage of the story.[8] My decision to use articles from the Italian daily press was not simply dictated by the accessibility of such material. As we shall see, Italian scientists made a significant contribution to the development of the controversy, thereby amplifying its resonance in the Italian media.

Signs of (con)fusion

The possibility of having nuclear fusion at low temperatures (room temperature or a few hundred degrees) has been known since the 1950s. But the story of interest to us here began in 1984, when the American chemist Stanley Pons (a professor at Utah University, Salt Lake City) and his British colleague Martin Fleischmann (from the University of Southampton, Fellow of the Royal Society of London) initiated a series of experiments to produce fusion by means of an electrolytic process.

Working with the minimum of resources, and mostly self financing their work and apparatus, they devised an experiment with a cell containing deuterium oxide (DO_2), a platinum anode and a palladium cathode. When fed with current, the electrolysis of deuterium oxide forced the deuterium to melt inside the palladium. In 1988, after four years of work, Pons and Fleischmann applied to the US Department of Energy for research funds. The Department of Energy put the physicist Steven Jones (from Brigham Young University at Provo, Utah, about forty miles from the University of Utah) in charge of evaluating their project. Jones himself had been studying cold fusion reactions since 1982, but his research had mainly been focused on the more traditional method known as 'muonic fusion', based on the catalytic properties of a leptonic particle (the muon). More recently, Jones and his collaborators had tried another cold fusion process ('piezonuclear fusion') based, like that of Pons and Fleischmann, on the compression of the deuterium nuclei by mean of an electrolytic process.

It is very difficult to tell what happened next, because the versions of events given by Jones on the one hand, and Pons and Fleischmann on the other, differ on many points. What is clear is that when the two research groups realized the similarities between their work, they met on at least a couple of occasions and they also considered producing a report in common. They finally decided to submit their papers simultaneously to the journal *Nature* on 24 March, 1989. The atmosphere at Utah University, however, was far from tranquil. On two different occasions (first through a legal office, later through the Vice-President) the University charged Jones with stealing information from Pons. Both charges were subsequently withdrawn.

On 11 March, Pons and Fleischmann sent their paper to the *Journal of Electroanalytical Chemistry*. On 23 March, a press conference was organized at which Pons and Fleischmann announced their results. What had taken place in their cell, they claimed, was by no means a chemical process but rather a 'hitherto unknown' fusion reaction. They had in fact detected the presence of gamma rays, neutrons, tritium and Helium-3. Moreover, they had obtained a heat power of 10 watt for each cm^3 of palladium, a measure which was only slightly less than the quantities which would guarantee large-scale industrial application. The claim caused great sensation all over the world: the *Wall Street Journal* and the *Financial Times* announced the discovery on the same day and CBS opened its evening news with the story. The scientific world, too, rapidly became highly excited. It was in fact difficult for the other researchers to judge Pons and Fleischmann's claims with the little information coming from the press conference. Nor had the two researchers been over-generous with details, apparently because of the several commercial patents at stake.

However, a preprint of their paper 'Electrochemically Induced Nuclear Fusion of Deuterium', became available via electronic mail within a few days. Objections were raised by other researchers, especially regarding the measurement of neutrons. Numerous researchers also complained that Pons and Fleischmann had not used a control cell with normal hydrogen in order to exclude the possibility of a simple chemical reaction. During the same days Jones' paper 'Observation of Cold Nuclear Fusion in Condensed Matter', mentioned since the day after Pons and Fleischmann press conference, now began to circulate. Comparison between the two papers revealed some significant differences. First, Jones was less concerned with the production of energy than with the explanation of certain phenomena on the basis of events within the electrolytic cell. According to Jones, in fact, sea water filtering into some region of the solid strata below the earth's surface is exposed to such pressures as to induce a fusion of deuterium nuclei, which are mainly responsible for the earth's heat. Indeed, the solution in his cell ('less efficient' compared with the one used by Pons and Fleischmann) contained the most common salts in the earth's crust.

In the week following the press conference, several laboratories set about replicating the experiment. Among them, was the important English centre at Harwell, which Fleischmann visited in order to provide some suggestions. The first replication, however, was claimed by two Hungarian scientists at Kossuth University, followed by a group of researchers from Texas State University and Georgia Tech Institute. In April, twelve other (at least partial) confirmations of Pons and Fleischmann's results were announced, although some were successively withdrawn by their authors because of mismeasurements. Within a short time, however, the number of confirmatory experiments exceeded sixty and had been conducted by American institutions such as Stanford, the University of Florida and the University of Washington as well as by international institutions in Brazil, Czechoslovakia, India and the Soviet Union.

In the meantime the first meetings and conferences on cold fusion were held (one of them in Italy, at Erice, where Jones gave a paper on 12 April 1989) and the first funds were allocated for further research (the Utah state government decided to finance experiments with five million dollars and asked the federal government for an additional 25 million fund). The journal *Nature*, after publishing an article which severely criticized the practice of claiming discoveries at press conferences before official publication,[9] returned Pons and Fleischmann's paper, asking them to make significant changes. The authors refused to do so and *Nature* published instead Jones'article on 27 April.

At this point Italian research also joined the fray. Italy has occupied a somewhat anomalous place in the history of nuclear fusion research. It was an Italian scientist, Bruno Coppi, who first suggested that experimental efforts should be directed at the understanding of the physical problems, rather than immediately concentrating on the production of utilizable fusion reactions. This idea engendered the *Ignitor* project to produce controlled nuclear fusion by the ignition of a deuterium-tritium plasma; a rather different process from the magnetic confinement on which the efforts of European research are focused. Also, following the national rejection of nuclear energy by referendum in 1987, Italian research resources have been more substantially directed to fusion than those of other European countries. There are centres for thermonuclear fusion research in Padua, Milan and Frascati (near Rome). At the time of Pons and Fleischmann's announcement, a special project was under way sponsored by CERN physicist and former Nobel prize for physics, Carlo Rubbia. The project's main aim was to use a sheaf of nuclear particles as the 'starter' for the fusion process instead of a laser beam.

A small number of Italian researchers, notably the physicists from the University of Bologna Antonio Bertin and Antonio Vitale, were also active in the field of muonic fusion. The two physicists called a press conference shortly after Pons and Fleischmann's announcement to announce that they had obtained similar results in recent years. Another physicist, Roberto Monti of the Bologna CNR (National Research Council) section, took part in a TV talk-show in early April and called journalists to publicly complain that his work on cold fusion carried out in recent years had been ignored by the Italian research community, forcing him to publish in non-scientific journals like *Frigidaire* or *Seagreen*.[10] In mid-April some publicity was also given to a commercial cold fusion patent allegedly registered some years before in 1974 by two Verona researchers. Another researcher at the University of Bologna, Francesco Premuda, claimed that he had found a theoretical explanation for Pons and Fleischmann's experiment well before M.I.T., which he had certified by a public notary and announced in a self-financed publication distributed among his colleagues.

On 18 April 1989 ENEA (The Italian National Institute for Energy and Environment, formerly National Institute for Nuclear Energy) called a press conference to announce that a group of researchers coordinated by physicist Francesco Scaramuzzi had obtained deuterium fusion at room temperature and had measured the related neutron emission. Unlike Jones and Pons and Fleischmann, Scaramuzzi 'blew' high pressure gaseous deuterium into an iron cylinder filled with 50 cm^3 of titanium-shavings. Scaramuzzi is a well known physicist in Italy and also in the United States, where he has been visiting professor at the California Institute of Technology

(Caltech) in Pasadena. He was also a good friend of the great American physicist Richard Feynman. In the days that followed, several other positive results from similar experiments were reported in Italy: one such experiment was conducted at the Department of Physics of Genoa University; another by a team directed by Perfetti at the Frascati CNR (National Research Council) laboratories; another at the National Institute of Nuclear Physics; and others by a CISE (Centre for Energy Development) laboratory in Milan and by three physicists in Perugia. Politicians expressed their interest in, and appreciation of, such accomplishments: the Minister for Scientific Research and the President of the Chamber of Deputies visited the National Institute of Nuclear Physics laboratory (located under the Gran Sasso mountain near L'Aquila specifically to minimize errors in neutron measurement). The ENEA president Umberto Colombo and Scaramuzzi were invited to a hearing by the Industrial Production Committee of the Italian Chamber of Deputies. A member of the Parliament also wrote a report on the matter in which he asked for the allocation of further research funds. The state grants to ENEA, which had been interrupted four years previously, were suddenly reactivated.

In the United States a congressional hearing on cold fusion was held on 26 April. Pons and Fleischmann, accompanied by the President of the University of Utah, Chase Peterson, appeared before the congressional subcommittee evaluating their application for $25 million to create a National Cold Fusion Institute. On watching the videotapes of the hearing, a number of researchers were angered by Pons and Fleischmann's failure to mention criticisms and counter-experiments. Jones was also heard by the subcommittee; he denied that his results corroborated Pons and Fleischmann's claims to any degree.

On the first and second of May two sessions on cold fusion were held during the meeting of the American Physical Society in Baltimore. The chemist Nathan Lewis and the physicist Steve Koonin harshly criticized Pons and Fleischmann's experimental results and conclusions and challenged some of those obtained by Jones. With regard to Pons and Fleischmann, in particular, Koonin spoke openly about 'incompetence and delusion'. At the end of the session, *at a press conference*, Jones asked all the researchers present to express their confidence in Pons and Fleischmann's results by ballot. The outcome was eight votes against Pons and Fleischmann and one 'abstention', Johann Rafelski, who invited those present to wait for further evidence. Jones also asked for a vote on his own results, obtaining a majority of votes in favour. Pons and Fleischmann were invited to the meeting, but declined to attend.

Thereafter, the interest of the general media in the cold fusion story declined. The scientific debate, however, continued. At the end of May a meeting entirely devoted to cold fusion was held in Santa Fe, at which all the technical aspects of the experiments were closely scrutinized. In particular, given a succession of contrasting results (some researchers detected neutrons but no heat production, others only heat), it was suggested that two phenomena might be involved: a minor fusion reaction such as documented by Jones and a more complex chemical reaction. Despite the events in Baltimore, there was still no consensus about what cold fusion is (or is not). In a report prepared for the United States Department of Energy, a group of researchers stressed that the relevance of the reaction for technical applications was scant, although they admitted that many aspects still required clarification ('there remain unresolved issues and scientifically interesting questions stemming from reported cold fusion efforts').[11] In the following months, specialized journals (such as the *Journal of Electroanalytical Chemistry and Interfacial Chemistry*, the *Journal of Fusion Energy* and *Fusion Technology*) continued to publish papers on the topic and meetings were held in several countries. By the end of 1991, almost 700 papers had been published on cold fusion.[12] In September, a conference entirely devoted to cold fusion was held in Varenna, Italy.

In June 1990, *Science* levelled charges of fraud against John Bockris, a researcher of Texas A&M who had been among the first to confirm Pons and Fleischmann's results. In October 1990, another conference was organized at Brigham Young University on 'Anomalous Effects in Deuterated Metals' which sought to shift the attention to a more respectable type of cold fusion, the Jones' variant: i.e. experiments focused more on neutron measurements and on the theoretical implications for geophysics rather than on heat production. However, interest in cold fusion research has inexorably declined over time: the United States Department of Energy has witheld its support since 1989 and the Cold Fusion Institute founded in Utah soon closed. The price of palladium, which rose from $145.60 an ounce to $170 (May 1989) has since fallen to $95 an ounce.

Today, scientists still work on cold fusion and positive results are reported from time to time. Interestingly, the decline has been more in the visibility (and especially in the public visibility) of the issue than in scientific activity as such. Researchers tend to avoid the dangerous label of 'cold fusion', preferring to speak of 'anomalous phenomena in the Palladium-Deuterium lattice'. Pons and Fleischmann's work is currently funded with Japanese money: according to the latest information available, they are working for the Japan firm Technova, a Toyota subsidiary, at a secret location in southern France. Japanese researchers and investors are apparently still confident about cold fusion, especially after a successful replication (neutron detection and energy production of 200 megawatt for each m^3 of electrode with some technical adjustments, i.e. larger electrodes and impulse rather than continuous current supply) claimed in 1992 by a group of researchers led by Hideo Ikegami at the University of Nagoya. Francesco Scaramuzzi continued to study cold fusion and to present his work at seminars and in publications until his recent retirement from research.

Cold fusion and public communication

As we have seen, the assumption at the core of the canonical account (and also quite common in the scientific field) is that science and the mass media are absolutely incompatible. According to this view, the media can offer at best an impoverished representation of science by picking up its more superficial and less significant elements. At worst, this impoverishment results in a deplorable sensationalization of actors and events involved in scientific issues and the related deception of the public due mainly to the emphasis placed on the possible commercial output of discoveries.[13]

The argument advanced here against this approach is that, in a case like cold fusion, it becomes particularly difficult to distinguish the areas of 'original' and 'pure' scientific communication from those in which science is publicly consumed and popularized.[14] Cold fusion was first included and then excluded from specialist debate by recourse to the public domain. Therefore, the need to recognize an important and active value with regard to scientific production and discussion emerges. A similar need applies to those presentations which, although taking place within the broader arena of non-specialistic communication, clearly involve and strongly influence the specialists themselves.[15]

Reference goes in the first place to the use made by scientists of the media. I have already tried to show that – even in general terms – scientists are by no means extraneous to the presentation of science by the daily press or by television.[16] First, because they are the sources and pre-selectors of such presentation; second, because they themselves rely on this level of communication as a source of information and professional legitimation. These and other 'uses' of public communication of science, however, are particularly visible in cases of deviation, when they become structurally part of the scientific debate and are employed to question and defend different layers of science boundaries in the most dramatic and 'theatrical' way possible. It can be easily shown that this was certainly the case with cold fusion.

From Pons and Fleischmann's announcement until the APS meeting, daily papers and TV news were the principal arena in which the issue was given meaning and discussed.[17] 'The first remarkable thing about the story', it was later noted by a BBC documentary on cold fusion, 'is that almost everybody who heard about it, scientists or not, heard about it on the same day.'[18]

The only information available to researchers wishing to verify or to replicate the experiment was provided by the daily papers and television images. For instance, several scientists declared that they had deduced the emissions of rays from a graph which appeared on television and that they had constructed their electrolytic cell on the basis of another picture, using Pons' fingers as a metrical reference.[19] 'There was no published paper from

Pons and Fleischmann to go on. It was impossible to contact them, so some of the world's most eminent fusion scientists ended up getting their data off a TV screen.'[20] A scientist recalls: 'The next day I had to pick up my dad at the airport. He had the *Financial Times* and he made me aware of an article and said what do you think about this?' I looked at it and said, 'That sounds so easy, I think I'm going to try that.'[21]

Only at a later time did researchers gain access to the preprints of articles (via fax and e-mail)[22] and to the news sections of weekly journals such as *Nature* and *Science*. Obviously, the confusion and the dubious confirmations of the first period have been widely attributed to this haphazard information. But this argument, too, can be fruitfully reconsidered from the perspective of scientific actors. Information instability allowed scientists to change their statements repeatedly, shuttling among different theoretical positions and alliances as the controversy developed.[23]

This applies in the first place to Pons and Fleischmann, who from the outset were not particularly forthcoming about their experimental results in order to protect their potential commercial patents. (This, at least is what they have declared: one could infer from subsequent events that they did not actually have a complete explanation of the results.) For instance, neither in their official publication nor at the first press conference, but only in subsequent talks with reporters did Pons reveal that he had recorded a helium-3 emission.[24]

Confirmations and denials were presented at the popular level, thereby transforming some journalists into brokers among different research groups. This was, for instance, the case of David Ansley, a reporter for the *San Jose Mercury News*, who submitted the doubts of other researchers to the researchers at Utah, and later reported their answers.

> I said, 'If you'll let me come watch you do this, I'll be happy to pass on any information I get on how this sucker works.' So when I got the manuscript [of the Jones paper] I faxed it to Huggins and to Lewis. And then I called them back to ask what they thought of it. . . . Everyone was scrambling for information. The day after we printed the story saying 'here's what the manuscript says', I got a call from SRI [a major consulting firm based near San Jose]. An electrochemist there said, 'Um, would you send us a copy of that [paper] I'm sort of unused asking this, but would you?'

> At one point, I called up [University of Utah Vice President for research James] Brophy and said, 'Look, this is making no sense. You say that all it takes is the simple description and that other researchers ought to be able to duplicate it . . . [but] here are the questions they're asking me. Can you answer any of these questions?' And he would give me the answers. I would call [the

researchers] back, and they would say 'That's so simplistic. That's just not enough. We need x, y, z. The way he's describing that doesn't do us any good.' I'd call [Brophy] back, and he'd say, 'No, really, that's how it works. It's that simple.'[25]

Phillip Schewe, of the American Physical Society Public Information Division, had to compile selections of newspaper clips and television cuts about cold fusion for the physicists.[26] In Italy the newspaper *La Repubblica* organized a telephone 'confrontation'[27] between Pons and Fleischmann and the Italian physicist of CERN, Carlo Rubbia, a former Nobel prize-winner in physics.

> With Sunday's issue of *La Repubblica* open on their table, ten experts on nuclear fusion read, reread, and try to interpret the report of the debate between Rubbia and Pons and Fleischmann.
> *La Repubblica*, 30 April 1989

'This week', a senior researcher from ENEA commented, 'I had to buy *Panorama* and *L'Espresso*[28] to keep myself updated on the cold fusion story. I haven't bought *Playboy* yet. . . . '[29]

Later, the article published in *Science* which overtly charged some of the researchers involved in the cold fusion experiments with fraud, was signed by a journalist, the freelance Gary Taubes.[30] The announcement made by Pons and Fleischmann at a press conference is also a clear example of the use of the popular level to foster the peer-review process, thereby securing the paternity of a discovery without having to wait for the usual publication and discussion procedures to be completed (which naturally also expose researchers to the risks of plagiarism, especially in cases such as cold fusion, where the commercial stakes are high).

Finally, the various parties involved in the controversy supported their views and results on television programmes and in the newspapers. It was especially the physicists working in institutions like CERN who found themselves forced to legitimate and defend their work against these revolutionary findings. They felt as if someone had pulled away the chair they were sitting on. 'Imagine that someone who designs aeroplanes is told that someone else has invented the antigravitational machine. They are obviously sceptical,' said Ian Hutchinson, a professor working on nuclear fusion at M.I.T.[31]

This first phase was essentially brought to a close by the American Physical Society Conference held in early May: on that occasion the criticisms brought against Pons and Fleischmann were so severe as to persuade almost all the journalists present. Thereafter, the general media were no longer one of the key arenas for the unfolding controversy and simply recorded its later developments. This was clearly evidenced by their growing dependence on events. Newspapers no longer sought out interviews and comments from the experts, and cold fusion only became 'news' again when a particular event was suitable for media coverage: a conference, for example, or the anniversary of the first announcement by Pons and Fleischmann. It was more and more a gaze 'from the external': the deviation process was over and so was cold fusion for the public.

Cold fusion and the Italian daily press

For the reasons set out earlier, the quantitative analysis of the Italian daily press material has been restricted to the first phase of the controversy and concentrates on the 197 articles that appeared in six newspapers (*La Repubblica, Il Corriere della Sera, La Stampa, L'Unità, Il Sole 24 Ore* – a financial newspaper – and *L'Osservatore Romano* – the Vatican newspaper) between 24 March 1989 (the day after the press conference, when the first articles were published) and 30 April. Bearing in mind that in the same period 166 articles appeared in the American daily press, the great importance attached to the event by the Italian press becomes clear.[32] On 24 March, cold fusion featured on the front pages of all leading Italian newspapers, although the story was accompanied by quite critical reactions from most of the Italian 'visible physicists'.

Given this large number of articles, a preliminary quantitative analysis was carried out in order to map the general features of daily press coverage. The complete results of the quantitative analysis are presented in Appendix 3.A.

Concerning the distribution of articles across time, the peaks in coverage occurred during the first days and in coincidence with the Italian experiments (Figure 3.1). That the issue was increasingly contextualized as an 'Italian' issue is shown also by Figure 3.2 and Figure 3.3. Cold fusion moved from a generic setting in the international scientific community to a near national setting through events like the Erice conference, Jones' visit and through the involvement of scientists like Francesco Scaramuzzi, Carlo Rubbia and Antonino Zichichi. An increasing amount of space was devoted to the presentation of confirmations and disconfirmations by Italian scientists, almost obscuring the debate on Pons and Fleischmann's original experiment.

The problem of sensationalism and of so-called 'spectacular science' is usually attributed by scientists and traditional models to the eagerness of journalists to emphasize the practical consequences of a discovery like cold fusion and their uncritical acceptance of it with banner headlines. In this regard, one notes that the presentation of cold fusion in Italian newspapers was dominated by the phases of verification and discussion. Unlike those in the US daily press, Italian articles expressed from the outset a remarkable scepticism concerning Pons and Fleischmann's discovery. The way the media presented cold fusion is shown in Table 3.1, and the front-page coverage in Figure 3.4.

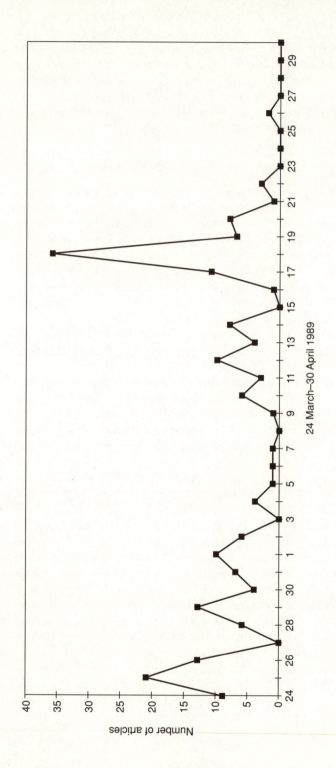

Figure 3.1 Press articles on cold fusion, March–April 1989

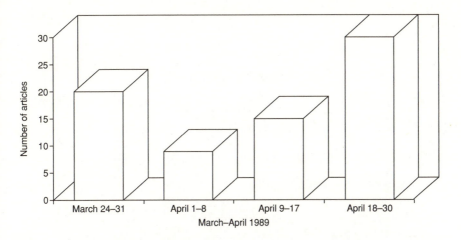

Figure 3.2 Cold fusion articles in national (Italian) news section, March–April 1989

Nuclear fusion in a test tube. The announcement from the United States with scepticism . . . the news has been received by European physicists with surprise and great perplexity.

La Repubblica, 24 March 1989

Rubbia: I do not believe it. Two scientists, one English and one American, have announced the achievement of a controlled fusion reaction. In Europe, however, there is still a great deal of scepticism.

L'Unità, 24 March 1989

A fusion to be checked . . . in the absence of more reliable data, this discovery seems too beautiful to be true.

Il Sole 24 Ore, 29 March 1989

From Switzerland and US doubts on the Fleischmann-Pons experiment: it is simply a chemical reaction . . . the English journal *Nature* has rejected Fleischmann and Pons's paper, as they were not able to provide the necessary clarifications.

La Stampa, 27 April 1989

Dreaming is beautiful but being cautious is necessary.

Il Corriere della Sera, 26 March 1989

Some articles were even published on pages dominated by the theme 'fraudulent science', together with renowned false discoveries of the past. A certain

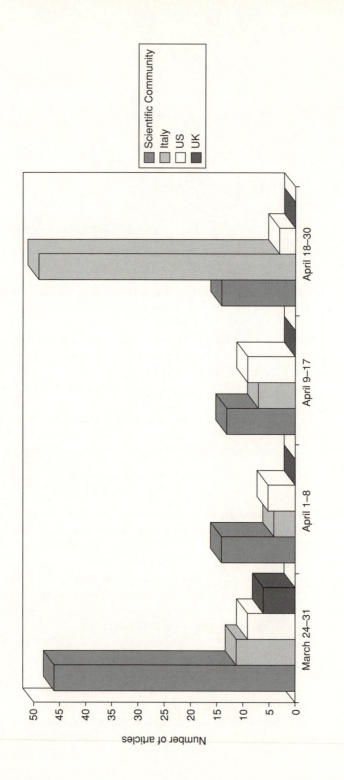

Figure 3.3 Dominant national context of cold fusion articles

Table 3.1 Representation of the scientific fact in its different phases

Stage of the story	Number of media reports
Research phases preceding discovery	34
Moment of discovery	53
Announcement of discovery	47
Phase of verification and discussion	140
Diffusion of discovery	39
Possible applications	63
Real applications	5

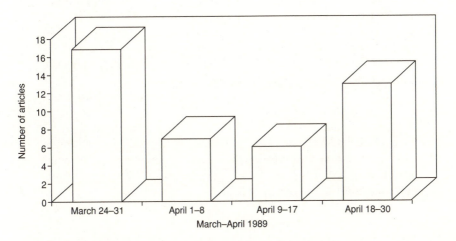

Figure 3.4 Cold fusion articles on the front page

trust came only with the results obtained by Scaramuzzi, considered 'a researcher above all suspicion', but from the end of April the issue was nonetheless considered by newspapers to be virtually closed.

> And fusion cooled down . . . in the laboratories of MIT and Caltech a proof that wipes out Fleischmann and Pons.
> *La Repubblica*, 3 May 1989

> The American daily press mocks the two scientists who were national heroes until a few days ago.
> *La Repubblica*, 4 May 1989

> Postfusion tepid, tepid.
> *L'Unità*, 13 September 1989

Moreover, many articles showed a considerable awareness of the risks of sensationalism arising from the reporting of science in the daily press.

> I do not think, however, that the daily press should have dedicated so many front page stories to the first discovery, because it has no practical outcome.
>
> *Il Corriere della Sera*, 10 April 1989

> Science should not run as fast as TV and newspapers.
>
> *Il Corriere della Sera*, 2 May 1989

> If I were to prepare a sensationalist headline for Scaramuzzi's experiment, I would write: 'The experiment in Frascati contradicts Fleischmann and Pons' results, not enough energy from cold fusion.' Instead, I see that the Italian daily press continues with its series of fanciful headlines that tell us that we shall soon have the production of home-made energy. This is an illusion.
>
> *L'Unità*, 19 April 1989

> Whereupon, the National Institute of Physics announced that the first results had been achieved at Gran Sasso as well. Everything is top secret. Partly because they are afraid of indulging in spectacular science and partly because there are still uncertainties about the evaluation of results.
>
> *L'Unità*, 21 April 1989

> Great joy, then: because it is the time for sensationalist physics, with all the dangers inherent in sensationalism.
>
> *La Repubblica*, 23 April 1989

> And the general public discovered science . . . even more surprising than the discovery, in my view, is the extraordinary response of the general public. An attitude that deserves closer attention.
>
> *La Repubblica*, 2 April 1989

The active involvement of scientists in the media discussion of cold fusion should not be ignored. Beside the several interviews and comments released, about one-sixth of the articles were signed by the researchers. The most visible Italian physicists, from Carlo Rubbia to Antonino Zichichi, Tullio Regge and Ugo Amaldi, commented daily on the story in newspaper columns. The financial newspaper *Il Sole 24 Ore* even published the whole of Jones' paper. Jones was also given an opportunity to replicate his experiment in front of the TV cameras when he was invited to a RAI (Italian Public Television) programme on 15 April. Table 3.2 shows the authorship of media articles.

Table 3.2 Authorship of articles

Author	Number of articles
Journalist	158
Researcher	29
Philosopher of science	6
Other commentator	2
Unidentified	2

A comparative analysis also demonstrates that journalists referred no more extensively to non-scientific elements (in particular, to the practical consequences of the discovery) than did researchers (Table 3.3).

With headlines, images were in general relevant to the article's content (even though they were often not essential). This did not apply to the relationship between images and headlines, as each tended to focus on different elements of the article (Tables 3.4 and 3.5).

Table 3.3 Predominant content of articles by author

Article content	Number of journalist articles	Number of researcher articles
Scientific	120	17
Technological	5	5
Economic	22	4
Other	11	2
Total	158	28

Table 3.4 Relevance of the images to the text of the article

Reference to article's content	Number of headlines
Non-relevant	15
Relevant unessential	44
Relevant useful	15
Relevant essential	6
No image	117

Table 3.5 Relevance of the images to the title of the article

Relevance of image	Number of headlines
Non-relevant	35
Relevant unessential	28
Relevant useful	11
Relevant essential	4
No image	117

Images, however, were not frequently employed. Photographs of researchers predominated, while graphs and explanatory schemes were almost entirely absent except in the earliest days of the story.[33] Moreover, researchers were quite often portrayed in non-research settings (e.g. with their families, during a conference – see Figure 3.5) and were instead rarely presented actually in the process of 'doing science' (e.g. in their laboratory). See Tables 3.6 and 3.7.

This type of portrait can be plausibly interpreted as an attempt to bring the scientist closer to everyday reality and therefore to the reader.[34] This impression is supported by other features. As the story proceeded, for instance, metaphors[35] were increasingly used to describe the relationships between scientists, or other non-scientific elements of the story, rather than to really elucidate theoretical or experimental problems. Whereas initially the reaction was widely explained by referring to a 'friendship between palladium and deuterium' or to a 'marriage between atoms', one increasingly finds later expressions like 'homemade fusion' or 'tepid fusion' (in order to highlight the cautiousness with which the announcement was received). The story was repeatedly compared to a 'thriller by Agatha Christie' or to a 'nuclear soap-opera'.[36]

> It happens as in crime stories: the detective has some clues left behind by the murderer; he must then check them, interview people, inspect places; in the end he finds that some clues fit and some do not.
>
> *L'Unità*, 18 April 1989

Figure 3.5 The American physicist Steven Jones with his wife

Source: La Repubblica, 15 April 1989, reproduced with permission

Table 3.6 Types of image in article

Image	Number of articles
Photograph	53
Drawing	17
Graph	9
Cartoon, comic strip	1
No image	117

Table 3.7 Subject of image

Image	Number of articles
Researchers at work	6
Press conference	7
Researchers (not working)	28
Politicians	4
Representatives of research institutions	1
Entrepreneurs	1
Experimental machinery	20
Applicative devices	5

> Is it possible that research by two scientists takes our breath away just like a crime novel? The answer is yes, if like a novel missing the last three pages, research is not finished ... An hypothesis remains, again suitable to a crime novel: what seem proofs are just clues, a sign that detectives have been hasty and superficial.
>
> *La Repubblica*, 28 March 1989[37]

Renato Angelo Ricci, President of the Italian Physics Society and of the European Physics Society, and project head of the study set out to explore the possibility of a particle ignited nuclear fusion, clearly excelled in this art of 'metaphorical redescription'.

> I believe it is now time to offer specifications on 'cold fusion', not least to help sensible people to find their way among the confusion of news, interpretations, facile judgements and ridiculous hypotheses, created by the *tom-tom of the new sorcerer's apprentices who pretend that science is a fairground sideshow*.
>
> *La Repubblica*, 4 May 1989, my emphasis

Overall, it seems that issue deconstruction was achieved by extensive use of such strategies: the scientific dimension of the story was underplayed and the focus was shifted to 'social/human' dimensions like, for instance, the shrewdness of Pons and Fleischmann (the latter being described as 'a

sly old fox' of science) or their financial ambitions. Rubbia himself emphasized this point, complaining during the teleconference organized by
Repubblica about the lack of a control cell in the original experiment: 'This
is a very important point. If you manage to do this, your pockets will soon
be full of money' (*La Repubblica*, 27 March 1989).

A journalist brilliantly summarized this shift of focus when he wrote:

> Perhaps the two are innocent scientists, fallen with their audacious
> experiment into the cogs of the 'brave new world' where publicity,
> dollars, glory, prizes, ambitions and the mass media boil together
> like the heavy water in the cloudy broth of the Utah bottle. An
> experiment that has triggered, if not atomic fusion, certainly a chain
> explosion in human vanities and weaknesses.
>
> *La Repubblica*, 29 April 1989

The long discussions of neutrons and heat measurement that had initially
filled the pages of the newspapers soon disappeared. One increasingly finds
talk *about* the scientific fact rather than discussion *of* the scientific fact.
Cold fusion left the science sections of newspapers and ended up in the
general news sections where it was treated virtually like any other political
or social theme or conflict. 'Amidst this brouhaha, with quasi-Nobel prize
scientists arguing like Sacchi and Trapattoni, what should the reader
think?'[38]

The 'cold fusion' controversy was therefore constructed not on the
opposition between different theoretical positions but on a series of political–social polarizations; in the first place, that between 'Little Science' and
'Big-Science'. Conflict among opinions, explanations and results developed
into conflict among parties and interest groups. The isolated ingeniousness
of Pons and Fleischmann, self-financed out of their own savings and put
into practice with a 'child's chemistry set' as apparatus, was ranged against
the huge and costly bureaucratic structures of particle physics, CERN in
particular. The emphasis was thus placed on the cheapness and simplicity
of the initial experiment.

> Nuclear fusion? Come in, I'll show it to you.
>
> Title on *L'Unità*, 26 March 1989

> By recovering that domestic dimension that it used to have until
> a few decades ago, science has again become a product of indi-
> vidual talent, that talent which couples bold imagination with
> thorough checks. It is the revenge taken by the individual against
> the hegemony of the group. Great ideas arise in one individual's
> mind, not programmed and generated in crowded corridors.
>
> *La Stampa*, 29 March 1989

Atomic energy from a battery.

La Stampa, 26 March 1989

Our fusion is like David's victory over Goliath.

Il Sole 24 Ore, 25 March 1989

The great revenge of little chemistry ... chemistry, ill-treated for so long, may have finally taken its revenge on high energy physics. That is: little science has defeated big science.

La Repubblica, 25 March 1989

The big bosses of scientific power shake.

La Repubblica, 29 March 1989

This is how the little mouse gave birth to a mountain.

La Repubblica, 3 April 1989

This 'isolated genius' frame, however, soon degenerated into a 'Dr Strangelove' scenario:

The whole story reminds me of some B-science fiction novel where the usual mad scientist defeats the big laboratories with a retired grocer's equipment, the only difference being that now everything seems so absurdly true.

La Stampa, 18 April 1989

A second contraposition was organized between European and American research, where Italy was projected as the unpredictable outsider: articles spoke of an 'Italian way to cold fusion', 'fusion with the taste of made-in-Italy', 'basil-flavoured fusion'. This emphasis on the 'political dimension' enabled the critics of cold fusion to gradually shift the frame of the story from a controversy between different theoretical claims and experimental approaches to a disciplinary conflict between the two main scientific groups involved, chemists and physicists: two categories particularly suited to be contrasted, since one is marked by low levels of theoretical consensus and by a high degree of accordance on technical methods, while the other bases its disciplinary integration on a limited number of shared theoretical paradigms[39] (see Figure 3.6).

This also endorsed the scientific community's ability to account for and thereby publicly justify the lack of consensus on the matter, a lack of consensus commonly held to be deleterious to scientific authority.[40] It was not that the physicists and the chemists were obtaining different results from the same measurements; they were in fact measuring different things. For physicists the approach was: 'We know what fusion looks like, we

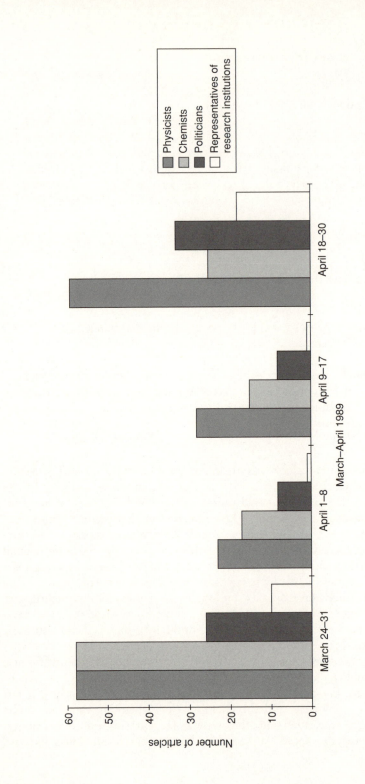

Figure 3.6 Cold fusion articles: representation of some categories

know that it produces neutrons, let's try to measure them.' Chemists, instead, started from the amount of heat produced in order to explain the phenomenon (see Figure 3.7).[41]

Chemists cheer, physicists are perplexed after Fleischmann's speech . . . A foregone success if one thinks that in his endeavour to rank among the great inventors, Fleischmann has chosen to 'play at home', as they say in the sports jargon.

Il Corriere della Sera, 31 March 1989

Fleischmann's triumph among his 'friends' the chemists . . . today, however he must reckon CERN in Geneva, the world temple of physics, the eternal rival of chemistry.

La Repubblica, 31 March 1989

Today, a repeat performance in the 'wolf's den', CERN in Geneva. Here everybody threatens to be much less understanding. Fleischmann will have to face an audience of physicists bearing a

Figure 3.7 'Fusion! Is it chemistry or physics?'

Source: Deseret News, 29 April 1989, © Danziger and *The Christian Science Monitor*, reproduced with permission

grudge against those seeking to change the set of certainties resulting from decades of research.

L'Unità, 31 March 1989

The chemist has charm but he does not persuade the physicists. In Geneva, in the 'wolf's den' of CERN, the scientist who announced cold temperature fusion has given a seminar. A number of doubts still remain.

La Repubblica, 1 April 1989

Rubbia remarked during his long-distance discussion with Fleischmann: 'It is curious that you, a chemist, are giving lessons to a nuclear physicist like me.' (*La Repubblica,* 27 March 1989). This was apparently not enough for physicists to reclaim their 'ownership rights' on the issue in public, and thereby assert their right to the last word on the subject. Perhaps, also, because the physics community was not fully united even in its public statements.

The final strategy, therefore, was once again to recontextualize the conflict in terms of a demarcation not just between different disciplines, but between science and non-science (i.e. orthodox scientists and heretics). Cold fusion was not presented merely as a dubious or unconfirmed scientific discovery; it was discussed as 'unscientific', as something which had nothing to do with the science community (just as Pons and Fleischmann were not simply 'wrong', they were 'non-scientists') and was likened to those neighbouring practices that most easily qualified as non-science in the public's mind, such as magic. 'Perhaps it's some sort of magic trick,' was Rubbia's first reaction to the announcement,[42] a comment followed by references to cold fusion as 'fool's gold', to Pons and Fleischmann as the 'sorcerer's apprentices', and to the whole story as 'paranormal science'.[43] 'Theories about cold fusion are nice,' said Koonin 'but I may nicely theorize about pigs with wings and pigs do not have wings' (*Il Corriere della Sera,* 3 May 1989).

Hence, both Pons and Fleischmann and their discovery had to be deconstructed and 'degraded' in Garfinkel's sense: 'The transformation of identities is the deconstruction of one social object and the constitution of another ... the denounced person becomes in the eye of the witnesses a different person.'[44] It was not sufficient to present them as 'wrong', they had to be 'ritually separated from a place in the legitimate order' and 'placed outside'.[45] The public, as witness and therefore as part of the degradation process was morally compelled to blame event and perpetrator as belonging to a completely different dimension.[46] A 'dialectical counterpart' was required for this purpose: i.e. there had to be an image of 'true science' and 'reliable scientists' available to be publicly contrasted with quackery.[47]

Although Mertonian[48] guidelines for a scientific ethos may not always be followed in science practice, in fact, they are still an important resource to be projected at the general public in problematic or ambiguous situations.[49] The distinction between those who are truly in pursuit of truth and 'false prophets' is not based on the validity of their theories and experimental results but on certain 'rules of the game', specific ways of behaving (e.g. suspending judgement, respecting the peer review system, not turning to the public before internal scrutiny has been thoroughly carried out) emphasized and idealized.[50]

> It was the scientist who was irresponsible; I think the scientist should not have gone to the press on March 23 and thereafter. It should have been done in the way science has been done. Science has to do its thing and its thing is working in publication, going to international meetings, having a scientific discussion, checking, rechecking, double checking, verifying everything and once, once it's true, then you can go to the press, IF it has any interest to the press.[51]

James A. Krumhnsl, President of the American Physical Society remarked that 'an ethical cloud has béen suspended over this subject [cold fusion] since the 23 March 1989 press conference called by the University of Utah to announce that Stanley Pons and Martin Fleischmann had achieved fusion of deuterium nuclei in a palladium lattice'.[52] The major lesson that CERN physicist Douglas Morrison drew from the whole story was that 'we should not call press conferences before doing all checks and controls'.[53]

Interestingly, it was Steven Jones, Pons and Fleischmann's former competitor in claiming paternity of cold fusion, who was often turned into the counterpart to the 'villains' Pons and Fleischmann, being presented as a 'real physicist' or a 'serious scientist'. Every trait of his character and of his conduct (including his looks, his family, the seriousness of his university), was described in a manner such that the public inevitably preferred him to the two electrochemists.

> So, who's the father of cold fusion? The bold sixty-two year old man who takes the floor as an accomplished actor [Pons], or the blonde Mormon with the 'All-American' looks sitting quietly, taking notes and, although he is forty-one years old, blushing when somebody asks him for clarification.
>
> *La Stampa*, 13 April 1989

> It was Jones himself, the day before yesterday, who gave the news to a large audience at Columbia University, New York, although he did not mean to do so. The meeting was to be for researchers only. But then some journalists sneaked into the room and spread

the news. The young American physicist, in his forties, with the looks of a good boy, had no intention of speaking to the press, not even after publication of his work in a scientific journal, a rule that is always respected by the most serious researchers. One perceives this, not just from the reserved demeanour acknowledged by Jones' collaborators, but most of all from the way in which he presented his discovery.

La Repubblica, 2 April 1989

The news coming from Brookhaven seems to shift the balance in favour of the cautious and quiet Jones, Professor at the Mormon university, forty years old, six children and another one on the way.

Il Corriere della Sera, 6 April 1989

At the Mormon University [BYU], in the town of Provo, there is no enthusiasm for the style of the Salt Lake City colleagues; the relaxed atmosphere that prevails there is replaced by a certain rigidity here. The 27 thousand students, mostly Mormons, must dress with decorum, swear not to cheat during examinations, and abide by the regulations.

Il Corriere della Sera, 30 March 1989

In mid-April 1989, while he was still arguing with Pons and Fleischmann over priority, Jones took pains to stress his greater deference to such rules:

Quietly and without fanfare, scientific break-even was achieved in a fusion experiment in 1982.[54]

The Italian press told Jones's story in similar terms:

Believing that truth has a place in this 'show society', Jones opens to his laboratory notebooks. On 22 May 1986, he accomplished the first cold nuclear fusion. A few days later, the Academic Council called him: 'Professor Jones, this is a revolutionary discovery; let us organize a press conference.' 'No, thanks,' Jones answered. 'I prefer to wait for peer controls.' He did not know that his style was outmoded.

Il Corriere della Sera, 2 April 1989

Later, even after he had reframed his own work as different from Pons and Fleischmann's, Jones nevertheless continued to pursue this argumentative strategy:

Douglas [Morrison] has maintained and published in *Physics World* that a press conference was held at BYU the day after the one at the University of Utah, that is, on March 24. Thus, he lumped our behaviour with that of Pons and Fleischmann. There is no basis in fact for his statement: at no time was a press conference relating to Cold Fusion held at BYU. Indeed, I took a planned trip with my family on March 24 for the Easter weekend and was not at all on BYU Campus that day.[55]

The boundary between 'proper' communication with the public and deviation[56] was therefore mobilized as one of the markers of scientific orthodoxy and therefore of public credibility. 'The most fundamental requirement of a scientist is that he or she talks like a scientist', writes Charles Taylor.[57] This requirement could be extended to the forms and occasions of scientific discourse: during the cold fusion controversy, the most fundamental requirement of a scientist was strategically posited to be his respect for the rules of scientific communication, namely talking only where and when a scientist is supposed to.

The eleventh commandment in the cold fusion controversy had become: 'thou shalt not hold a press conference'.[58]

Utah's fusion fuels heated debate. While scientists worldwide labor to verify or debunk claims of cold fusion, *controversy centers on how news of the coup was broken.*
                                        Title on *The Scientist*, 1 May 1989, my emphasis

The importance of ritual fulfilment of the communication rules was almost grotesquely highlighted on the occasion of Scaramuzzi's announcement: Scaramuzzi had agreed to call a press conference on condition that he could present his results to his colleagues first. Thus a 'helter-skelter' seminar was organized for that same day, with researchers from other Rome laboratories invited.[59] This may not be deviation *strictu sensu*, but it looks very much like it: the presentation to one's scientific peers becomes only a formal pre-condition that enables one to access legitimately the public arena, i.e. the level that really matters in such a case. Bertin and Vitale, the two Bologna physicists, cited as proof of their neutron production that it had been demonstrated on a television show:

We have seen them [the neutrons], we have even shown them on TV, at Mino Damato's programme.
                                        La Repubblica, 29 March 1989

'There are really two cold fusion controversies,' appropriately commented Marcel C. La Follette in early 1990, 'one is the technical debate over how to achieve and sustain a room temperature

61

fusion reaction. The other debate ... clearly shows how news about the research has been communicated, among scientists and by journalists.'[60]

However, the former controversy was gradually flattened on the latter by cold fusion critics.

The way the controversy was handled also provided opportunities to show the public that the 'scientific house' could clean itself by ruling out cold fusion as an 'isolated instance of individual illness',[61] banishing those responsible for it and thereby reaffirming the general well-being of the scientific establishment[62] and its related ability to eliminate heretical behaviour.[63]

Religious metaphors (e.g. heresy and orthodoxy, excommunication and inquisition) thus formed an ideal framework within which to read the issue:

> The 'holy war' of cold fusion. Orthodox, heretical and skeptics have convened to discuss and argue over the 'sun in a bottle' ... Just as during the Nicea Council, as in the discussions between early Christians on the nature of angels and on the divine substance of Christ, the debate on the Utah experiment is entering the realm of metaphysics and faith ... The Wise Men fly back home, without clear answers, divided between faith in heat, i.e. in the energy that mysteriously springs from a bottle, and the skepticism of the helium-4 party.
>
> La Repubblica, 27 April 1989

> More than a month has passed since Holy Thursday [day of the announcement], and still no fusion Passover is in sight.
>
> Il Corriere della Sera, 3 May 1989

> Nobody congratulates the prophets of nuclear fusion: 1557 chemists, gathered in L.A. with the enthusiasm of believers to see the skeptics finally converted by evidence, are disillusioned.
>
> Il Corriere della Sera, 11 May 1989

> Faxes have become the weapon in this war between religions fought by phoning xeroxes sent from one side of the US and of the world to the other ... The two heretics are visibly afraid, they deserve neither the sarcasm of the 'holy inquisitors' nor blind trust.
>
> La Repubblica, 11 May 1989

As was stated with another clearly religious metaphor: 'Be merciful to electrochemists as they know not what they do'.[64] After the Pons and Fleischmann affair, cold fusion is 'taboo', as a journalist declared in an article written in 1995 about a similar discovery claimed by three Italian physicists at the University of Siena – Sergio Focardi, Francesco Piantelli and Roberto Habel.[65]

At work here are the main mechanisms that Mary Douglas identifies as typical of a culture when it must preserve its integrity in the presence of ambiguous/anomalous events: strengthening of definitions of normality to exclude the event, the labelling of the event as 'monstrous' or 'dangerous', even the physical suppression of the event.[66]

The Italian media reported a joke played on Pons and Fleischmann at the University of Utah: somebody put a newspaper clip about their discovery on their laboratory noticeboard and glued to it a headline cut from the *National Enquirer* which read 'Baby born with wooden leg'.[67] Rubbia immediately warned the public about the dangers of Pons and Fleischmann's experiment:

> For such an amount of energy produced by nuclear fusion the neutron emission will kill us all. During the Manhattan project, a scientist did something whose consequences he could not know, because they were unknown at that time. The poor guy placed two pieces of plutonium next to each other on a table. This triggered a chain reaction of the same type as they were trying to make for the bomb . . . The scientist died two days later from the effects of the large number of neutrons he had been exposed to.
>
> *La Repubblica*, 28 March 1989

The message is clear: those who touch cold fusion, will die. Physical suppression was obviously envisaged only rhetorically, although in very strong terms: several articles (those published by *Nature*, the bulwark of scientific orthodoxy against the cold fusion heresy) presented themselves as 'obituaries' for cold fusion. When interviewed for the NOVA documentary *Confusion in a Jar*, John Maddox commented: 'Ah, I think that broadly speaking, [cold fusion] *it's dead, and it'll remain dead for a long, long time*'.[68]

> Caporetto[69] in Los Angeles for Pons and Fleischmann. *Slaughtered* by the physicists' criticisms ten days ago in Baltimore, Pons and Fleischmann were playing at home, last Monday, in front of the chemists.
>
> *Il Corriere della Sera*, 11 May 1989, my emphasis

In the same article, Nathan Lewis is said to have been 'quite pleased with his role as a "cold fusion killer"'. 'Some kind of monster of science', wrote physicist Eugene Mallove, 'had to be killed with a stake through its heart, lest it rise once more to cause trouble.'[70]

An important signal of the 'deconstruction' of Pons and Fleischmann and their discovery is to be found in the several cartoons and comic strips published in the popular press during the cold fusion story.[71] Humorous devices such as caricature, parody and 'unmasking' (this latter being the opposite of travesty) result in what Freud calls *Heraubsetzung*, the degradation of an object or individual.[72] Unmasking, especially, seems to be of relevance here since it is employed against 'someone who has seized dignity and authority through deception and these have to be taken from him in reality'; it therefore seeks to 'degrade something that was otherwise praised' and 'diminish the dignity of an individual by directing attention to the frailties that he shares with all humanity, but in particular the dependence of their mental functions on bodily needs'.[73]

Thus, the claim to 'purity' (i.e. to be dealing with science and truth, supposedly untouched by 'human' elements such as interest, error, insanity) by the advocates of cold fusion was ridiculed and their supposedly revolutionary object was cut down to size – portrayed as the result of unskilled cookery or alcohol abuse (Figures 3.8 and 3.9).

Several scientists commented on the original announcement as an early 'Fools' day joke' (remember the story began in late March), and Pons and Fleischmann were later described as slipping from the status of 'Nobel prize candidates' to 'the joke of the scientific community'.[74] 'The general opinion of scientists around the country is that [cold fusion] is all a joke, and it's terribly funny that people should do any work on it, because it was a gigantic mistake, which was made by two fine fellows in Utah. It's all finished now and we can look back at those times and laugh', was John Bockris' conclusion at a meeting of chemists in 1990.[75]

The following piece of doggerel was composed by Stanford physicist Walter Meyerhof:

> Tens of millions of dollars at stake, dear brother,
> Because some scientists put a thermometer at one place and not another.[76]

Although Meyerhof's couplet was originally intended to lampoon the temperature measurements taken by his colleague Robert Huggins, it was widely quoted by newspapers as referring to Pons and Fleischmann or even to cold fusion believers as a whole. Some doctoral students of the Department of Physics, University of Parma, wrote a fake letter signed by the Italian nineteenth century scientist Macedonio Melloni, describing an experiment very similar to the cold fusion one.

These comics and jokes embody what I earlier sought to describe as the essence of the deconstructive process with regard to cold fusion: the public level was used to invade its *backstage* privacy,[77] thereby exposing that more contingent dimension of scientific activity usually concealed from the public.

Figure 3.8 'You're right … a bunch of money grabbing physicists and chemists do generate more heat than fusion'

Source: Ogden Standard Examiner, 4 May 1989, reproduced with permission

Figure 3.9 '. . . and if you think Utah fusion is impossible, just try getting a *drink*
there . . .'

Source: The Salt Lake Tribune, 1 May 1989, © Pat Bagley, *The Salt Lake Tribune*, 1989,
reproduced with permission

If you examine any scientific episode in detail, reconstruct what
the scientists did on a particular occasion, and re-narrate the story
in a particular way – in what I call the 'bumbling boffin narra-
tion', such that the scientists appear to be incompetent and not
fully in control of what they did – then, of course, that bit of
science starts to fall apart. It looks more like everyday life, subject
to the fables and foibles of everyday life.[78]

To put it in Goffmanian terms, a process of downkeying and delamina-
tion of the reference frame occurred, from the world of intellectual activity
down to a 'joke' dimension or even to primary frameworks such as the
natural and the social domain.[79] Comparison here is again the key element.
Cold fusion research was contrasted with an idealized *frontstage*, i.e. the
shiny, glazed and bold layer of scientific consensual and disinterested performance usually projected to the public eye. It was thus denied citizenship
of this unsullied realm and instead likened by analogies, metaphors and
related discursive devices, to non-scientific practices.[80] 'Knowledge about
nature is treated as rather like knowledge about art, politics, or the law'[81]

but also degraded to the level of other more mundane practices such as cookery.

The reduction of science to cookery, in particular, which is a classical tool in critical and degradation strategies of scientific facts,[82] often emerged with regard to cold fusion:

What's cooking in that test tube.
Title of one of Rubbia's articles on
La Repubblica, 29 March 1989

The whole story began when Pons and Fleischmann hastily called a press conference at the University of Utah, to announce to the press they had obtained cold nuclear fusion in a glass *as big as a cocktail shaker.*
Il Corriere della Sera, 6 April 1989,
my emphasis

I learn that physicists are divided into two largely mythologized families: the big science family, the billionaire physics of giant machines requiring budgets on a state scale; and the cellar physicists, those that with four tanks, two liras and a socket take out from the oven cold fusion, a cold fusion which everybody can make on his own kitchen balcony.
La Repubblica, 23 April 1989

This cold fusion ... makes us think of cream and chocolate ice cream cone ... It may be the discovery of the century, or of the whole history of mankind, but this is why it is so nice to think of it in a household context. Titanium? They sell it at Crocetta's market! Deuterium? Tuscany farmers undersell it! There is a smell of ratatouille to this story, just as if experiment after experiment one could obtain cold fusion using aubergines, carrots, and some basil.
La Stampa, 23 April 1989

One month ago it was a mythical dream and now everybody cooks it, like a humdrum *risotto* ... Quite understandable: if mothers jealously hand the recipes for nocino macaroni pie down to their daughters, why be surprised about this race for patents that are worth billions?
Il Corriere della Sera, 21 April 1989

As failures to replicate the experiment multiplied, a scientific journalist noted:

67

Fusion is not like whipped cream, which rises or does not rise for reasons unknown to the cook.

La Stampa, 27 April 1989

Pons and Fleischmann were eventually accused of 'having simply warmed up old soup' with reference to a similar discovery announced in the early decades of the century by the German inventor Johan Bodereiner.

The two Utah researchers had laid themselves open to application of the cookery metaphor when, in the first days of the affair, they had told journalists about their having begun experiments in Pons' kitchen:

We were so enthusiastic about it that we decided to try it in the kitchen of my house.

Il Sole 24 Ore, 25 March 1989

So we decided to dive into this adventure, beginning immediately in my kitchen.

La Repubblica, 25 March 1989

How is it possible to obtain in a domestic kitchen, using a 'child's chemistry set', paying out of one's own pockets, a result that the best and most highly paid brains in the world have been frantically searching for since the '50s with billion-dollar investments?

L'Unità, 25 March 1989

Legend has it that, during the decisive meeting at Pons's house in Salt Lake City, a bottle of Jack Daniel bourbon whisky was passed around a number of times, acting as a catalyst.

Il Corriere della Sera, 28 March 1989

At the time of the Los Angeles meeting, when scepticism already largely prevailed, Fleischmann explained his unwillingness to provide complete details: 'A good cook never reveals all the ingredients he has used' (*La Repubblica*, 11 May 1989).

It should be stressed that, although this excommunication and ritualized degradation was carried out in public, the boundary between the 'right' type of public involvement in the scientific debate (as passive spectators) and the 'wrong' type of involvement (i.e. as active participants) was also strategically reaffirmed.

In general, the whole process of deconstruction by the progressive extension of the boundaries at stake had to be accompanied and reinforced by the redefinition of another boundary, that between science and the public. Only when the public has been driven back outside the borders of the scientific discussion, can the distinction no longer be drawn in terms of 'right theories' and 'wrong theories', but rather in terms of scientists and non-scientists. 'Ironically, the public seem to be insiders, expected to agree with the verdict on cold fusion, and yet the public are excluded from science, told not to interfere with science policy.'[83]

That the boundary between the two types of participation was displaced *ad hoc* according to the specific needs and situations is confirmed, for instance, by the different reactions of different groups of scientists to the closed NSF-EPRI workshop of late 1989. On 16–18 October 1989, a workshop on 'Anomalous effects in deuterated materials' was organized in Washington under the patronage of the National Science Foundation and EPRI (the Electric Power Research Institute). It was a closed meeting, whose participants (including Stanley Pons, Martin Fleischmann, Steven Jones, Nathan Lewis and John Bockris) were admitted on condition that they would not make announcements to the press. During the meeting, experimental results were presented which purported to be evidence for cold fusion, and the general conclusion of the workshop was favourable to continuation of research on the subject. The President of the American Physical Society, James H. Kruhmnsl, expressed his concern to Mary L. Good, chair of the National Science Board:

> The APS society has consistently affirmed its support of the unfettered communication of all unclassified scientific ideas and knowledge, and we are heartened that the NSB has also taken a strong position by adopting the eloquent Report of the NSB committee on the openness of scientific communication. We recognize, of course, that there are certain circumstances under which the NSF quite properly operates behind closed doors. We would therefore be grateful if the NSB could examine the circumstances surrounding the NSF sponsorship of the meeting on 'Anomalous effects in deuterated materials' and inform us of the Board's findings prior to the November meeting of our council.[84]

In response to this letter, Eric Bloch, director of the National Science Foundation, wrote:

> The idea [of limiting discussions with the press until the official press conference] was to discourage publicizing conclusions before the issues were discussed. Also, in keeping with normal scientific etiquette, the workshop participants themselves agreed not to discuss openly each other's work until that work had been subject to the peer review process and accepted for publication.[85]

At this point in the controversy, control over the public level had already been regained by the cold fusion critics who wanted the issue to remain public until its deconstruction and the related sentencing of the guilty had taken place. Thus the initial attitudes to 'deviation' or 'making science in public' were clearly reversed: while the sceptics were now ready to play with it, cold fusion advocates sensed that it was a source of danger. In March 1990, when the first annual conference on Cold Fusion was held at Utah University, Pons and Fleischmann declined to answer questions from journalists.[86] Nobody, on the other hand, blamed the CalTech scientists for using press conferences at the time of the Baltimore meeting to continue their attack on the two Utah scientists.[87]

As the Utah University research manager Ted Brophy pointed out, 'If Pons and Fleischmann have made mistakes, they will publicly acknowledge them. But up to now not one of their critics has dared to publish his criticisms officially. Everybody prefers to hold press conferences, just as we have been accused of doing' (*La Repubblica*, 4 May 1989).

In and out of the public level

The scientific fact known as 'cold fusion' was first created and later substantially dissolved by deviation to the level of public communication. Pons and Fleischmann were obliged to bring their discovery into the public forum because otherwise it would have had little chances of receiving attention. Despite their personal good reputation, the peculiar and quite unconventional nature of their work (in terms of approach and results) would obviously have hampered its reception for scientific discussion and attempts at replication. Moreover, the findings of Pons and Fleischmann, *as chemists*, would have been difficult to accept on a topic such as fusion, which has traditionally been the province of the *physics community* – arguably one of the most powerful professional groups in science today. When the science reporter of the *Wall Street Journal*, Jerry Bishop, was informed by Pamela Bogle, the information officer of Utah University, that a conference on cold fusion was scheduled to take place on 23 March and was given a preview of the announcement, he asked some physicists he knew at M.I.T. what they would have thought if someone announced cold fusion. 'I'd be very excited', one of them replied. 'What if it went on for more than one second?' 'Then I'd be very suspicious.' 'What if it went on for 100 hours?' 'That's ridiculous.'[88]

Given the 'boundary nature' of their object, Pons and Fleischmann had to speak simultaneously to different categories of scientific practitioners within science (not just physicists or chemists, but internal categories like nuclear physicists and plasma physicists, electrochemists, and so on) as well as to research managers, policy makers, businessmen and the general public. It may be argued that, in their awareness of the difficulties awaiting them when they submitted their results to the scientific community (as outsiders to the field, as diverting from traditional approaches to the problem, as having not fully clear results), they tried to shift the discussion to a 'broader' context where their results would appear more attractive (e.g. as home-made creative cheap science versus bureaucratic, expensive science), while leaving technical aspects (which they were unwilling or unable to publicize) unaddressed. Here we find a quite peculiar effect that arises when scientific issues are turned to the public. Turning to the public only *apparently* leads to 'more' information and communication openness. In actual fact, by virtue of the selective processes governing access to such a forum, it serves to exclude arguments and actors from the scientific debate.[89] The public level also promised to reward Pons and Fleischmann by ratifying their priority over the discovery, given their ongoing quarrel with Jones.

However, once in the public arena, cold fusion as a boundary object was not sufficiently resilient to counteract the enormous weight of the institutions, visible scientists and experimental machinery that attacked it. Especially in Italy, cold fusion enjoyed public confidence for a very brief span of time, around mid-April; confidence driven by some sort of nationalistic aspiration invested in the work of Scaramuzzi and other Italian physicists. As to the rest, the public level of communication was largely dominated by cold fusion critics, most notably by the high energy physicists, who used it to set the issue at the specialist level as well.

Under such pressure, the internal boundary of scientific controversy was overwhelmed – in the first place by the disciplinary boundary chemistry–physics, and then by a thicker, and therefore more publicly visible, boundary: that which separates science from non-science, the good scientists from the quacks. Rubbia himself summed up this boundary shift very well when he introduced Fleischmann's lecture at CERN and he apparently committed a Freudian *lapsus*:

> 'This man is not a scientist, but a chemist', thundered Rubbia, provoking hilarity among the participants. And then he immediately corrected himself: 'He is not a physicist, he is a chemist.'
> *Il Corriere della Sera*, 1 April 1989

By placing appropriate emphasis on the formal misconduct of its supporters, the critics of cold fusion pushed it across the borders of science and confined it to the realm of non-science. Thus the costs of 'hanging out the dirty laundry for all to see'[90] to the public credibility of scientists were minimized and internal solidarity was reinforced by placing the source of all troubles outside the borders of science. As soon as such task was accomplished and those responsible for the 'contamination'[91] of scientific orthodoxy had been publicly marginalized, degraded and excommunicated,[92] the issue could be removed from the public forum.

This was achieved mainly by disentangling the scientific dimension from the public dimension with which it had originally been merged by Pons and Fleischmann's initial announcement, and by information exchanges among researchers performed at the public level. The public level was used to remove the scientific issue from the public debate itself, thereby remitting the evaluation of the claim to the closed circles of specialist discourse. There it could be more easily settled in the terms preferred by those who dominate such discourse (i.e. high energy physicists) without interference by non-scientific actors.

Thus, deviation was 'neutralized', and popularization was re-established as the unidirectional, uncontroversial, science-oriented, top-down flow of communication that is described by the continuity models, being almost entirely restricted to the procedural shell of scientific practice (the human, social, anecdotal dimension) without affecting the core scientific debate. The public and scientific dimensions were artificially separated and the issue split into two facets: the public (journalistic) facet and the scientific one.

'Dear *Horizon* viewer, cold fusion is "the biggest science story" of the century.' That statement is only true if one uses the journalistic sense of big story and measures size in terms of column inches and seconds of airtime. There seems to be every likelihood that, viewed from a purely scientific standpoint, it will turn out to be a very small story.'[93] The public stage was eventually left, and media actors were allowed to play with only the peripheral and more pictoresque elements of the object cold fusion.[94]

The removal of the scientific problem from public debate was thus finally complete: 'science is reduced to a rhetorical resource to construct a credible story' and can serve at the same time as an 'interpretative black-box for uncontested use'.[95] Cold fusion in its turn was employed as a metaphor to elucidate non-scientific issues: for example, an article in the *Money* weekly supplement of *Il Corriere della Sera* (24 March 1989) talked about 'hot fusions' with regard to the agreement between the publishing groups Mondadori and L'Espresso (the page featured a drawing of an electrolytic cell). Later, an advertisement for a new bank (the Banca di Roma) resulting from the merger of two smaller ones appeared in the same newspaper claiming, 'This fusion will set free a gigantic energy' (Figure 3.10). In the USA, a press release to launch the new perfume *Kelvin* presented it as: 'Absolutely Cool', created by Bruno Klodandhauer 'who allegedly stumbled upon the first truly unisex fragrance in his rush to verify the Fleischmann and Pons cold fusion experiments'.[96]

The ways of deconstruction

It is all too tempting to describe the public construction of cold fusion and (especially) its public deconstruction as a rational and preorganized plan devised first by Utah researchers and later by their critics. However, this description fails to do justice to the complex array of actions and reactions, commitments and negotiations that made up these processes. It is

Figure 3.10 'This fusion will set free a gigantic energy'

Source: Banca di Roma, from *Il Corriere della Sera*, 3 July 1992, reproduced with permission

important to stress that cold fusion deconstruction was achieved also because the main aims and strategies pursued by its critics largely coincided with newsmaking practices and media needs with regard to science issues. Apart from the (clearly important) dominant position in terms of visibility and authority enjoyed by its critics in the public arena (in the Italian public arena in particular), this also applies to the 'personalization' of the issue – held to be a quite typical feature of public communication of science[97] – which made it possible to collapse the deconstruction of cold fusion with Pons and Fleischmann's excommunication. Another important element, one I have already mentioned, was the tendency by the media to present scientific controversies as balanced between pairs of extreme positions by emphasizing oppositions such as chemists versus physicists, heat versus neutrons, the good guys versus the bad guys. Finally, the elimination of cold fusion as an object of public debate found a perfect correspondence in the tendency of the public perception to remain agnostic with regard to scientific matters, and doing no more than picking 'nice' elements from them in terms of metaphors, stories, and characters. Although such exceptional deviation situations may open the scientific black-box to public scrutiny and have the public itself contribute to shape the scientific fact, these situations cannot last for very long: the state of equilibrium is still to be found in the popularization pattern. 'One of the problems the fusioneers have is that their experiments last far longer than the media's attention span' (*The Economist*, 30 September 1989). Since this work is focused primarily on the role of scientists in the public communication of science, I shall not dwell further on this topic, turning instead to another aspect which seems crucial to proper understanding of the cold fusion affair.

In previous pages I have tried to show that massive effort was devoted to public deconstruction of cold fusion. Exemplifying the endeavour to cancel the very existence of cold fusion, was *Nature*'s mention of cold fusion as a 'non-event of 1989'[98] and the failure of The American Institute of Physics to mention it in the 1989 edition of its annual publication *Physics News*. However, all of these efforts did not straightforwardly reduce the cold fusion fact to a zero, non-existent status; therefore, the 'deconstruction' of the scientific fact known as cold fusion is to be understood as a matter of degree and not in absolutist terms. If we were to plot the cold fusion fact in a two-dimensional space with its existence as a matter of degree on one axis and a time scale on the other, what we would presumably see is the fact gradually approaching zero but never entirely disappearing. As I have mentioned, cold fusion is still cautiously practised and discussed in restricted communicative forums: an international Cold Fusion conference is still held approximately once a year and several journals entirely devoted to cold fusion research are published at the time of writing.[99]

Moreover, although one clearly prevailed in the early part of the story and the other one in the later stage, the two processes of construction and deconstruction were ongoing from the beginning.[100] Even at the outset, when newspapers reported the announcement on their front pages, the cold fusion object was not accepted at face value but accompanied by the sceptical comments and criticisms of several scientists. With one of those ironies that seemingly mark the existence of scientific issues at the public level throughout different media and communicative situations,[101] the same elements used to bring cold fusion into the public arena were also used to degrade it. I have given some examples: for instance, the presentation of cold fusion as a 'cheap', 'home-made' discovery, put together in a kitchen lab as a new and appetizing dish, clearly appealed to the public's distrust and suspicion of huge and costly research institutions. A domestic, creative type of science was set against the awesome machines run by men in white coats. But this proximity to 'everyday life' settings gradually compromised the status itself of cold fusion as a scientific fact; cookery became synonymous with sloppiness and the isolated genius became the Frankenstein-like 'mad professor':

> A sorcerer's apprentice, [Fleischmann] is victim of the machine he himself as awakened.
>
> *Il Corriere della Sera*, 25 April 1989

An approach to public communication of science in cases of deviation such as the one developed here requires, among other things, forgoing the idea that negotiation at the public level – however much it may be dominated by a science part and successful in influencing the specialist discussion – will result in the clear-cut closure of controversies. I have already emphasized that a theory or a result may enjoy different statuses at different levels of scientific communication. For instance, cold fusion may be currently denied at the specialist level, moderately taken into account at the inter-specialist levels, neglected at the pedagogic level and occasionally mentioned (mainly as a 'curious story') at the public level. Compared to the other levels, moreover, the public level is characterized by the greatest variety and dispersion of discourse forums as well as by the utmost heterogeneity of its participant actors. Which means that it is rather unlikely that a scientific fact will be granted homogeneous and consistent status throughout the level.

> The two scientific subcultures of cold fusion and anti-cold fusion are now firmly in place, so that one can have personal preferences and cultural meanings confirmed without having to consider counter-arguments. Even if the subculture of cold fusion is much more modest than that of the sceptics, who have conquered most of mainstream science, it still possesses enough resources to nurture hope for those who want hope nurtured.[102]

The very thought of a scientific fact or theory as a homogeneous object, a 'black box' whose status (e.g. in terms of acceptance or denial, success or failure) can be at any point assessed by insiders and outsiders, clearly makes sense only with regard to those few facts whose contours have been steadily reinforced by diachronic and synchronic sedimentation (i.e. through historical trajectories in time and standard popularization trajectories across communication levels). It surely does not make much sense regarding 'boundary objects' such as cold fusion, which have their core existence shaped and negotiated within the turbulence of public discourse. It may not be appealing or even possible, at a certain point, to give a 'yes/no' categorization to these objects simply because *per se* they no longer exist in the public sphere, having been reduced to single pieces (e.g. metaphors, images, personalities) or recontextualized in broader thematic areas. In a later chapter I shall try to provide a clearer idea of this process, showing how even an authoritatively sponsored scientific 'fact' may be selectively appropriated at the public level.

This proves once again that it is impossible to separate the public side of cold fusion from its scientific side, a split that only the cold fusion sceptics could employ as a strategic rhetorical resource by cold fusion sceptics. For all scientists, 'cold fusion' today inevitably evokes much more than a wrong, dead or simply bizarre hypothesis: it is vested with an 'aura' (an 'ethical cloud' as Krumhnsl would say)[103] of danger resulting more from its public vicissitudes than from any thorough critique of it in ordinary scientific settings; an aura that will inevitably condition its discussion in every forum for many years to come, however specialized and 'purely scientific' such discussion may claim to be. On the one hand, this aura has evident effects in terms of resistance to cold fusion claims in the future.

> It is now virtually impossible to publish positive results in certain journals because the editors or their chosen peer reviewers are convinced that the effect is bogus. This creates a catch-22: the journals will not accept papers until more papers published in such journals show evidence for the effect.[104]

On the other hand, however, it may be suggested that the public exposure and negotiation of cold fusion will have more subtle effects on core scientific practice: for instance in the already suggested 'agenda setting' terms. Put very simply, there are very few scientific facts that are familiar (as cold fusion is) to such a wide variety of scientific fields and communities. In 1992, in the preface to his university thesis *Study of the Anomalous Nuclear Effects in Solid-Deuterium Systems*, Japanese student Taku Ishida grounded his choice of the topic in the curiosity aroused in him by the public resonance of the Pons and Fleischmann story.[105]

One of the lessons to be learned from the cold fusion story is that just as it is hard to bring a scientific fact into being by resorting to the public level, it is equally difficult – no matter how powerful a party may be – to take complete control of this level and use it to disintegrate the fact. As Nate Hoffmann of California Technology Institute said: 'You can't kill cold fusion by an edict in a newspaper.'[106]

APPENDICES

Appendix 3.A: data

General information

Number of articles in various newspapers

La Repubblica	45
Il Corriere della Sera	55
La Stampa	29
L'Unità	48
Il Sole 24 Ore	18
L'Osservatore Romano	2
Total	197

Distribution of the articles across the four sub-periods

24–31 March	73
1–8 April	24
9–17 April	32
18–30 April	68

Placement in the newspaper

Front page	43
National news section	74
International news section	5
Science section	40
Entire page on cold fusion	31
Other	4

Type of article

Story	137
Interview	20
Box	7
Short news	33

Genre of article

National news	63
International news	49
Culture	3

Science	73
Economics	9

Size of article (columns)

Number of columns	Number of articles
1	40
2	32
3	24
4	32
5	31
6	24
7	11
8	0
9	3

Elements emphasized by title

Scientific	117
Technological	14
Economic	20
Political	7
Ethical	10
Religious	5
Everyday life elements	14
Other	10

Relevance of title to text

Non-relevant	26
Relevant unessential	97
Relevant useful	57
Relevant essential	17

Iconography

Type of image

Photography	53
Drawing	17
Graph	9
Cartoon	1
No image	117

Relevance of image to text

Non-relevant	15
Relevant unessential	44
Relevant useful	15
Relevant essential	6

Relevance of image to title

Non-relevant	35
Relevant unessential	28
Relevant useful	11
Relevant essential	4

Subject of image

Researchers at work	6
Press conference	7
Researchers (not working)	28
Politicians	4
Research institution managers	1
Entrepreneurs	1
Experimental machinery	20
Applicative machinery	5

Author of article

Journalist	158
Researcher	29
Philosopher of science	6
Other intellectual	2
Unidentified	2

Representation of various categories in articles

Category	Number of articles in which it is present
Chemist	115
Physicist	168
Manager of research institutions	75
Politician	30
Philosopher of science	6
Other intellectual	2
Businessman	18

Dominant frame

Scientific	144
Technological	9
Economic	25
Political	3
Ethical	9
Unspecified	7

Dominant national context in article

Italy	71
United States	26
United Kingdom	6
Japan	1
Other countries	5
Generic (International Scientific Community)	87
None	1

Representation of the scientific fact

Phases portrayed in article

Phase	Number of articles in which it is present
Research stages prior to discovery	34
Moment of discovery	53
Announcement of discovery	47
Diffusion of discovery	39
Possible applications	63
Real applications	5

Appendix 3.B: some metaphors and analogies in cold fusion articles

Metaphors from the natural sciences

The earth's heart	Blossoming of neutrons
Muons as fat electrons	Migration of ions
Hunger for energy	Theories like dinosaurs
Swarms of muons	

Metaphors from technology

Palladium as pump absorbing deuterium
Tunnel is formed within dueton barriers
Palladium as a swamp

Metaphors from economics

Energetic balance
Fusion 'made in Italy'

Metaphors from everyday life

Deuterium as a guest
Metals eating hydrogen
Heavy water
Atoms = rubber balls or
    Christmas tree balls
Fathers of fusion
Magnetic bottles
Atoms as parents
Atoms married
Cosmic silence

Deuterons trapped
Wall of energy
Muon's work
Nuclei as drops of water
Home-made fusion
Nuclear Owen
Neutrons leaving their signature
Palladium 'devourer'
Life of metals
Noble and plebeian metals

Other

Thriller (the scientific intrigue)
Mystery (the scientific problem)
Cheated detectors
Laboratory-bunker

Analogies

Cold fusion discovery = revolution like that of superconductors
Cold fusion = fraud like polywater
Cold fusion = case of public interest in science as recombinant DNA
Pons and Fleischmann machinery similar to a pocket battery or a car battery
Palladium similar to platinum

A PUBLIC EXPLOSION: BIG BANG THEORY IN THE UK DAILY PRESS

> Imagine doing just what the Big Bang did/
> The whole world/ Knew it was loaded
> Wave bye-bye 'cause it ain't never coming down now
>> The Breeders, 'I just wanna get along',
>> Last Splash, 4AD Records, 1993

A public explosion

At 10 a.m. on Thursday, 23 April 1992, David Whitehouse of BBC Radio news informed his listeners that a NASA satellite – the COBE, Cosmic Background Explorer – had detected 'ripples' in the cosmic background radiation which provided the conclusive evidence that the universe began with the explosion known as the Big Bang.

The following morning all the British 'quality' newspapers (the *Independent, The Times,* the *Guardian* and the *Daily Telegraph*), as well as some tabloids, featured the COBE story on their front pages. For several weeks, the story was one of the hottest items in the news, at least in the English media, becoming the subject of editorials, comment and humorous pieces.[107] George Smoot, the physicist in charge of the COBE team, was offered several million dollars to write a book about the discovery.[108] Wide publicity was given to Smoot's remark that he and his colleagues had found the oldest and largest structures ever seen in the early universe, 'primordial seeds of modern-day structures such as galaxies, clusters of galaxies . . . if you are religious is like seeing God'.[109] These as well as other comments by Stephen Hawking,[110] who claimed this was 'the discovery of the century if not of all time', and by cosmologist Michael Turner ('they have found the Holy Grail of cosmology') doubtlessly attracted public interest to the discovery and fuelled a more general debate on science, religion and their mutual relations in the human quest for truth.

So, what was all the fuss about? Just another example of 'sensational' or 'spectacular' science as in the cold fusion case? Not really. Although Smoot and his staff skilfully managed their access to the public arena through press releases and press conferences from the earliest days of the COBE enterprise, nobody ever charged them with fraud or blamed them for hastily seeking publicity before the scientific community had had time to carefully review their findings.[111] Why, then, did a rather esoteric, abstract finding with no apparent practical implications have such a big impact in the media?

Explanations have been proposed that emphasize the role of media practices and the element of public resonance.[112] According to such explanations, the media, and the British media in particular, had already been 'sensitized' to the issue by ongoing debates about science and its achievements. While acknowledging the importance of these factors, it can be easily argued that in this perspective the role of scientists in making science public is largely left aside as unproblematic.

What I offer here is an attempt to focus on the other side of the process. What were the conditions that made it possible and appealing for the COBE scientists to go public and what were the consequences for the scientific debate? Why were the COBE scientists not sanctioned for 'going public' as Pons and Fleischmann had been? In other words, how was science actually 'made in public' in this case?

A brief history of the universe[113]

Until the 1920s, despite the changes introduced by Einstein's theories, the predominant scientific picture of the universe was that of a static, immutable entity. Between 1922 and 1924, the Russian mathematician Aleksandr Fridman proposed the first non-static solutions of Einstein's general relativity equations. In 1927 Georges Lemaître, a Belgian mathematician and Catholic priest, hypothesized that the universe may have resulted from the gradual expansion of an original 'cosmic egg', a primeval atom (*atome primitif*) which divided itself into smaller and smaller atoms by virtue of a powerful radioactive process. These ideas, however, were either strongly criticized or entirely ignored by the most visible scientists of the time, including Einstein, who promptly rejected Fridman's theory and always refused to discuss Lemaître's model. It took some time for these ideas to be coupled with the observations made by Edwin Hubble, the American astronomer who discovered in 1929 that the other galaxies are moving away from our galaxy at a speed that is directly proportional to their distance. This became known as Hubble's law, and its constant of proportionality is accordingly known as Hubble's constant, H_0. Nevertheless in 1931, in a speech to the Mathematical Association in Cambridge, Arthur Eddington expressed his 'philosophical repugnance' toward the very notion of a beginning of the universe.[114] It was only in the late 1940s that George Gamow and his colleagues further elaborated on the idea by devising a cosmic 'singularity', i.e. a situation characterized by an extreme density, exceptionally high temperature and zero dimension that triggered the expansion process by its explosion.

Interestingly, the label 'Big Bang' was coined in 1950 by English astronomer Fred Hoyle during his radio programme 'The Nature of the Universe', and it was originally intended to ridicule the idea that the universe could originate from a primordial explosion. Nevertheless, 'Big Bang' became the standard term to identify this model of the universe's origin and expansion, a model which met with increasing success in the following years. In 1948 Hoyle himself, together with two Austrian refugees, Thomas Gold and Hermann Bondi, had elaborated an alternative model for the evolution of the universe, the so-called 'steady-state theory'. As their critics especially emphasized, these researchers had their idea for this model when watching the movie *The Dead of the Night*, which ends by reverting to its beginning. They thus conceived a model in which the universe has no beginning but remains generally the same forever, the continuous creation of new matter off-setting the dilution caused by expansion.

The experimental result often held to have settled the matter between the two models was the discovery of the cosmic background radiation by Arno Penzias and Robert Wilson in 1965. Working as researchers for the Bell Laboratories, Penzias and Wilson had had problems in eliminating a background noise from their reception of a satellite transmission. Later measurements led them to identify this noise as the radiation that – according to Gamow, Alpher and Herman – was a residual of the intense radiation produced by the initial Big Bang explosion. For this discovery Penzias and Wilson were awarded the Nobel prize, but only in 1978.

Problems nonetheless remained with the model. In particular, it was difficult to explain the regularity observable in the universe. Since light (and therefore all other types of 'information') would not have had time to travel from one region to another of the forming universe, how did these regions all end up with the same temperature and expansion rate? In 1981 an American physicist, Alan Guth, proposed a solution to accommodate these and other difficulties: the idea of an 'inflationary' universe. In its very first phase, the universe passed through a period of accelerated expansion, which allows us to conceive of an original region of such a small size that light would have been able to cross it in the time available. The inflationary theory, however, required gravity to be negative within the short span of accelerated expansion; an idea that was strange in the 1960s, but which has become acceptable in the last two decades due to the work of particle physicists. Since 1979, the inflationary model has stimulated the efforts of scholars from different disciplines. It has been further developed by hypothesizing, like Linde in 1983 for instance, a chaotic inflationary universe (with the inflation process being potentially different in different regions of the growing universe).

COBE takes off

According to the predictions made by Big Bang theorists, Cosmic Background Radiation (CBR) should have a bell-shaped curve as its spectrum – typical of an electro-magnetic radiation. Extensive efforts have therefore been devoted to obtaining accurate measurements of the CBR.

In 1987, a group of researchers from the University of California at Berkeley and from the University of Nagoya (Japan) used an orbiting spectrometer for this purpose. The instrument detected a background radiation some-what different from that expected, and which exhibited a number of spectral distortions. Physicists and astronomers wrestled with assorted interpreta-tions of this result until 1989, when NASA launched a satellite named COBE (Cosmic Background Explorer). The launch had been planned since 1974, and its aim was to measure the spectrum of CBR without interfer-ence from the earth's atmosphere.

The launch was announced at a press conference on 17 November 1989. Larry Caroff from NASA stated that COBE and other planned space obser-vatories were going 'to provide us with an unprecedented, unbelievable view of the universe'.[115] More cautiously, scientist John Maher said that he was 'not expecting to overturn Big Bang theory with what we see, because it is a good theory and works well. However, we could get a big surprise'.[116]

The first results of the COBE enterprise were presented before the American Astronomical Society in January 1990. The CBR measurement was a reasonably good match with the theoretical graph for blackbody radiation. Thanks to this measurement, according to Smoot, 'the Big Bang was still on track'.[117] Thus, the CBR was homogeneous and therefore consis-tent with the expanding universe envisaged by the theory. However, it was *too* homogeneous, because COBE had failed to detect the expected 'ripples', fluctuations in radiation interpreted as the echoes of the initial perturba-tion that gave rise to the cosmos, its 'primordial seeds'.

It was only two years later that Smoot was able to announce to his colleagues and the general public that COBE had finally detected fluctua-tions in the microwave background radiation to the order of a few parts per million. On 23 April, at 8 a.m., he delivered a short communication at the American Astronomical Society in Washington. About four hours later, the result was presented to the media, and for the rest of the day Smoot and his partners had to satisfy the curiosity of journalists from all over the world.

More Big than Bang

What is the current status of the Big Bang model and what role have the COBE results played with regard to this status?

> Once almost everybody believed that the universe had been created several billions of years ago, in a gigantic explosion known as the big bang. This theory enjoyed its greatest popularity in the two decades between 1965 and 1985. In those years quite a few dissenting voices came either from theoretical scientists or from the general public, against the doctrine that Big Bang had really taken place.[118]

Until the second half of the 1980s, as Boslough suggests, criticism of the Big Bang model was almost entirely confined to scientists like Fred Hoyle, one of the original proponents of the steady state model. But by the end of that decade the situation was beginning to change. In 1988 Stephen Hawking, whose work with Roger Penrose helped to consolidate the model in the early 1970s, wrote in his bestseller *A Brief History of Time* that although everybody accepted now the hypothesis that the universe had begun with the singularity of Big Bang, he had, 'ironically', 'changed his mind' about it and was trying to persuade other physicists that there was actually no singularity at the beginning of the universe.[119]

About one year later, John Maddox, the influential editor of *Nature*, declared that 'The Big Bang is an over-simple view of how the universe began, and is unlikely to survive the decade ahead. In all respects, save that of convenience, it is thoroughly unsatisfactory. It is an effect whose cause cannot be identified or even discussed.'[120]

Various contributions have since appeared which both questioned the Big Bang model and reacted to these criticisms. Halton Arp, together with Fred Hoyle and other 'well known dissenters from the Big Bang'[121] wrote an article for *Nature* in 1991 in which they based their criticism on experimental results judged inconsistent with the model, namely exceedingly high values for the Hubble constant (implying that the age of the universe is rather younger than required by the Big Bang model) and COBE's initial failure to detect fluctuations. In that same year, physicist Eric J. Lerner published a book with the eloquent title *The Big Bang Never Happened*. Even the second COBE announcement, claiming that ripples had been detected in cosmic background radiation, did not seem to settle the matter. Continuing debate was prompted by new data gathered by the Hubble Space Telescope, and from which three different teams estimated the age of the universe at 8 billion years, which is much less than the known ages of some stars.

Today, while some claim that the COBE and related results lend further support to a model that was already well-founded, others seem more critical of such explanations. 'Big Bang not yet dead but in decline' was the title of a more recent article by John Maddox.

> The result, the third of its kind in under a year, makes a nonsense of the standard Big Bang view of how the universe began. But even those who were persuaded on other grounds that Big Bang is a fairy story, perhaps for no better reason than that it is 'too good to be true', had better conduct themselves with circumspection in the months ahead. . . . In short, the new measurements of H_0 [Hubble's constant] are not the death of the Big Bang, but merely a further sign of its fragility. . . . The minute it is suggested that these structures are so exceptional that they must

be survivors from an earlier stage in the evolution, the Big Bang will have given way to continuous creation. That will be a turn-up for the book.[122]

While some react bitterly to these attacks – 'I think the damn Big Bang model works', declares Allan Sandage of Carnegie Observatories in Pasadena[123] – others more cautiously claim that the Big Bang need not be straightforwardly accepted or discarded; rather, it should be integrated with additional theories such as inflationary models.[124] However, neither is there complete agreement even on the relation of inflationary models to the Big Bang model. Is inflation to be regarded as a further specification of the Big Bang or as a model alternative to it, as some of its leading theorists seem to suggest?[125] This problem gains considerably in interest when one considers the close relation between the COBE findings and the inflation approach. Some researchers have even questioned the idea that the existence of a Big Bang is the most crucial problem to investigate.[126]

One could conclude with Bradley E. Schaefer that simply 'there is no consensus out there'.[127] But it is probably worth emphasizing that establishing whether the Big Bang is still generally accepted by cosmologists is also made difficult by its blurred status: should it be regarded as a single, definite model or rather as a group of theories and models,[128] or as a general thought framework – a paradigm, in Kuhn's terminology – lying behind a number of different theories and data collections?[129]

Big Bang and the public

The Big Bang model – the idea of an enormous explosion as the starting point of the universe as we know it today – has been the dominant model used by the general public to understand the origin of the universe in the second half of this century. Moreover, in the 1950s and early 1960s, when consensus on the Big Bang was still far from being reached within the scientific community, the public played an evident role in establishing it as the leading explanation in cosmology.[130] The idea of a 'singularity', an instant creation burst, was far more appealing to common sense than any other model like Hoyle's steady-state theory.[131] It was also more easily reconciled with religious beliefs. In 1951, Pope Pius XII, after having been informed about the Big Bang hypothesis, proclaimed that it was in perfect accordance with the Christian idea of religious creation. 'True science to an ever increasing degree discovers God, as though God were waiting behind each door opened by science.'[132] In an address to the Pontifical Academy of Sciences, the Pope wrote: 'In fact, it seems that present-day science, with one sweeping step back across millions of centuries, has succeeded in bearing witness to that primordial "Fiat Lux" uttered at the moment when, along with matter, there burst forth from nothing a sea of light and radiation, while the particles of the chemical elements split and formed into millions of galaxies. . . . Hence, creation took place in time: therefore there is a Creator, therefore, God exists!'.[133] More recently, the scientist and theologian Stanley L. Jaki has forcefully argued in a number of books and articles against those researchers who still question the Big Bang by envisaging a steady and eternal universe. In fact, it is precisely the contingent dimension that the Big Bang gives to the universe that makes it possible to believe in Creation.[134] However, as early as 1991, Lerner noticed that 'while the Big Bang as a scientific theory is less and less supported by data, its prominence in our culture has increased'.[135] It should come as no surprise, therefore, to find that the public level was closely involved in the controversy over the Big Bang that ensued in recent years and which focused on the COBE story as one of its central issues.

Crisis, what crisis?

The term 'controversy', however, might not be appropriate to describe the treatment of the Big Bang–COBE story in the daily press. Although the COBE findings attracted considerable public attention, their principal effect was to reinforce public confidence in the Big Bang model. Despite some contrary statements by some researchers involved in the issue,[136] previous COBE results (even those which reported homogeneous radiation with no ripples) and other criticisms did not in fact generate public distrust or suspicion regarding the model.[137]

> To many people, the finding may seem less than earth shattering.
> *The Times*, 25 April 1992

> This discovery not only proves that the Big Bang took place – for there is still a minority of doubters . . .
> *Daily Telegraph*, 24 April 1992

> In a way, it would have been more exciting not to have found it.
> Jasper Wall, quoted in the
> *Daily Telegraph*, 25 April 1992

> A triumph for conservatism.
> Arnold Wolfendale, quoted in the
> *Daily Telegraph*, 25 April 1992

> The Big Bang theory was so well developed in other ways that it would have been more exciting, in one respect, if the small signals had not been present.
> *The Times*, 25 April 1992

Already in January, more than three months before the COBE announcement, a reviewer of Dennis Overbye's book *The Star Gazers who Wait and Measure: Lonely Hearts of the Cosmos* clearly stated this confidence:

> Today . . . the idea that everything began in a Big Bang has become part of our culture.
>
> *Independent*, 11 January 1992

> 'Even before the discovery in April by the COBE satellite,' wrote Adrian Berry in a harsh review of Lerner's book, 'the consensus of cosmologists was that the universe had a beginning in the form of a gigantic explosion, the Big Bang, which created space, time and matter.'
>
> *Daily Telegraph*, 9 May 1992

This is not to imply that the discovery was not generally held to be important, especially insofar as it elucidated the development of the universe after the Big Bang. The Big Bang model *per se*, however, was rarely discussed and rather taken as ascertained fact on which other reflections and debates could be built. Big Bang was also set as a zero reference point in time: a number of articles concerned themselves with what came before it and what is going to happen to our universe in the end (a Big Crunch?).

> Most astronomers cringe if you ask them what came before the Big Bang.
>
> *Independent*, 25 April 1992

> But this is not the end of the Big Bang story. Emboldened by this evidence that theories were right all along, astronomers are already speculating on what happened before the Big Bang . . . With the Big Bang theory itself on a secure foundation, it is questions like those that now provide scope for cosmological speculation, and which will make headline news in the years to come.
>
> John Gribbin, cosmologist, *The Times*, 26 April 1992

That the Big Bang concept was, so to speak, ready to be decontextualized and 'black-boxed' for different uses is evidenced by the number of occasions on which it was used to elucidate non-scientific issues. 'Prof. Hawking's Big Bang came in 1988,' ran an article on the English mathematician's huge success as a writer with his bestseller *A Brief History of Time*.[138] The defeat of the Labour party in the 9 April 1992 elections was described as a 'political Big Bang' while the deregulation of the securities market became a 'financial Big Bang'. There was a 'Big Bang' in the prison service and a 'Big Bang' in former Yugoslavia.

This widespread tendency to exploit the appeal of Big Bang was lampooned by Henry Cockburn in *The Times*:

'Clearly, the whole basis of the universe is devolution,' the Rev. Murdo McGurr, the hard-left minister of Letterbeg and Girnmore, told reporters last night. 'What we see in the universe is a metaphor for an assembly with tax-raising powers . . . What the scientists call Big Bang is the original multi-option referendum, even though it only lasted a fraction of a second. . . . Provost Willie McFouter, leader of the ruling Labour group of Dunfreeble Dunstable College, took a similar view. In a 564-page fax from the Seychelles . . . he claimed that the ever-expanding universe was a symbol of man's destiny to travel even farther afield. 'We are all atoms in transit,' he said . . . Sadie McClarty, the crusading Easterhouse grandmother, was more openly dismissive: 'Oarigins of the universe? A load o' bluidy havers! Whit'a that God tae dae wi' the price o' mince? See thae Scientists – they're a bunch of bluidy scanners.'

The Times, 26 April 1992

An interpretation of the COBE story might be the following: communication at the public level provided an opportunity to deal with the problems and the criticisms that the Big Bang paradigm was encountering at the specialist and interspecialist levels. As in other cases, the public level offered here a discursive forum with fewer constraints and controls in comparison with specialist ones. It was a forum in which the Big Bang was still supported as strongly resonating with broad cultural and religious explanations; even more important, a forum in which the Big Bang was still an issue capable of raising momentous questions (What came before the Big Bang? Who made the Big Bang happen? Will another Big Bang mark the end of the universe?). David Whitehouse from the BBC acutely argued that 'the COBE story made the splash it did because the scientific community needed the satellite's results to preserve a cherished theory'.[139]

One could elaborate on this argument by pointing out that this had to be coordinated with the exigencies and constraints of public discourse. In short, the general paradigm comprising a constellation of measurements, models and theories (e.g. Hubble constant, Dark Matter, Inflation in its original formulation) mobilized its most immediate and appealing image and linguistic label, Big Bang, to reactivate public support against the unbelievers.[140]

The COBE results, appropriately translated as Big Bang (which in turn is often synonymous with Creation and ultimately with God) provided an opportunity to strengthen and defend the boundaries of the paradigm. The Big Bang thus became a sort of metonym which played a pivotal role in anchoring the paradigm in public culture, thereby providing umbrella protection for all those elements that in specialist arenas were each subject to separate and detailed criticism.

Thus, the first similarities and differences with respect to another case of deviation – cold fusion. The similarities concern mainly the information role played by the public media for scientists, especially in the first phase of the story. Smoot's press conference urged scientists to interest themselves in the issue and to discuss the results of the COBE enterprise without an official publication to hand. As the British astronomer Michael Rowan Robinson explained in an article in the *Guardian*:

> Almost uniquely in the history of big discoveries, the first news reached the scientists via the Associated Press wire services ... scientists had to respond to journalists off the cuff, without knowing the details of the COBE announcement.
>
> *Guardian*, 1 May 1992

As to the principal difference, it has to do with the fact that cold fusion was a case of controversy conducted in public, where one party devoted its most intense efforts to restoring the issue to the specialist arena. The COBE story was instead a case of deviation to the public level as a source of consensus which would help settle a debate carried out at the specialist level or at least back up a position. This also explains why the COBE deviation was not blamed, and ultimately sanctioned, as happened in the cold fusion case: the distinction between 'proper' popularization and inappropriate spectacularization is itself a political resource available to scientific actors. Smoot, for instance, took great pains to present his 'turn to the public' as authorized, appropriate communication with the public by emphasizing 1) the quality of the media coverage, quite rarely acknowledged by scientists and 2) his substantially passive participation in the process, claiming that he was forced to communicate by media pressure.

> He had expected the scientific community would be excited. *He had not expected the public reaction. 'I walked round the corner and came into this exhibition hall. There was this row of TV cameras, and there were as many press people as there were scientists to hear my talk. Then I realised it was a little out of hand.'* ... He was plunged into a welter of questions, hyperbole, telephone calls and TV shows. *Oddly enough, he was understood. 'I was quite impressed by how well the press did in getting the point across.'* That may be because cosmologists are used to talking in grandiose terms and the press liked it. *It's amazing how well the press did cover it, particularly the British press.*
>
> *Guardian*, 12 May 1992, my emphasis

However, internal struggle around a paradigm was not the only discursive boundary dealt with in the public arena. Articles in the daily press treated COBE and Big Bang as representative of cosmology as a whole, and therefore presented the findings as validating the discipline's prestige and achievements.

> Cosmological theory, like the universe itself, develops slowly.
> *Independent*, 3 May 1992

Once again, we are dealing with a relatively young discipline that still lacks certain features of institutional recognition. There are not yet chairs in cosmology, nor it is possible for a graduate student to earn a Ph.D. in cosmology but only, for instance, in astrophysics, a sub-sector of astronomy. Researchers nevertheless define themselves as cosmologists in the media and are defined as such by journalists; their comments and articles trace the rather short history of their field from Hubble's discovery to COBE results.

> It is worth recalling the other great landmarks in 20th century cosmology: the discovery of the expansion of the universe by Edwin Hubble in 1929; the invention of the Hot Big Bang model by George Gamow in 1945; the discovery of the cosmic microwave background radiation by Arno Penzias and Bob Wilson in 1965; the explanation of the abundance of the primordial light elements, helium, deuterium and lithium by Bob Wagoner, Willy Fowler and Fred Hoyle; and the discovery of the motion of our galaxy through microwave background radiation in 1979 by George Smoot, David Wilkinson and colleagues at Berkeley and Princeton.
> Michael Rowan Robinson, *Guardian*, 1 May 1992

As I have already pointed out,[141] in this phase of disciplinary definition the level of public communication acquires particular significance in at least two senses.

First, because it enables the attraction and coordination of the converging approaches and interests of researchers from different fields. This would not be possible by means of sectorial and specialized communication alone (which would in any case have to be performed in other disciplinary contexts, the discipline still lacking its own institutional channels of communication). In the case of cosmology, for instance, it is important to address at once physicists, astronomers and mathematicians. Moreover, in this phase of 'institutional fluidity' the public stage is also used by these diversified specialists to negotiate their authority over a common subject such as the origin of the universe. This topic, originally 'owned' by astronomers, has been increasingly appropriated by physicists and mathematicians since the end of the nineteenth century. It is therefore not difficult to understand why astronomers hailed the COBE results as one of the most important discoveries ever: Smoot (an astronomer) was finally able to join Hawking (a mathematician) and Davies (a physicist) as a public guru of the universe.

Second, public communication mobilizes the public recognition and support crucially required to establish a discipline as such and thus obtaining such resources as funds, Ph.D. programmes, and chairs. It is therefore only an apparent paradox that cosmology's disciplinary identity appears as more well-defined and established in media accounts than it does in specialist discourses. Perhaps further discussion of the character of this presentation in public is required. By its nature, in fact, cosmology cannot legitimate its activity in terms of technical/economical achievements, as nuclear physics or physiology can. Cosmology makes no promise that it will benefit society in terms of cheaper welfare or enhanced physical well-being, and now that the Cold War is over neither can it offer opportunities to display political and military strength.

Instead, what cosmology can bring to the public arena is something more subtle and non-material, namely attempted answers to humanity's profoundest questions: where do we come from? What will become of us in the end? By claiming some ability to answer such questions, cosmology must not only appear in public as 'science' but (as publicly representing 'science') it must define its role with regard to other activities giving inter-pretation to the meaning of existence, namely religion and art.

This brings me to the third, most general, and perhaps most interesting, boundary at stake in the COBE issue: that between science and other practices – religion in the first place. Expressions such as the 'Holy Grail of cosmology', 'sign of creation', 'mystery of creation', 'message of creation', 'evidence of creation' and 'fingerprint of creation' employed by the researchers themselves to describe the COBE findings (recall the initial comment by Smoot, 'If you are religious, it's like seeing God,') highlight that the significance of such findings, and therefore, of cosmology, was projected well beyond their value in terms of confirming a scientific theory.

The Big Bang that launched creation.

Guardian, 16 June 1992

It is difficult to know what an appropriate reaction to such mind-expanding discoveries should be except to get down on one's knees in total humility and give thanks to God or Big Bang, or both.

Guardian, 24 April 1992

The first definitive evidence of the Creation has been discovered by astronomy.

Daily Telegraph, 24 April 1992

The scientists conducting the NASA experiment announced that they had found the unevennesses – loops and whorls and serrations that made up the fingerprint of Creation itself.

Guardian, 16 June 1992

The whole universe is sacred, from the Big Bang that began it to every particle of what he calls energy/matter.

Guardian, 25 April 1992

The most recent headlines about the Big Bang have brought physicists even closer to what Buddhists and other mystics have known all along; that all forms of life are connected and interdependent.

Guardian, 20 May 1992

Despite their readiness to incorporate and adjust scientific findings to religious beliefs, as shown by the Vatican's early acceptance of the Big Bang model in 1951,[142] religious readers and Church representatives were also careful to cut down science's aspirations to hegemonize Creation discourse evident in pieces such as the following:

The second verse of the Bible, that speaks of space at the beginning as being 'void' is therefore inaccurate. The great explosion some 15,000 million years did not emerge into empty space. It emerged into 'nothingness'.

Daily Telegraph, 25 April 1992

Berry and others quoted scientists claiming that inquiring into the causes of Big Bang itself or about what came before it was no more than a pointless 'unscientific' exercise.

'Sir,' a reader replied, 'Would you please point out to Adrian Berry that the Bible is accurate in its second verse. Mr Berry is inaccurate. . . . The Genesis account of creation does not deal with the creation of the matter, but the later-in-time action of taking a formless earth, and, in several stages, making it into a home for man and animal life. Not all scientists believe it wrong to talk about the "cause" of the Big Bang and where it came from. . . . Why does the universe reveal such order and harmony? Why are there transcendent laws ruling it? . . . The conclusion that there must be a supernatural lawgiver is confirmed by our improving understanding of the origin of the universe.

Daily Telegraph, 30 April 1992

Revd Bill Westwood, Bishop of Peterborough, declared to the *Daily Telegraph*:

94

This doesn't make any difference to God. If anything, it makes him even more amazing.

Daily Telegraph, 25 April 1992

The Revd Dr John Polkinghorne, a former professor of physics later ordained a priest, currently president of Queens' College in Cambridge and therefore a key actor in the debate, clearly restated the respective roles of science and religion:

Scientifically the result is very, very interesting. It helps to explain why the universe is so lumpy when it started out so smooth. Theologically, it's not very significant. We're concerned with *why* the universe began, not *how*. Our view is not greatly affected by this discovery. What's more important is the future of the universe. It's been known for a long time that it's facing a very dismal future. But Christians have never believed that our purpose is fulfilled only in this life. Our universe will have a destiny beyond its death.

Daily Telegraph, 25 April 1992, my emphasis

This 'division of labour', assigning to science the task of inquiring into the hows and to religion that of answering the whys, was an argumentative strategy frequently used on the religious side throughout the debate:

At bottom there is no argument between science and religion. Science is about what can or may be known or demonstrated: scientists have to leave God out of the equation.

Guardian, 24 April 1992

To my mind there is no conflict between science and religion. Rather, scientific discovery enhances theology. Science asks how things happen, theology asks why. Faith is not a matter of choosing between science and religion, of believing either in God the creator or the Big Bang ... It takes a two-eyed vision of religion and science to see the world as a whole ... Therefore religion has nothing to fear from science. Science liberates rather than constricts or conflicts with the Bible ... Our new knowledge of the beginnings of the universe fills a larger piece of the scientific jigsaw, but theology is concerned with the whole picture.

Sunday Times, 26 April 1992

The comforting point is that the cosmologists still have no answers. Each scientific step towards explaining the ultimate creation always leaves the ultimate questions wide open.

Daily Telegraph, 25 April 1992

If you're there, God, come back. New Big Bang theories about creation are seeing scientists again trying to deal with a Creator. But he is still moving in mysterious ways. And thanks to them, further away from us.

Guardian, 18 May 1992

If a creator God existed for the sake of big bang and then had no further role ... then the search for a relationship with God is a waste of time ... In my foolishness, I shall continue to prefer a faith I cannot entirely understand.

The Times, 3 August 1992

Was the touch-paper for the Big Bang lit by God? That is the sort of question the faithful are facing but the scientists, without knowing it, are having an even harder time. On the one hand, they are proclaiming the existence of a 'dark cold matter' while on the other refuting the existence of a light warm God. Science appears to be increasingly steeped in the devout acceptance of its own faith.

Guardian, 9 May 1992

Specific researchers involved in the controversy and scientists in general were labelled as 'high priests of scientism':

Physicists may be the high priests of reductionism, but nevertheless they conjure up in the name of God with surprising frequency.

The Times 7 May 1992

Much discussion, no longer restricted to the relationship between science and religion, turned into a general questioning of science's role in society. At a debate held at the London Institute of Education in May, which received extensive coverage in the daily press, novelist Fay Weldon 'accused scientists of the responsibility for the death of religion, asserting that belief in cosmological theories such as the Big Bang would leave mankind diminished and wretched' (*The Times*, 12 May 1992).

With our radio telescopes, listening to the faint echoes of the big bang ... we seem to be drawing ever closer to the final outer and inner extremities of existence. This leads science to the brink of asking the forbidden question: why? ... new science is invading the final stronghold of philosophy and faith, the first of the barriers to the final triumph of classical science.

The Times, 25 April 1992

Lewis Wolpert, a biologist who has achieved fame in recent years as a pugnacious advocate of the scientific enterprise against its alleged critics, including many historians and sociologists of science, strongly reacted to such attacks in a speech that was reported in its entirety by *The Times*. Quite interestingly, his defence was largely based on the aesthetic value of scientific experience:

> No less remarkable and beautiful has been the progress in physics, in areas such as cosmology, the Big Bang and the search for fundamental theories based on superstrings. I use the word beautiful intentionally ... understanding the principles in no way makes it less wonderful. But for Bryan Appleyard these ideas are profoundly depressing. He sees no beauty in science, enjoys no intellectual thrill as he understands it.
>
> *The Times*, 12 May 1992

Thus, science does not content itself with being just 'useful': it yields deep wonder and beauty just as religion and art do. In their book, Smoot and Davidson similarly remark:

> Cosmologists and artists have much in common: both seek beauty, one in the sky and the other on canvas or in stone. When a cosmologist perceives how the laws and principles of the cosmos begin to fit together, how they are intertwined, how they display a symmetry that ancient mythologies reserved for their gods – indeed, how they imply that the universe must be expanding, must be flat, must be all that it is, then he or she perceives pure, unadulterated beauty.
>
> Smoot and Davidson, 1993: 297

> The Cold Dark Matter theory is a very beautiful one.
>
> Astronomer Michael Rowan Robinson in the *Independent*, 24 April 1992

> 'I have an aesthetic bias against the Big Bang', reacted in turn Sir Fred Hoyle to the COBE announcement.
>
> *Daily Telegraph*, 11 May 1992

Cosmology therefore attempts to ground its legitimation on its cultural relevance at large:

> 'It is now very difficult', lamented physicist Joe Schwartz, 'for us to understand and experience science in the same way we see other aspects of our culture – music, writing, poetry, architecture; cultural

endeavours we engage with and to which we bring strong aesthetic and emotional responses.'

Guardian, 13 June 1992

'I have sacrificed a lot to science,' explained Smoot in an interview, 'just like people do to their concepts of art or religion . . . I do think that Cosmology is about philosophy and religion as well as science. Our work changes culture, like the first Moon landing did: people see themselves in a different perspective.

Independent, 13 May 1992

Smoot subsequently gave greater explicitness to this need for cosmology (that he of course equates with science at large) to adapt to the new demands of public opinion by stating his objective of ' . . . improving the public image of science. I want to make it more popular, to get away from the idea that technology equals weapons and to help school children get involved in astrophysics' (*Independent*, 13 May 1992).

Astronomer Arnold Wolfendale similarly acknowledged:

Of the physical sciences, astronomy is unique in its popular appeal, and within it cosmology stands supreme. Just how did the universe start? How did galaxies form and stars, and planets and . . . ? No one who has looked at the sky on a dark moonless night can fail to be moved by the vastness and beauty of the heavens or not want to know more about it.

The Times, 25 April 1992

Big Bang as a boundary object

The COBE story enables us to address several features of deviation of scientific discourse to the public level at once. As I have shown, it provided in the first place an opportunity to evade increasing criticism at the specialist levels by shifting to a level where Big Bang orthodoxy was still strong and appealing, a level almost inaccessible to the subtleties of critics and alternative models (e.g. chaotic inflation). But deviation not only served the interests of a group, however large and influential, of astronomers; it also enabled different actors to engage in multilayered boundary work. By lying at the core of a metonymy chain that begins with the COBE measurements, Big Bang turns out, in this respect, to be an ideal 'boundary object'. It enabled different categories of actors to interact at the public level by providing a common set of images, a reservoir of rhetorical practices to be used at several levels of discussion and boundary negotiation.

One layer of boundary work concerned the boundaries of the Big Bang paradigm as such, its status and capacity to incorporate new models. Another concerned ownership rights and competencies with regard to the disciplinary field of cosmology. Being a discipline still in the making, cosmology's boundary work had to be performed in public so researchers with different backgrounds (i.e. astronomers, physicists and mathematicians) could participate, and the necessary public recognition and support for the field be established.

Finally, at the most general level, Big Bang metonymically stood for science as a whole, being taken as a 'touchstone of the scientific outlook' with a vigour only otherwise possessed by evolution theory. In a 1990 study of the scientific literacy of the American and British public, two questions were used to test acceptance of the scientific world picture. People were asked to agree or disagree with the propositions 'the universe began with a huge explosion' and 'human beings developed from earlier species of animal'.[143] When criticizing Hoyle's reluctance to accept the Big Bang, a *Daily Telegraph* writer claimed that Hoyle also 'disbelieves Darwin's theory of evolution by natural selection'.

Big Bang was therefore employed to question, define and defend the boundaries between science and other forms of knowledge such as religion: as a kind of watershed, it marked the borders between what can be studied by science and what was to be left to religion. 'Is this theology or physics?', wondered *The Times*' science correspondent, Nigel Hawkes.

In 1981, when a conference on cosmology was organized by the Jesuits at the Vatican, the Pope received the scientists participating and urged them to enquire into what happened after the Big Bang. They were not to investigate the Big Bang itself, since this was the moment of creation and therefore the work of God.[144] In this sense, the public debate triggered by COBE fitted with a longstanding tradition of boundary negotiation between science and religion centred on the Big Bang model: books written for the general public like Isaac Asimov's *In the Beginning . . .* and Gerald Schroeder's *Genesis and the Big Bang* sought either to shape the Bible according to scientific theories, as in Asimov's case (who actually 'rewrites' the first book of the Bible to adapt it to the scientific view)[145] or to place scientific research within a general religious framework. This is what Schroeder does when he writes that 'astrophysics is part of the super-search for the Creator' (1990: 81). The Italian physicist Tullio Regge takes the Biblical term *Berescit* to be the equivalent of Big Bang.[146]

In order to delegitimate Big Bang, therefore, its critics had to try to have it publicly trespass the border by pushing it into the realm of faith and mythology. Hannes Alfvén, a Nobel prize-winning physicist, claimed for instance, that 'the Big Bang supporters, being aware as they are of some of its problems, are cautious. A Christian does not go to Mecca and become convert overnight.'[147] 'What theory is this', Hoyle wondered once, 'which has been "proposed by a priest and endorsed by the Pope"?'.[148]

All cultures have creation myths and the Big Bang is ours.
Letter to *Independent*, 3 May 1992

The same strategy was used by Big Bang supporters with regard to alternative models. As Regge again wrote, 'At this level the personal *theologies* prevail of those who want to organize the cosmos according to a great design. We have thus been provided with cyclical universes that contract or expand periodically or stationary cosmologies variously revised such as Hoyle's and Narlikar's.'[149]

As a boundary object, Big Bang provides continuity through the different stages of scientific discourse; at the specialist as well as at the interspecialist and popular levels (not to mention the pedagogic, where it stands as the uncontested origin of the universe) it is valid currency and an obligatory passage point for all participants in the debate, whatever their view and approach. Its flexibility allows it to assume different statuses at each of these levels: it can be considered as a single model, as the paradigm of cosmology or even as a synonym of science. As Sir Michael Atiyah, President of the Royal Society, said in a speech shortly before the COBE announcement: 'The standard of exposition and illustration [of science in the press] is now so high that even biologists can understand all about the Big Bang.'[150]

The 'universal' value of Big Bang as a boundary object is evidenced even more clearly by the fact that the metonymical chain illustrated (from COBE to 'Science') is not the only one centred upon it. Although the initial emphasis on the COBE results was envisaged by NASA as an opportunity to deviate and thereby improve its public image (ravaged in earlier years by the Shuttle tragedy and by the initial problems with the Hubble telescope); and although astronomers saw it as a chance to restate their authority within cosmology; and although cosmologists sought to use it to enhance their prestige within science, and scientists in general to enhance theirs within society, Big Bang was also 'translated' in a number of other ways to provide a handy interpretative framework for political or economic events.

The COBE discovery thus acted as a sort of quick-match by revivifying the networks of discourse strategy and competition that at the time were ready to be activated within the British public arena. Cosequently, concepts such as the 'sensitization' of public opinion do not do justice to the active manipulation of scientific results performed at the public level.

THE PUBLIC SCIENCE OF LOUIS PASTEUR: THE EXPERIMENT ON ANTHRAX IN THE POPULAR PRESS OF THE TIME

Foreword

This section was originally intended to be an analysis of the coverage of the Pouilly-le-Fort experiment in the English and French daily press of the time. I was interested in the public view and discussion of a public experiment, and in its relation both to specialist discussions of the principle of immunization and to widespread popular ideas on contagion and its prevention. Gradually, the connection of the topic at hand with other public issues of the time (vaccination, homeopathy and vivisection) emerged as inevitably requiring treatment. Accordingly, tracing the debates in their multiple interrelations provided the opportunity of considering other nonspecialist sources such as popular scientific magazines (e.g. *La Revue Scientifique*) as well as the association bulletins and pamphlets in which the opinions of the groups involved in the debates set out their views.

I have tried as far as possibile to let the actors speak for themselves, since it is what they say and how they say it that provides insight and supporting evidence for my interpretation. One last cautionary remark: the following is not yet another attempt to explain Pasteur's 'success'. Although Pasteur and his experiment at Pouilly-le-Fort are the starting point of the analysis, the real focus of the work is the public framing and appropriation of a scientific experiment at a time when the relationship between science and the public was in a crucial phase of its development.

Prologue: a short account of the Pouilly-le-Fort trial

Since the beginning of 1880, Pasteur had been trying to extend his work on chicken colera to other contagious diseases by formulating a general principle of immunization.[151] Some successful experiments conducted by Toussaint (a professor at the Veterinary School of Toulouse) on immunization against anthrax during that year stimulated his enthusiasm and efforts. On 28 February 1881, he delivered an important paper, 'De l'atténuation des virus et de leur retour à la virulence', in which he sketched one such principle and at the same time urged an experiment on a large scale.[152] This opportunity was offered to him in April by the Société d'Agriculture de Melun. Pasteur was already famous among French farmers, whose society had awarded him a gold medal.[153]

Rossignol, a veterinary surgeon somewhat sceptical about Pasteur's ideas and laboratory results, challenged him to replicate them on his own farm. The Société would provide Pasteur with the necessary animals. Although the results of his efforts in attenuating the anthrax bacillus to atmospheric action were not yet completely satisfactory, Pasteur felt himself obliged to take up the challenge. On the twenty-eighth of April, he signed the agreement with the society and the related experimental protocol, subsequently modified at the request of the society, that asked him to add ten cows. He accepted, warning at the same time that vaccination tests on cows were not yet as advanced as those on sheep, and therefore that the results may have been less convincing than those achieved with sheep. However, he expressed his gratitude to the Melun society for providing him with the ten cows.[154] Just before the beginning of the experiment, two of the sheep were replaced by goats.

The first inoculation of twenty-four sheep, one goat and six cows with an attenuated culture of anthrax took place on the fifth of May. The second inoculation was performed on May seventeenth. On the thirty-first of May, the final inoculation was administered to thirty-one vaccinated animals and to another twenty-nine non-vaccinated animals (twenty-four sheep, one goat, six cows). The final session was held on the second of June, when those present saw that twenty-one non-vaccinated sheep had perished together with the goat. The cows had not died, although they were suffering from severe infections. The vaccinated animals, instead, were all perfectly healthy except for one goat, which was found dead on the following day. A later examination by the veterinary surgeons Rossignol and Garrousse identified the cause of its death as complications in its state of pregnancy.

Pasteur himself, reporting to the Académie des Sciences on the thirteenth of June, 1881, described the experimental results as depending in part on chance.

> Ce programme, j'en conviens, avait des hardiesses de prophétie q'un éclatant succès pouvait seul faire excuser. Plusiers personnes eurent l'obligeance de m'en faire la remarque, non sans y meler quelque reproche d'imprudence scientifique. Toutefois, l'Académie doit comprendre que nous n'avions pas libellé un tel programme sans avoir de solides appuis dans des expériences préalables, bien qu'aucune de ces dernier n'eut l'ampleur de celle qui se préparait. Le hasard, d'ailleur, favorise les esprits préparés, et c'est dans ce sens, je crois, qu'il faut entendre la parole inspirée du poète: *audentes fortuna iuvat*.[155]

It is clear from his letters and from his notebooks as retrieved by historians that Pasteur was nervous and uncertain about the outcome of his experiment until the very last hours. His assistants in a certain sense 'saved' his reputation by employing a more efficient chemical method of attenuation[156] (although it was less consistent with Pasteur's biological explanation).

A celebrated experiment

> An invitation having been sent to me, I went today to Pouilly-le-Fort to see some very important experiments on the farm of M. Rossignol, a veterinary surgeon. Pouilly-le-Fort, which is a few miles from Melun, in the Department of Seine et Marne, is a large farm reached by one of the splendid roads, lined with limes and acacias, which intersect that flourishing department. Just now a harvest is expected that is called 'electoral', the peasants often being influenced in their votes by a good or bad harvest, voting, according as it turns out, for or against the government.
>
> M. Pasteur, one of the scientific glories of France, made to-day experiments in connexion with his latest researches on that malady dreaded by agriculturists, called 'charbon', a sickness which rages more especially among sheep, the mortality of which produced by it is estimated in France at several million francs a year.
>
> *The Times*, 3 June 1881: 4

Thus begins the report on Pasteur's public experiment at Pouilly-le-Fort written for *The Times* by its French correspondent Henri de Blowitz.[157]

The event obviously attracted the attention of the French daily press as well, expecially the Paris newspaper *Le Temps* and local newspapers such as the *Journal de Seine et Marne*; the latter covered the experiment right from the start. On 11 May, the *Journal* published an article entitled 'La vaccination des animaux', almost entirely devoted to listing the most notable witnesses to the experiment, from

> MM. Tisserand, directeur au Ministére de l'Agriculture' to 'environ cinquante vétérinaires de Paris et du département, et un grand nombre de cultivateurs le plus distingués de la région s'étaient également empressés de suivre ces expériences dont les resultats sont appelés à rendre les plus grands services à l'agriculture.
>
> *Journal de Seine et Marne*, 11 May 1881: 2[158]

On 17 June, the *Journal* gave a final, enthusiastic account of the experiment under the title 'Les expériences de M. Pasteur à Pouilly-le-Fort'.

> Les curieuses expériences de Pouilly-le-Fort ont été couronnées d'un succès complet. Après l'inoculation du virus charbonneux violent, les animaux non vaccinés ont succombés, les autres se portent à merveille. Les belles experiences de Pasteur sont concluantes et décisives. Nos cultivateurs de la Brie ont aujourd'hui un remède tout trouvé contre le charbon: pour cela faire, il ne reste plus qu'a faire vacciner leurs moutons avec le virus atténuè de M. Pasteur.

L'expérience faite *in campo* par M. Pasteur est appelée à devenir mémorable, elle est la consécration de ses expériences nombreuses de laboratoire, et on peut dire sans ambages, que ce célebre chimiste vient de doter son pays d'un grand bienfait. Ce sera l'éternel honneur de la Société d'Agriculture de Melun d'avoir provoqué des expériences qui auront des conséquences heureuses non-seule-ment pour notre pays, mais encore pour le monde entier.

Journal de Seine et Marne, 17 June 1881: 2

Le Temps first reported on the experiment through the communication given by Pasteur at the Académie des Sciences on 13 June:

Trés importante communication de M.Pasteur rendant compte des expériences faites ... Ces résultats confirmaient de la manière la plus rigoreuse les prévisions èmises par le savant expérimentateur ... M. Pasteur concluait en disant: ' Nous avons donnè aujour-d'hui pour la maladie charbonneuse, comme pour le choléra des poules, une sorte de virus attenué qui est facile de reproduire avec l'intensité voulue, qu'il est facile de transporter et d'inoculer. Chacun de ces virus est un vaccin par rapport à celui qui le precede dans l'échelle de la virulence.[159]

A few days later, *Le Temps* continued in the same vein, documenting Pasteur's presentation of his experiment to the Académie de Médecine:

L'immunité conférée par les procédés de M. Pasteur offre une précieuse ressource à l'agriculture, en donnant aux éleveurs le moyen certain de soustraire leurs troupeaux aux ravages des epizooties charbonneuses. La certitude du moyen consiste surtout en ce que le virus préservateur est obtenu expérimentalement et qu'on peut doser et mesurer son énergie, par consequent ses effets: ce vaccin, mantenable et transportable, devra être preparè dans le laboratoire de M. Pasteur dans les premiers temps, pour éviter toute chance d'accident.

Le Temps, 20 June 1881: 3

Only towards the end of the article is a brief reference made to a priority claim by Gabriel Colin, a veterinary surgeon who had strongly opposed Pasteur's microbiological theories over the years:

C'est moi, dit-il, qui a le premier decouvert, même avant M. Toussaint, que les inoculations fractionnés, pratiquées avec les matières charbonneuses, étaient préservatrices.

Le Temps, 20 June 1881: 3

The debate resumed a few days later, this time in an article almost entirely devoted to Colin's priority claims. One notes with interest that neither article mentioned the most substantial criticisms brought by Colin against the experiment: why had Pasteur not used blood taken from one of the dead animals for the last inoculation instead of his own culture.[160] Finally, Colin questions at large the originality of Pasteur's method.

> M. Colin revient à la charge: la recherche des virus atténués est vielle d'un siècle; on a pratiquè des inoculations contre la peste bovine, contre la clavelée, contre la syphilis.
>
> *Le Temps*, 24 June 1881: 2[161]

But the conclusion was once more favourable for Pasteur:

> M. Bouley termine ses observations par un éloge très vif des travaux de M. Pasteur, éloge accueilli par des applaudissements reitérés.
>
> *Le Temps*, 24 June 1881: 2

On 12 July, the story of Pouilly-le-Fort appeared on the first page, replacing the usual episode of fiction in the section 'Feuilleton du Temps'. The article again recalled the communication of 28 February and the agreement between Pasteur and the Agricultural Society:

> M. Pasteur *prophétisait*[162] que les vingt-cinq moutons non-vaccinés mourraient tous de charbon et que les vingt-cinq vaccinés ne mour-raient pas.
>
> *Le Temps*, 12 July 1881: 1, my emphasis

The article emphasized the difficulties that Pasteur had to cope with, especially since he had had to replace two rams with goats in order to comply with the Society's requests:

> Ainsi, tous les animaux non-vaccinés périrent sans exception, comme l'avait *prédit*[163] M. Pasteur; tous les animaux vaccinés, sauf un, furont sauvés.
>
> *Le Temps*, 12 July 1881: 1, my emphasis

Le Temps, however, had been publishing articles about experiments and debates on anthrax long before the Pouilly-le-Fort trial. Most of them were occasioned by an announcement made by Toussaint, a professor at the Veterinary School of Toulouse, whose claim to have discovered a vaccine for anthrax was reported by Bouley at a meeting of the Académie de Médecine in July, 1880.

An article published at the beginning of March gave great importance to the criticisms brought by Pasteur against the attenuation method used by Toussaint, which consisted in heating the blood infected by anthrax.[164]

> M. Pasteur éstime que sa méthode est bien supérieure à celle de M. Toussaint. Le virus attenué, peut il revenir a la virulence? Oui, repond M. Pasteur, et voilà comment.
>
> *Le Temps*, 2 March 1881: 3

Again, about twenty days later,

> M. Pasteur critique les procédé, bien connu des nos lecteurs, par lequel M. Toussaint avait annoncé qu'il dépouillait le sang charbonneux de sa virulence. ... Tout récentement, avec la collaboration de MM. Chamberland et Roux, M. Pasteur a perfectionné encore ses procédés de cultures atténuantes et les a rendues aussi simples qu'on peut le désirer. Deux cultures et quelques semaines suffisent pour réaliser le degré de virulence qu'on cherche.
>
> *Le Temps*, 23 March 1881: 3

Even a few months after Pouilly-le-Fort, every opportunity was taken to celebrate Pasteur:

> On annonce que l'honorable M. Pasteur, le savant à qui l'industrie et l'humanité sont déjà redevables de tant de découvertes utiles, aurait l'intention de se rendre au lazaret de Pauillac Gironde pour y étudier la fièvre jaune et rechercher si cette maladie ne serait pas elle aussi, causée par un parasite spècial. On n'aurait plus alors qu'à rechercher les moyens de préservation. Ce serait un bienfait de plus à inscrire à l'actif de M. Pasteur et de la science française.
>
> *Le Temps*, 27 October 1881: 3

> M. Bouley, au nom de l'Académie des sciences, a célébré la grande decouverte d'un de nos plus éminents physiologistes, M. Pasteur. Dans les comptes rendus que nous donnons chaque semaine des séances de l'Académie des Sciences, nous avons signalé les interessantes discussions qui s'y sont produites au sûjet de la nouvelle vaccination. Nous nous contenterons de citer le passage ou M. Bouley, un des juges les plus compétents en cette matière, résume à grands traits la découverte de son collègue.
>
> *Le Temps*, 27 October 1881: 3

One might thus conclude that the level of public communication provided important support for Pasteur's ideas[165] and played an important role in constructing the Pouilly-le-Fort experiment as a spectacular *experimentum crucis*.[166] In fact, although Pasteur's ideas were still being debated by a number of his colleagues[167], they aroused great interest and received enthusiastic acceptance in the daily press. However, many of Pasteur's colleagues were unable to accept two implications of his last experiments in particular:

1   that explanation of a disease could be reduced to a microscopic external agent, thereby minimizing the importance of studying the entire organism affected; and
2   most of all, the idea that appropriate inoculation with the same agent could prevent an individual from getting the disease.

At that time, the dominant paradigm in the medical field was that of 'morbid spontaneity': the ubiquity of disease which could only be prevented by sanitation and the moralization of society.[168] 'La maladie est en nous, de nous, pour nous', was the efficient synopsis provided by Pidoux.[169]

It is interesting to note that immunization[170] (i.e. protection against a disease afforded by a mild form of the same disease) and the related practice of inoculation had nevertheless long been familiar to popular culture.[171] Moreover, the daily press was a *locus* where the theoretical explanation – still unclear at the time – mattered less than the practical and (as Pasteur himself emphasized), economic[172] results:

> Mais les resultats les plus importants sont dûs aux inoculations préventives dont le type bien connu est la vaccination qui met à l'abri des attaques ulterieures de la variole. Dans ce cas, on obtient l'immunité par l'inoculation du virus de même famille, mais beaucoup moins énergique, qui vous donne une petite maladie passagère: celle-ci rend l'organisme impropre à nourrir le virus de la maladie mortelle, sans qu'on connaisse d'ailleurs la cause de ce fait singulier. La science, on le voit, a montré une fois de plus que les découvertes théoriques sont toujours fécondes pour la pratique. Mais, par une bizzarrerie singulière, elle ne peut pas expliquer l'immunité qu'elle sait cépendant produire. Quand un sol a été epuisé par une culture, le repos lui rend bien vite la fécondité; quand une espèce quelconque de parasites a ravagé une première fois un organisme, rien ne l'empêche de le ravager du nouveau: pourquoi donc le virus est-il incapable de se developper dans le terrain où il a vecu déjà?
>
> *Le Temps*, 24 April 1881: 2

This is not to argue that Pasteur consciously mobilized popular knowledge against the experts; instead, I am trying to show how these two levels of communication were combined in his discourse.[173]

I have already pointed out the close similarity, often in terms of identical sentences, between Pasteur's communications to the scientific community and those intended to reach the wider public (the influence between the two being reciprocal). One also notes, with regard for instance to his dispute with Toussaint, that Pasteur was granted a pride of place in the reports (the dispute is always documented through his words) by virtue of his position within the specialist milieu: unlike Toussaint, he was a member of the Académie, and articles drew heavily on the sessions at the Académie.

The law of similars

I shall now slightly complicate this picture. An issue discussed in the public arena never exists in a vacuum. It is also framed and given meaning by being related to other issues. This applies equally to Pasteur's experiment of 1881 and the connected debate on immunization. In *The Times* especially, there were three topics that attracted the attention of the public during the same period: homeopathy, vivisection and vaccination.

In early 1881, an event occurred which fuelled the debate about homeopathy in both the medical and the daily press. At the time when Lord Beaconsfield (Disraeli) entered his last illness, his attendant physician was a certain Dr Kidd, who had certainly practised homeopathy over the years and who, according to *The Times*, was 'more or less identified in the public mind with what is called homeopathy, and that he holds, or did hold, office as a physician to what is called the Homeopathic Hospital' (*The Times*, 15 April 1881: 6).

The Queen requested the attendance of an additional doctor and therefore asked for Jenner, who refused. Dr Quain accepted, but only after receiving a written assurance from Kidd that he was treating Disraeli with regular medicine only, and that he would consent to being directed by Quain himself. Quain's decision was eventually endorsed by the Royal College of Physicians, but the collaboration nonetheless provoked considerable discussion.

An article by a *Times* correspondent justified Quain's decision on two grounds. The first was the urgent need to try to save 'an illustrious life'. The second is of much greater interest to our analysis. *The Times*' correspondent argued that the fact that Dr Kidd had signed an official document admitting that he was not treating Disraeli with homeopathy consituted a clear proof that homeopathy was just a 'fashionable mode of treatment' now being made increasingly irrelevant by advances in regular medicine.

> Regular medicine has advanced with enormous strides, and has made great progress in the treatment of diseases previously known to be curable, as well as in bringing under subjection others which had been reputed to be incurable. Of this knowledge, which was in

entire opposition to the principles that they professed, homeopathists became possessed as students; because in order to practise medicine or surgery at all, they were compelled to pass through the ordinary medical curriculum, and to obtain one of the ordinary qualifications.

The Times, 15 April 1881: 6

The following day, *The Times* published five letters replying to the article, the first signed by Kidd himself. Kidd argued that the two principles 'similia similibus curantur' and 'contraria contrariis curantur' were not antagonistic and could be profitably employed in the treatment of various diseases. Dr Dudgeon went further, claiming that:

If 'regular medicine' has advanced with 'enormous strides', it has only done so insofar as it has discarded its useless and injurious methods and assimilated itself to the scientific specific method of homoeopathy.

The Times, 16 April 1881: 7

Other comments and replies followed, and the correspondent himself felt obliged to restate his argument:

Why cannot the homoeopaths, even now, take advantage of the late events to admit that their professions are no longer tenable, and that everything which is true in the doctrine of similars is the property of all the world?

The Times, 18 April 1881: 10

In sum, the debate saw the adversaries of homeopathy arguing that advances in medicine had made the homeopaths' claims to difference obsolete; on the other hand, the advocates of homoeopathy claimed that those same advances had been made possible by the acceptance of some central ideas of homeopathy itself. In the course of the debate, both parties regarded the 'law of similars' (i.e. the principle that it is possible to cure a disease using the disease itself – 'like cures like') as embodying the essence of homeopathy. It is difficult to ignore the affinity between this principle – which to *The Times'* correspondent seemed to be 'contradicting both science and common sense' – and the concept of immunization itself against contagious diseases which lay at the basis of Pasteur's anthrax experiment. Moreover, one of the items of evidence that homeopaths adduced in support of their practice was the demonstrably superior efficacity of homeopathic treatment during the cholera epidemic in Vienna, compared with allopathic treatments.

A few years later, Deane Butcher wrote in a homeopathic journal: 'At all events, I think we may fairly take as proved, that the researches of Pasteur do support the doctrines of our school.'[174] A similar point was

made in the Presidential Address delivered before the Homeopathic Society
for the 1903–4 session:

> Our law of cure – the law of similars – misunderstood as it still
> is, wilfully or unwilfully, misrepresented as it often has been, volun-
> tarily or involuntarily yet holds the field as the one therapeutic law
> which has survived the protean changes of medical opinion during
> the last century. ... We recognise the fact, that in many of the
> publications of the so-called dominant school during the past half
> century, our therapeutic law has been to a greater or less degree
> acknowledged. ... The development of serum therapy has arisen
> pretty directly from the influence of bacteriology on treatment
> ... there is nothing in the method which bears any relationship
> with any other therapeutic law than that of similars'.[175]

Homeopaths were also keen to emphasize the originality and 'difference'
of their methods compared with those of regular medicine, in order to
highlight that it was this latter practice that was borrowing their ideas and
therapeutics, and not vice versa. In the 'Varietés' section of another homeopathic journal, Hermann documents the case of a shepherd whose sheep
were threatened by smallpox. He was provided with a homeopathic vaccine
('mercurius, sulphur, thuya and variolin') and the success was so complete
(none of the animals fell sick) that the shepherd later passed the vaccine
to a friend of his.

The author of the article makes two main points in favour of the homeopathic vaccine: its lower price (3.40 francs against 21.88 francs) and its
less aggressive nature compared with enforced vaccination: 'Comment se
ose encore imposer aux populations le vaccine, comme une mesure forcé,
lorsque d'autres présérvatifs, beaucoup plus certains et moins dangereux,
existent?'[176] However, this strategy did not prove to be particularly successful
in the long run, and the debate over immunization can now be interpreted
as one of the crucial stages in homeopathy's loss of a specific identity and
ultimately its decline.[177] Pushing interpretation to its extremes, one could
argue that interest in Pasteur's experiments was partly aroused by the possibility of using them to incorporate a moderate amount of homeopathic
principles and therapeutics into regular medical practice, thereby reducing
the need to maintain homeopathy as an alternative to medicine.[178]

On animals, for animals

During the very same days that comments and rejoinders on homeopathy
abounded in the pages of *The Times*, several letters and articles were also
published on vivisection, one of the topics of greatest interest to the public
in the Victorian age.[179]

On 18 April, *The Times* published a letter addressed by Darwin to the Swedish professor Holmgren, 'in answer to a request for an expression of his opinion on the question of the right to make experiments on living animals for scientific purposes – a question which is now being much discussed in Sweden'. As he had done on many other occasions,[180] Darwin expressed his aversion to cruelty to animals but at the same time voiced concern that progress in physiology might be affected by restrictive legislation on the matter:

> No one, unless he is grossly ignorant of what science has done for mankind, can entertain any doubt of the incalculable benefits which will hereafter be derived from physiology, not only by man, but by the lower animals. Look, for instance, at Pasteur's results in modifying the germs of the most malignant diseases, from which, as it so happens, animals will in the first place receive more relief than man.
>
> *The Times*, 18 April 1881: 10

Several other letters followed, including one signed by Frances Power Cobbe, secretary of the Society for the Protection of Animals from Vivisection:

> As to Mr Darwin's concluding observations respecting the benefits derived already from vivisection, I am, of course, not competent to argue with so great an authority. It sometimes would appear, however, that men of science mistake the discovery of the cause of a disease and the means of its transmission for the very different discovery of an available remedy. . . . We seem to be always condemned to listen to a repetition of the story of the old Egyptian magicians who succeded in reproducing the plagues, but failed to cure them.
>
> *The Times*, 19 April 1881: 8

This was one of the two main argumentative strategies employed by anti-vivisectionists against animal experiments: the 'technical' one (i.e. to question its actual contribution to the development of more efficient treatments). The second argument was the moral one,[181] which Cobbe introduced at the end of her letter:

> But lastly, Sir, I beg to ask whether the principles of the evolution philosophy require us to believe that the advancement of the 'noble science of physiology' is so supreme an object of human effort that the corresponding retreat and the disappearance of the sentiments of compassion and sympathy must be accounted as of no consequence to the balance?
>
> *The Times*, 19 April 1881: 8

Scientists and members of the medical profession generally ignored this latter argument, focusing their replies on the advances made possible by experimentation on animals as the letter by Darwin clearly shows.[182]

The Medical Congress

Vivisection was one of the key topics discussed at the International Medical Congress of London, in August 1881, another important event for the English daily press given the attendance of such distinguished participants as Darwin, Virchow and Pasteur. Despite *The Times*' generally sympathetic treatment of anti-vivisection movements until a few years previously, it reported a long speech against them by Virchow and passed favourable comment on it.

> So far as it is possible to appraise the feeling of the public on a subject it has not studied, and is not competent to study, it appears not inclined to take the responsibility of approving and disapproving. When philosophers like Mr Darwin and Dr Virchow pronounce the practice essential to the advance of medical science, nations will be hardly induced to choose darkness.
>
> *The Times*, 6 August 1881: 9

Similar emphasis was given to the concluding resolution by the Congress on vivisection:

> 'This congress records its conviction that experiments upon living animals have proved of the utmost service to medicine, and are indispensable for further progress; that, accordingly, while strongly deprecating the infliction of unnecessary pain, it is of opinion that, *alike in the interest of man and of animals*, it is not desirable to restrict competent persons in the performance of such experiments.' This resolution was received with loud cheers, and was declared carried without a single dissent.
>
> *The Times*, 10 August 1881: 4, my italics[183]

Successes like those achieved in animal vaccination by Pasteur at Pouilly-le-Fort, with their public resonance and their promise of benefiting the animals themselves which had been the subject of the experiment, were an ideal rhetorical resource in this strategy.

> There is no argument on which the vivisectionists have relied so confidently as showing the success of the experimental method of investigating disease, as the inoculations of M. Pasteur and his school.
>
> Joseph Collinson, letter to the *Vaccination Inquirer*, July 1897: 53

As French has pointed out: 'It was the accomplishments of bacteriology and immunology during the last two decades of the XIXth century that provided the example required by spokesmen for experimental medicine.'[184]

It is not unlikely, as French suggests, that it was precisely this perception of Pasteur's activity as threatening their cause that fostered the anti-vivisectionists's increasing hostility towards him. Although Pasteur had been a target for their attacks since his first experiments on animals in his studies on contagious diseases, criticism of his work rose to a crescendo when he turned to examination of rabies.[185] Under the title of 'Pasteur Necrology' anti-vivisectionists published annotated lists of the animals dying in the course of his experiments,[186] labelling his Institute a 'hell of animals' and his achievements the 'diabolus of atheism-scientism'.[187]

Homeopathy and vivisection

I have considered the relationship between the publicity given to Pasteur's work on virus-vaccines and two other prominent issues such as homoeopathy and vivisection. A question now inevitably arises: was there any reciprocal relation between these latter two debates?

The answer seems in the affirmative. One of the main problems for anti-vivisectionists was for long their inability to provide 'institutional alternatives to vivisecting hospitals and medical schools';[188] they consequently warmly approved homeopathy and other unorthodox medical practices. Still in 1906, the chairman of the Second Royal Commission on Vivisection passed the following comment on the deposition by Mr G. Burford, M.B., of the World League of Opponents of Vivisection:

> I understand that the important point that you wish to bring before us is your objection to experiments for purposes of pharmacology and the statement that experimentation might be superseded altogether without any cruelty and with as good effect by following the method of homoeopathy.[189]

The witness gave further explanation of the homeopathic method for testing drugs, which entailed always 'healthy, conscious and volunteer human beings' and no vivisectional procedure: 'Homoeopathy finds that experiments on healthy human beings yield results more ample, more direct, more fertile and more reliable than the details obtained by experiments on animals.'[190]

> Sir William Church asked witness if he did not agree that serum therapy is of use, and if it could have been arrived at without experiments on animals? Witness admitted that *as a private individual* he believed in serum therapy, but he added: 'It is quite possible that it could have been arrived at in another way, and

that the same properties which are utilized in serum therapy might have been used without having recourse to animal experimentation. I will cite one instance of that – the virus of consumption, that is to say the tubercular virus was prepared by homeopathists, and employed by homeopathists, long before Koch's discovery of the tubercle bacillus.[191]

A complementary attitude was apparent among homeopathists with regard to vivisection:

The vaunted success of this mode of discovering the powers of drugs by torturing stupid frogs and rabbits with them will hardly have the effect of convincing us of its superiority over the Hahnemannian method of testing them on intelligent human beings, more especially when we observe the exceeding diversity of opinion with regard to the mode of action of almost every drug arrived at by our most intelligent vivisectors.[192]

The vaccination debate

It is clear how the experiment at Pouilly-le-Fort could be straightforwardly related to the ongoing debate on vaccination, with its particular focus on compulsory smallpox vaccination and on the use of animal vaccines. *Le Temps* reported extensively on the long discussions held at the Académie de Médecine, and *The Times* hosted several discussions and letters on such topics. Also, a great number of pamphlets were produced both in favour of vaccination and against it, citing Pasteur's inoculations either as final evidence of the necessity and usefulness of vaccination or as additional proof of its perils.[193]

Dr Klein has arrived at conclusions adverse to the general adoption in this country of Pasteur's proposal to inoculate cattle with anthrax as a prophylactic measure against that disastrous disease ... This country is comparatively free from anthrax and therefore the introduction and use of this so-called 'vaccin charbonneux' seems to me most dangerous, and capable of producing incalculable mischief.

Report by Dr Klein to the Veterinary Dept of the Privy Council, published in *The Veterinarian* and quoted by *The Vaccination Inquirer and Health Review*, October 1881: 112–13

In France, but especially in England and in the USA, resistance against vaccination by no means subsided immediately after Pouilly-le-Fort.[194] *The Vaccination Inquirer and Health Review*, the official organ of the London

Society for the Abolition of Compulsory Vaccination, constantly surveyed the French press in search of reported failures of Pasteur' vaccines, taking every opportunity to attack him[195] and to deny that his results confirmed the validity of vaccination:

> Pasteur's inoculations may be accepted as affording analogy and support to the theory of vaccination, or not. If they be accepted, then the theory of vaccination still remains without a single shred of scientific evidence to back it up.
>
> *The Vaccination Inquirer*, April 1882: 6

> His [Pasteur's] inoculations have by no means conformed to the expectations excited, and none who know the gulf which exists between the laboratory of the man of science and the practice of common life, feel surprise when 'discoveries' with far better show of reason than M. Pasteur's come to naught.
>
> *The Vaccination Inquirer*, June 1882: 35

> The haste and desperation with which medical men have clutched at Pasteur are highly significant. They prove how wide and deep is the distrust in vaccination, and how welcome is assistance, however shadowy, for their sinking faith. Nevertheless, greater composure would be more becoming, as well as a more exact appreciation of what Pasteur had done and taught. Our Pasteurians exceed Pasteur as the Wilkesites did Wilkes. So far, Pasteur has done nothing in mitigation of the cattle plague ... Many such furores have we witnessed, but after a little season they pass away. Rarely indeed is the science that is true born into the world with such instant recognition and uproarious acclaim.
>
> *The Vaccination Inquirer*, September 1881: 95

Published in France, the official bulletin of the International League of anti-vaccinators, the weekly *Réveil Médical*, attacked Pasteur in even more picturesque terms, by labelling him 'bacteriocole', 'tête microbiophile' or 'ami des microbes'.[196]

Dr William J. Collins[147] did not fail to mention Pasteur in his address at the Annual Meeting of the London Society for the Abolition of Compulsory Vaccination:

> What relation do Pasteur's experiments bear to the subject of vaccination? The advocates of vaccination seek to make capital out of his experiments, in order to bolster up vaccination; and in doing so, they make use of most unwarrantable analogy, and push the theory to an extravagant extreme. Pasteur himself says there is a

great difference between the two classes of facts, and that his use of the term is intended rather as a compliment to Jenner than from belief in the analogy of his experiments with vaccination.

The Vaccination Inquirer, June 1882: 47

It is no coincidence that one of the main accusers of Pasteur, the anti-vivisectionist Anna Kingsford, was also present at the meeting. In spite of their inevitable individual differences,[198] the anti-vaccination, anti-vivisection and homoeopathic movements were all expressions of a struggle against the increasing institutionalization, 'scientification' and technicization of medical studies and practice,[199] which advocated sanitation and moral virtue as opposed to animal experimentation and germ theory.[200] Activists like John Clarke or Edward Berdoe were at the same time anti-vivisectionists and anti-vaccinationists as well as being highly sympathetic to homoeopathy and the same parliamentary spokesmen ranged among the three issues.[201] In his essay on 'The law of similars: the scientific principle of vaccination', Dr J. Compton Burnett explicitly coupled vaccination with homeopathy:

> Homeopathy is such an unwelcome subject, and vaccination is another. Speaking generally, nobody wants to hear anything about either, and still less to have them brought into correlation.
>
> Burnett, 1884: 3

Anti-vivisectionist Frances Power Cobbe did the same for vivisection and vaccination in an article entitled 'Whither is Pasteurism to lead us?':

> Is it really to be believed that the order of things has been so perversely constituted as that the health of men and beasts is to be sought, not, as we fondly believed, by pure and sober living and cleanliness, but by the pollution of the very fountains of life with the confluent streams of a dozen filthy diseases? . . . Are we, then, our oxen, our sheep, our pigs, our fowls (that is to say, our own bodies and the food which nourishes them) all to be vaccinated, porcinated, equinated, caninized, felinized, and bovinated, once, twice, twenty times in our lives, or in a year? Are we to be converted into so many living nests for the confortable incubation of disease germs? Is our meat to be saturated with virus, our milk drawn from inoculated cows, our eggs laid by diseased hens – in short, are we to breakfast, dine and soup upon disease by way of securing the perfection of health? Surely, when this last medical bubble has burst, it will be deemed the emptiest and the ugliest of the long series of which potable gold and the Elixir of Life formed the beginning.
>
> *Contemporary Review*, April 1882, repr. in
> *The Vaccination Inquirer*, April 1882: 28

M. Pasteur acknowledges that up to present time he has only found out how to kill the horses and half the sheep and cattle he vaccinates, and no doubt he will go on with his experiments till the latter have shared the fate of the former.

The Vaccination Inquirer, October 1882: 121[202]

Vaccination and vivisection were alike favoured, and so were the various anti-toxin serums and lymphs which are now being used and experimented with. All such practices have their origin and bear no more relationship to sanitation and hygiene than does cheese to the moon.

Joseph Collinson, letter to *The Vaccination Inquirer*, July 1897: 53

Despite all these argumentative efforts, however, the anti-vaccinators largely failed to wrest the experiments of Pasteur from the hands of their 'enemies'. In a late anti-vaccination pamphlet, Swan justified the decline of the movement:

Why did not the criticisms of Drs Creighton and Crookshank[203] secure the downfall of vaccination? . . . Another contributory cause was the concurrent rise into fame of the investigations of Pasteur, and the introduction of the method of treating diseases by sera, vaccines and antitoxins. The vaccinists astutely utilised these developments to bolster up their tottering idol.[204]

The uses of a public experiment

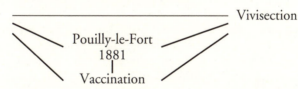

In what sense was Poully-le-Fort a public experiment, and what role did it play with regard to the immunization debate?

Collins[205] has introduced a typology of 'scientific manipulations' in public, in order to solve what he regards as two paradoxes:

1   Public experiments require a firm conclusion, from a public of non-experts, on scientific matters which are still debated among experts; and
2   the public should draw certain conclusions from these experiments, while according to Collins' and other related models[206] proximity leads to uncertainty, and certainty is exactly a matter of distancing from the research front ('distance leads to enchantment', as Collins aptly puts it).

He then resolves the paradox by introducing a typology of scientific manipulations which distinguishes true experiments from 'demonstrations, epidictic displays of virtuosity and downright entertainment'. He then argues that true experiments are usually not performed in public. Just as Faraday would prepare his experiments in the basement of the Royal Institution, and then demonstrate his accomplished results in the lecture theatre, so scientists only offer the public a 'second-hand' witnessing by selectively replicating experiments and representing only one party's view.

It is not easy to conceptualize Pouilly-le-Fort within the framework offered by Collins, since it was surely not just a display of virtuosity. As we have seen, Pasteur's ideas were still contested in 1881; in fact, the experiment was organized by Rossignol (one of his adversaries) so that definitive counter-evidence would be forthcoming.

With the public resonance that it enjoyed, Pasteur's experiment of 1881 was not simply a further step in establishing himself as one of the leading and most visible scientists of the time.[207] Rather, the level of public communication was crucial in shaping the very form of the experiment (the conditions of which had to be extensively negotiated with non-scientific actors like the agricultural society), and its meaning for the scientific community.

Since a stable disciplinary frame for his work on the virus-vaccines did not yet exist, Pasteur had to position himself in a 'central' (and generally accessible) discursive space (the public arena) from which he could simultaneously address several different categories of actors, all in their own way relevant to the topic (physicians, veterinary surgeons, chemists). Also, communication at the public level enabled him to underplay still unclear theoretical aspects by emphasizing practical ones such as the effectiveness and the cheapness of his method.

He was therefore able to direct the attention of different sectors of research and practice within a common arena. Latour[208] has shown how, throughout his career, Pasteur moved from one discipline to another, in each case transferring his previous experience and achieving innovation by linking concepts and problems from different areas.

An event like Pouilly-le-Fort was clearly an important factor in consolidating the new experimental programme in medicine.[209] By enlarging his laboratory to the size of a farm, and by moving it towards the public front, Pasteur perfectly embodied this process of reorganization centred on the laboratory as the privileged *locus* for medical investigation and practice[210] and on the growing importance of fields like chemistry and bacteriology.[211] Appeal to the public was important because it activated, from 'outside' the specialist debate, popular ideas and alternative practices (e.g. homeopathy) which variously supported the principle of immunization against the paradigm of 'morbid spontaneity'.[212] This 'over-extension' of the scientific debate to non-scientific actors and arguments[213] was not uncommon for Pasteur, who on several occasions used political arguments to discredit other theories and scientific achievements or to emphasize his work.[214]

At a more general level, affinities and distinctions were continuously reshaped between science and non-science, e.g. orthodox practice and homeopathy. The public space generated around Pasteur's enterprises was a key arena in the negotiation of respective authorities and in the selective appropriation of each other's concepts and prestige.[215]

Finally, the public stage was essential for the negotiation of the degree of public involvement in the scientific debate. A frequent matter of discussion in press articles on all the debates analysed here, is whether and to what extent account should be taken of the public (often represented by its philosophical incarnation – common sense) when scientific issues are at stake. Depending on the specific needs of the parties involved, the public is summoned *ad hoc* as the ultimate source of authority[216] or in turn rejected as unreliable and irresponsible.

> Everybody appeals to common-sense, but what is common-sense? Common-sense is reason as evolved from common experience. What the multitude of men have found to be true in the course of life, that is common-sense, which to question or resist is folly or fanaticism.
>
> *The Vaccination Inquirer*, March 1881: 170

> It is amusing to observe the readiness with which the unscientific literary class flop upon their knees at anything in the name of science. It is the etiquette of the vulgar among that numerous body. For example, a writer in the *Christian World* of 11th August, professes to have been 'stimulated' by Pasteur's lecture at the Medical Congress, and inspired with the hope that 'the force of many fearful diseases may be broken by vaccination'.
>
> *The Vaccination Inquirer*, September 1881: 95

> Apart from the general consideration that in this matter physiologists and physicians must be the best judges, it is obvious to common sense that if physiology is the foundation of medicine, and if it is the science of vital processes, neither physiology nor medicine can advance in any important degree, save by the study of organisms into living state, when alone these processes are in operation. It would be as reasonable to tell a child to learn to read from a closed book as to expect a physiologist to advance his knowledge while denying him the only method which nature has provided.
>
> George J. Romanes, surgeon, in a letter to
> *The Times*, 25 April 1881: 10

The demands of this poor public are not reasonable but they are quite simple. It dreads disease and desires to be protected against it. . . . What the public wants, therefore, is a cheap magic charm to prevent, and a cheap pill or potion to cure all disease. . . . Thus it was really the public and not the medical profession that took up vaccination with irresistible faith.[217]

In broad terms, it could be argued that the Pouilly-le-Fort experiment and the related concepts introduced by Pasteur furnished a key opportunity to question, protect and strengthen scientific boundaries against the intrusion and competition of other systems, practices and actors.[218]

In spite of these achievements, it is not completely satisfactory to portray the process described above as deliberate strategy woven together by Pasteur and his fellows in order to construct a network of supporters by enrolling the greatest possible number of actors.[219] The complex array of relations and reciprocal influences among different issues and movements that I have outlined should be sufficient evidence to show that it is almost impossible, even for so powerful a scientific actor as Pasteur, to control completely the fate of his ideas and practices once they have entered the public arena. Therefore, 'Pouilly-le-Fort' and Pasteur's germs were not only enrolling supporters, but were being enrolled[220] from time to time by various groups and bent according to their different needs and purposes.[221] Understanding of this process also requires a recognition of the 'fundamental ambivalence and chronic instability in the identification of actors with the networks to which they have been enrolled'.[222]

Pasteur's experiment was presented as providing proof of the strength of homeopathy and its weakness in relation to ordinary medical practice; as an experiment of cruelty to animals and as showing the benefits of animal experimentation; as an argument for compulsory vaccination and providing evidence for its dangers. The borders of the laboratory were not just extended to include external actors; they were forced open by these actors and tailored to their own taste and demands. The writings of the advocates of homeopathy and the anti-vaccinationists provide many examples of this 'selective appropriation' of Pasteur's results. I have already mentioned that the former emphasized both the affinities of their method with Pasteur's ('the law of similars' and immunization) and their differences, their method being more precise and less violent.[223] The latter often distinguished two elements in Pasteur's work, and although they praised the idea that the causes of disease might be destroyed by atmospheric oxygen (which clearly fitted with their sanitation programme), they strongly opposed the principle that inoculation conferred 'absolute resistance'.[224]

Pouilly-le-Fort was not merely a display of public virtuosity, nor was it simply a rallying point in the relentless rise of Pasteur's prestige and in the institutionalization of experimental medicine. It was a publicly negotiated and manipulated resource in the discursive strategies of different practitioners and public movements. There was no experiment prior to going public, just as there was no 'external public' out there, passively and naively[225] waiting to be persuaded in order to lend its support. The public dimension was articulated into multiple networks, which reciprocally crosscut one another in terms of actors, topics and rhetorical arguments.[226]

There was no straightforward victory but a series of battlefields[227] and unstable alliances in which the experiment was framed and its meaning extended well beyond its scientific significance, as can be seen in this passage from a speech that the socialist leader Gambetta addressed to the workers of Le Havre:

> Eh, bien? qu'ai-je vu? J'ai vu que vous avez les germes et les éléments de la fortune, mais qu'ils n'avaient reçu ni l'impulsion, ni la chaleur necessaire pour leur faire véritablement produire tous leurs fruits.
>
> *Le Temps*, 27 October 1881: 2

A few years later, the Italian statesman Sonnino wrote:[228]

> As brilliantly expressed by Eugène Melchior de Vogüé, according to the theory and method of Pasteur, it is not possible to fight the dangers of intrusive socialism without inoculating into the social organism, as well as into the state organism, a germ extracted from its own doctrine, a virus attenuated and purified; that is, an element, a more active and intense feeling of social charity and solidarity.[229]

There may be those who are tempted to dismiss these uses and appropriations of a scientific fact in the public arena as nothing but 'misuses', recasting them under the old scheme of 'public science as distortion of science'. I have already addressed this problem in the first two chapters. Concerning the case discussed here, one notes that Pasteur himself employed the metaphor of immunization in other contexts:

> Je croirais manquer à tante bienséance si je ne vous exprimais toute ma gratitude pour l'article que vous avez consacré aux élections académiques de demain. Vous m' avez vengé, *vacciné*, contre le virus de M. Cuvillier Fleury, virus affaibli singulièrement par vous, Monsieur, et qui, je n'ai la confiance, ne sera pas mortel.[230]

In his own account of the experiments at Pouilly-le-Fort, he commented on the sudden 'conversion' of some sceptical witnesses thus:

La confiance de l'un d'eux [Biot], le plus sceptique au début, allait jusqu'à vouloir se faire vacciner. C'est un bon augure. Ils deviendront les *propagateurs* de la vaccination charbonneuse.[231]

4

LINES AND TENSIONS

Deviation as an exposure of the backstage

The notion of *backstage* as introduced by Goffman[1] seems of particular importance to proper understanding of the process of deviation. Elaborating on his metaphor of social interaction as a theatrical performance, Goffman argues that every performance has a 'front region', i.e. the place where the performance is given, and a 'back region' or backstage. The backstage 'may be defined as a place ... where the impression fostered by a given performance is knowingly contradicted as a matter of course'.[2] Specific aspects of the activity are accentuated in the front region in order to make a certain impression on the spectators while other aspects 'which might discredit the fostered impression, are suppressed'.[3] The backstage is the region where these suppressed aspects resurface and they must therefore be concealed from the performance spectators. Here the performance is rehearsed, the necessary arrangements and adjustment are made, and the 'dirty laundry' is hidden to be washed afterwards.

For instance, restaurant workers usually behave and talk in quite different ways when they are in the kitchen compared to when they are in the presence of the restaurant's guests, where the impressions and performance are sustained. The managers and employees of a firm have places where they can relax from the performance they are carrying out in front of each other, freely comment on a previous performance, or arrange for the next with other members of their team and indulge in gossip and small talk.

Although Goffman's main concern was with situations of face-to-face interaction, his conceptualization lends itself extremely well to description of the standard relationship between scientists and the public as recounted by the sociological/continuity models of public communication of science. It is surprising that no study in this area has ever explicitly applied Goffman's model to science, although probably this tells us a considerable amount about the reluctance of the sociology of science to confront general sociological theory, especially since the so-called 'cognitive turn'.

However, what Goffman so elegantly explains with practical examples is essentially what the continuity model of science communication is about:

1   There are places/situations in which science is crafted, quite often by assembling disparate items of knowledge and machinery in a chaotic process of successive adjustments shaped by social and personal factors (e.g. interests, non-scientific beliefs, etc.).

2   When this process is recalled in front of an audience, i.e. when a discovery or experimental result is presented, this everyday life dimension is carefully removed. All possible incongruities, unorthodox methods and inappropriate behaviours are dropped and the scientific fact is ready to be served up[4] as a polished, objectified, linear and persuasive story.[5]

As an historian of science has acutely noted: 'Between the process of discovery and its later description the same relationship exists, in a certain way, as that which exists between life and its theatre representation.'[6]

Mulkay and other scholars concerned with the study of scientific discourse[7] have accordingly identified two main discursive repertoires used by scientists: a contingent repertoire that predominates in 'backstage situations', characterized by loose terminology, confidential expressions and emphasis on the observer/experimenter as actively manipulating objects and on the social and personal contingencies shaping his/her actions and beliefs. On the other hand, an empiricist repertoire is used in front-stage settings, with the emphasis on rational argumentation, specialized terminology and conventional impersonality, i.e. complete passivity and anonymity on the part of the observer/experimenter, who is only supposed to record natural phenomena without interfering with them. 'The scientist is regarded as only a messenger relaying the truth from Nature.'[8]

This process, as I have mentioned, is described as a funnel through which scientific knowledge increases in certainty and facticity stage by stage. To use Collins' terminology, the ship is eventually bottled and any observer – especially a lay observer – would have difficulty in removing it and dismantling it into its original pieces.[9] Therefore, the continuity approach clearly underestimates the possibility that scientists may find themselves in the situation of introducing the public to their backstage; a public (following Goffman's metaphor of theatre) which is comfortably sitting in the last rows of the theatre, to their backstage. Should this happen, the status of an object or result as a scientific fact is placed in serious danger and the reputation of the related researchers greatly undermined.[10] After all, as Goffman well explains: 'It is here [in the backstage] that the capacity of a performance to express something beyond itself may be painstakingly fabricated.'[11]

There are many examples of the selective use of these 'backstage visits' and 'backstage exposures' to the public eye as a strategy to dissolve the scientific pretensions of certain claims, with journalists usually more than ready to support such a strategy. Apart from events during the cold fusion saga, one recalls the 'task force' sent to inspect Benveniste's laboratory during the memory of water story, a task-force comprising not just a group of scientists but also *Nature*'s editor John Maddox and some journalists,[12] or the investigation and replication of experiments organized by committees for the investigation of the paranormal, which are usually boldly announced in the general media.[13]

Once again, however, I would argue that the process whereby scientists bring the public to the backstage requires more serious analysis for at least two reasons:

1   It is not an inconceivable event, as the cases mentioned in this work prove. Consider, for instance, the biomedical researcher who summons journalists to watch him injecting blood taken from a HIV-patient into his own arm, or Pasteur testing his vaccine in public or to the COBE scientists inviting the public to share their marvellous journey through the mysteries of the universe; and

2   it does not necessarily entail the deconstruction of facts and reputations.

Like other levels of scientific communication (but clearly in different ways and intensity, with rules that are to some extent peculiar) which have deserved much greater consideration by science studies, the public level is a level of open negotiation, enrolment and counter-enrolment of actors whose effects in terms of the construction/deconstruction of a scientific fact can be complex and manifold, stratified in time and space and diversified according to different expository and communicative situations. This should have emerged from the analysis of the cold fusion case, in which the deconstructing effect of backstage exposure was predominant but still quite distant from a clear-cut solution of the controversy. The Pasteur case and the COBE case can by no means be fitted into the traditional framework which identifies backstage exposure with the collapsing of scientific certainty. Let me once again stress that this identification is vitiated by the continuity model's emphasis on the predominance and control of the specialist levels over the 'terminal', popular ones. In reacting to the canonical account's claim of incompatibility between science and public communication of science, the latter has been entirely absorbed by the former and the recognition of its specific features overwhelmingly neglected. Such recognition does not obviously mean questioning its close connection to the core scientific enterprise.

For instance, the process of 'objectification' and 'certainty-building' regarding a scientific fact clearly unfolds in different ways at the level of specialized communication and at the level of public communication. At the specialist levels, objectification is achieved by laying a patina of anonymity and conventional passivity over any possible reference to the author and his/her personal inclinations. At the public level, objectification is produced largely in the opposite way, i.e. by the personalization and identification of theories and results with the faces and names of visible scientists.[14] Einstein *is* relativity and the need to identify Stephen Hawking with the Big Bang gives rise to a rather elastic reconstruction of the history of cosmology, as when he is said by journalists to have 'developed the Big Bang theory about the beginning of the world and (!) the Big Crunch theory about its end'.[15] The status of a result is often concentrated in the physical appearance of its proponents: George Smoot, leader of the COBE team, is described as 'clever, charming and handsome'[16] while Fleischmann is 'a short, unpleasant man'.[17]

Similarly, narratives of discoveries at the public level employ a 'genius' repertoire more frequently than do corresponding accounts at the specialist levels, where a 'cultural maturation' repertoire is predominant.[18] To give a last example, whereas at the specialist level a priority dispute may have an objectivity-reinforcing effect (by implicitly confirming that a discovered object exists and that it is relevant to scientific research),[19] at the public level it may sow suspicion concerning the real commitment of scientific actors to the disinterested pursuit of knowledge.

The following remarks should sharpen the focus on the problem. First of all, not every instance of scientists turning to the public entails the same degree of backstage exposure. Goffman notes that a region may function in certain situations as a backstage and in other situations as a frontstage; an example being a television or radio broadcasting studio (depending on whether the microphones and cameras are switched on or off). Even one of the most concealed backstage areas of a house, the bathroom, can be arranged as a frontstage when a guest is invited.

One can similarly conceive different layers of backstage access in the relationship between science and the public. The level of scientific debate and controversy, which works as a frontstage for scientists and their colleagues (being the site in which the performance privately rehearsed in the laboratory is carefully presented) is usually a backstage for the public, which is denied access to this 'region' until consensus has been reached.[20] It is here that the necessary arrangements are made for later presentations to the general public. As Goffman suggests, 'here poor members of the team, who are expressively inept, can be schooled or dropped from the performance'.[21] The cold fusion case displays some dynamics of, and motives for, having the public admitted to such region.

From this point of view, however, the laboratory is an even more remote region, the 'primary' backstage where diverse fragments begin to coalesce into a scientific story that can be plausibly narrated in a scientific forum. Quite rarely is the public granted access to this region; and in this sense Pasteur's anthrax experiment clearly represents an extreme situation of backstage exposure.

This distinction between different layers of backstages, with first-order backstages and second-order backstages (backstages of backstages) also suggests that a region can sometimes be presented as a backstage when it is actually a frontstage. This is arguably the same distinction that Collins draws between public experiments and displays of virtuosity: in the latter case the public is only apparently allowed to witness science at the bench, because what takes place in public is only a carefully rehearsed performance designed to impress the spectators,[22] an example being provided by physicist Steven Jones when he brought his test tubes to an Italian TV show during the cold fusion controversy.

This 'institutionalization' of the backstage is not only a feature of public communication of science: candid cameras and 'behind the scenes' TV shows exploit the same mechanism with regard to other areas of social life, fostering an artificial effect of spontaneity and authenticity. Thus, the dressing rooms in which a football player or a soubrette are interviewed by a TV troupe before or after a match/show are switched from their backstage status into a frontstage dimension.

Displays of scientific virtuosity can be interpreted as attempts to turn to the public 'softly', i.e. to obtain proximity and familiarity with the public without incurring the risks of deconstruction and thorough exposure entailed by strong forms of deviation, and especially by public experiments. The turn to the public remains substantially under the control of the scientists concerned.[23] On the other hand, this strategy may escape the control of the scientific actors fostering it, who suddenly find themselves 'naked' in front of the public, as happened to Pons and Fleischmann during the cold fusion controversy.

This point can perhaps be refined further. Imagining the process of scientific communication as a *continuum* of backstages and frontstages which proceeds from the laboratory workbench to public performances, with every frontstage functioning as a backstage to the next communicative situation, does not take us much beyond the shortcomings of continuity models. We are still largely trapped in the analytical fiction that places communication stages in strict temporal sequence. While this might work for the linear, popularization processes of scientific communication to the public, it cannot fully account for our deviation cases, in which the public is not always addressed after the routine scientific scrutiny of ideas, but in parallel with, and even prior to, specialist debating.

Goffman once again has a useful suggestion. He points out that, just as access to the back region must be controlled in order to prevent 'dramaturgical problems', so too must access to the front region be monitored and controlled by performers. A performance, in fact, does not have only a backstage and a frontstage; it also has a residual region, 'the outside'. For instance, a performance in a house will have its internal backstages and frontstages separated from the outside world by the walls of the building.

Accordingly, the outsiders are those persons excluded from a given performance. However, the performer now acting for an audience may also be preparing a show similar to or different from the one being staged for those temporarily outside.[24] We have already seen how the same researchers often give performances for variously differentiated audiences of colleagues and also for the general public, e.g. by granting interviews to journalists or signing daily press articles as well as publishing specialized articles or giving talks at conferences.

The interesting situation arises when different audiences and related performances intersect, i.e. 'when outsiders enter the front or the back region of a particular performance-in-progress'.[25] The consequences of this intersection inform all the different types of communicative situation involved because every performance, at the time when it is given, claims some sort of exclusive character:

> Performers tend to give the impression, or tend not to contradict the impression, that the role they are playing at the time is their most important role and that the attributes claimed by or imputed to them are the most essential and characteristic attributes. When individuals witness a show that was not meant for them, they may, then, become disillusioned about this show as well as about the show that was meant for them.[26]

Performers normally seek to avoid this situation by 'segregating audiences', i.e. by arranging for their shows to take place in different regions or in the same region but with a different time schedule. A scientist may try to ensure that the lay audience to one of his public communicative performances does not include any of his colleagues, and vice versa, since he is aware that some of the aspects emphasized in one performance will not be compatible with the aspects emphasized in another. For instance, the anonymity and cultural maturation repertoires of the specialist performance may collide with the personalization and 'genius' repertoires of the public performance.[27] To this end, some researchers publish their popular contributions or fiction writings under pseudonyms.[28] While this segregation of audiences seems feasible for routine popularization, it seems less so for the public communication of science to general media like newspapers and television news (the content of which is likely to be generally accessible to other researchers), and especially as regards deviation cases, i.e. those public performances which are used as part and parcel of the scientific debate and to some extent as a substitute for specialized communication. It is precisely the intersection of audiences and communicative practices in such cases that enables scientists to shape scientific discourse, although it is obviously still a potential source of 'danger', e.g. in terms of professional misalignment or failure to comply with the profession's communicative standards.

By condensing communicative situations usually kept separated in terms of time, space and participants, deviation introduces an 'essential tension' between different performances and discursive repertoires. Apparently innocent mechanisms such as humour are often the best markers of such tension. The greater the usual distance between the situations that are condensed, the higher the tension is, the climax being theoretically reached when one or more than one front region is sharply contrasted with its original, 'primary', backstage. I say 'theoretically' because I have given to the expressions backstage and frontstage here only a relative meaning within the framework of scientific communication: each backstage is potentially a frontstage for another communicative situation and vice versa. Even the laboratory, as the 'primary' backstage *par excellence*, may be eventually reaccommodated as a frontstage.

How far this tension can be sustained depends not only on the specific strategies pursued by scientific actors, but also on non-scientific elements such as the attention span available in media arenas, the possible competition by other issues, and so on.[29] In the long run, different teams of participants are likely to apply pressure to release the tension by disentangling performances, separating audiences or at any rate collapsing this multidimensional configuration into a one-dimensional space (i.e. by re-establishing the routine orderly sequence of performances).

Negotiations are thus likely to centre on the status accorded to a situation:[30] critical scientists may refuse to accept that a performance is also directed to the specialized community (i.e. as truly 'scientific') and reframe it as a performance merely fabricated for public consumption. This happened for instance in the cold fusion case, when Pons and Fleischmann's work was labelled as 'science by press conference' or 'showbiz science'. When Willner injected himself with HIV-infected blood, the definition itself of the performance as an experiment was questioned: doubt was cast on the actual HIV-positivity of the subject from whom the blood was taken, who was described as a 'self-described HIV-positive man'.[31] Instead, Richard Feynman's simple fiddling with clamps and ice water before the press and the TV cameras is framed as a true experiment and translated into conclusive evidence of the causes of the Shuttle accident.[32]

I previously questioned the idea that public communication of science necessarily strengthens the solidity of a scientific fact through a cumulative process of subsequent filtering and distancing from the research front. I showed that this process might generally be applied to routine popularization but not to cases of more 'active' and dramatic public address. In this section I have similarly questioned the related assumption that an interruption in this cumulative chain, by backstage exposure, for example, will necessarily result in the disintegration of scientific facts and reputations.

In short, as an element potentially embedded in deviation processes, backstage exposure does not *per se* guarantee a straightforward outcome.

Just as the public is not out there only to say 'yes', it is not out there only to say 'no'. To avoid the misleading 'outcome' perspective, one may hypothesize that consequences depend on the ways in which this exposure is, more or less selectively, applied to human and non-human actors,[33] how it is framed and placed within the general context of scientific discourse and the extent to which different audiences and performances encroach on each other. Attention should also be paid to the shifting composition of audiences in the course of a debate[34] as well as to the multiple memberships of both performers and spectators during a single performance.[35]

Public communication and boundary configurations

In examining the three case studies presented here, I have attempted to show that not only is deviation related to 'marginal' situations requiring boundary negotiation, but also that this 'boundary-work' is articulated into a number of layers common to each case, although clearly expressed with different intensities and features. I shall now summarize these dimensions, further highlight common elements and specificities, and finally set out a model that sums up my view of the process of deviation and its importance in relation to boundary-work in particular.

Three general layers of boundary conditions have been identified as associated with deviation to the public level: they are examined in the next three sections.

Problems of demarcation between science and non-science

This is the most general layer of boundary work. It comprises all those cases in which demarcation concerns the 'external boundaries' that separate science from other activities (which may be competing practices such as mechanics, other areas of human endeavour like art or religion, fringe sciences like parapsychology). This layer of boundary work is activated when one such activity applies pressure on the external borders of science for inclusion, but is also mobilized to expand these borders by 'invading' other areas. One of the forms of boundary negotiation involved in the COBE/Big Bang case lay precisely at this level, with respect to the boundary between science on one side and religion and art on the other. A model such as Big Bang and a field such as cosmology must obviously compete side by side against other activities offering answers to mankind's fundamental questions. Scientists increasingly claim that research is to be praised by the public not only for its technological achievements but also, and especially, for its contributions in terms of cultural and aesthetic richness and pleasure.[36] One may also argue that this shift of emphasis to the 'cultural' contribution of scientific research is a strategy with which to counteract growing criticism that scientists are unable to provide 'harmless' solutions to practical problems.[37]

Problems of demarcation between different disciplines

At stake here is the more 'internal' type of boundary that separates one field of scientific activity from another. Disciplinary fields often intersect and must therefore compete with neighbouring areas over ownership of a certain problem, over the most appropriate approach to a phenomenon, and over the related distribution of resources (funds, recruits, respectability and audiences). Both the COBE case (which was framed within a long-standing tradition of boundary negotiation among disciplinary fields such as astronomy, physics and mathematics over their models of the universe) and the cold fusion case (with physicists and chemists publicly debating which measurements should be used to assess the existence of cold fusion and physicists gradually regaining control over an issue they felt was their own) are significant examples of this process; a process that takes place at even more internal levels, i.e. between subdisciplines within a discipline (e.g. biochemistry, electrochemistry, and so on) and within more specific segments of scientific activity within a subdiscipline. To comprise all these different levels of partitioning, Gerson[38] has proposed the use of the general expression 'lines of work'.

> The various segments of a tradition will always be engaged to some degree, in competing for recognition and prestige both within and outside the discipline. There is almost always a differential distribution of prestige among different subdisciplines, and as a result there is almost always some degree of jockeying for position. This often involves distancing and differentiating lines of work from one another as it does the positive assertion of legitimacy for a particular tradition.[39]

Boundaries around paradigms

The third, and most internal degree of boundary negotiation involved in deviation to the public level is that concerning the questioning and/or protection of the basic conceptualization (paradigm) to which research work in a particular line or set of lines is anchored. Examples of this negotiation are provided by both the COBE case (in which turning to the public was clearly important to shield the Big Bang model against increasing criticism developing at the specialist levels) and the Pasteur case (in which the paradigm of 'morbid spontaneity' was eventually overthrown). During these strong controversies or tensions, which are most acute in the periods of conflict over a possible paradigm shift and 'revolution', participation of 'external actors' may prove crucial in fostering or counter-acting the establishment of a new paradigm.

The foregoing is not an exhaustive classification of all the boundary layers involved in deviation processes. Infinite degrees of boundary negotiation exist among these three broad types and within each type. Nevertheless, they provide an overall framework into which I shall now introduce some important specifications.

First, it is perhaps necessary to emphasize that these boundary negotiations in public do not merely set margins and reinforce boundaries between different lines of work. In the second type of negotiation especially, what is generally at stake is the process whereby disciplines and lines of work intersect. In this process, competing and displacing the borders that separate one line from another is just as important as crossing or making these boundaries more flexible. As new research problems and themes arise, they must be handled using a combination of methods, techniques and theoretical models available from different lines of work. In these cases, it is crucially important for scientists to have a common space for the communication and exchange of ideas, techniques and experimental results, a space which cannot be provided by traditional, specialized forums. Again, the COBE and the cold fusion cases aid understanding, because in both of them the public arena provided a space that was rapidly and simultaneously accessible to researchers working in different fields. The negotiation of 'ownership rights' over cold fusion between physicists and chemists and their public confrontation would have been impossible if this space had not been available.

In all of the three cases presented here, but in the Pasteur case especially, this intersection assumes an even wider form, by bringing not only different categories of practitioners together but also different scientific audiences. In Pasteur's case, for example, the audiences participating in negotiation of the experiment included not only chemists and biologists but also farmers, veterinary surgeons and physicians. In the cold fusion case, both policy makers and managers of scientific research were closely involved in defining the issue. I have already mentioned Epstein's insightful analysis of the importance of pressure groups like gay activist movements in the shaping of AIDS research.[40]

The public level, I have argued, is the ideal stage for this intersection, bridging and negotiation between 'social worlds' to occur since all the participants combine their memberships in a specific arena with membership in this space.[41] As other scholars have pointed out, 'A public space is vital to resolve doubts that cannot be resolved within a field to settle issues pertaining to interfield relationship'.[42]

This role of 'common arena' where issues are taken whose resolution cannot be dealt with entirely within the border of a specific arena (be it an arena defined by a specific paradigm, or a disciplinary arena, or the scientific arena at large) is usually marked by the existence of specific discursive items for which I have used Star and Griesemer's term 'boundary objects'.[43] A boundary object is the pivotal linguistic and conceptual reference around which negotiation between different audiences rotates: the

Big Bang, the Cold Fusion and the Germ are respectively the boundary objects of the COBE debate, of the cold fusion debate and of the anthrax vaccine debate. They are what the actor–network model identifies as 'obligatory passage points' in the translating of interests and enrolling supporters for a scientific claim,[44] or what Moscovici locates at the heart of a social representation (its 'zero degree'). In the perspective adopted here, however, is less clear (contrary to what the actor-network model seems to suggest) that a scientific actor can entirely control the 'functioning' of these objects by forcing other actors to pass through them in order to support his own views. Boundary objects are translated and manipulated at different levels of communication with different intensities and meanings by the various groups involved. The label 'Big Bang' may denote a number of models addressing the problem of the origin of the universe to cosmologists, a single explanation to scientists not directly involved in this research area or a benevolent act of creation to lay readers. This flexibility of boundary objects and the possibility that they might escape the hands of their creators has been shown with regard to both the Big Bang and Pasteur cases: their adaptation to the specific needs of a group may go as far as to turn them upside down and use them against the actors initially responsible for them. Consider again the label 'Big Bang' coined by Fred Hoyle to make fun of the model, or Pasteur's germ being eventually enrolled by anti-vaccinationists. Moreover, as for Big Bang and Cold Fusion, such labels often do originate in, or are shaped at, the public level. The acronym initially used to denote the AIDS disease, GRID (Gay Related Immunodeficiency Disease) had to be discarded after protests by gay organizations.[45]

Thus, boundary objects do not matter here as supporting a theory or enrolling allies but simply as central elements in making communication between levels and arenas possible; indeed, their disappearance is associated with the interruption of such communication, as the development of the cold fusion story illustrates. Like flags, they are planted at the intersection of territories and help actors locate the boundary layers at stake. For instance, the Big Bang identifies at one level the border between science and religion, at another level that between physics and astronomy and at a more internal level Big Bang supporters and their opponents. Cold Fusion similarly separates science from quackery, chemists from physicists and critics from believers.

A cluster of other linguistic elements like metaphors and paradoxes usually surrounds a boundary object and guarantees connection to individual levels, in a chain of translations which further anchor it to the representations and frameworks specific to each social world. Thus, cold fusion is described as a 'marriage between neutrons' and a germ as an 'invader of the body'. It is not uncommon for a metaphor or a paradox to form the core of a boundary object, as in the expressions 'Big Bang' and 'cold fusion'.

Mapping deviation

I now introduce into the model two axes which cut across the above classification of boundary layers: the first of them is vertical, the second cuts
each of the three layers horizontally. Deviation to the public frequently
entails the joint negotiation of the three boundary layers; a combination
to be observed in each of our cases. The public, however, is obviously more
responsive to the more visible boundaries; that is, it is more aware of
disciplinary demarcation than of paradigm shift, and more aware of the
demarcations separating science from non-science more than of disciplinary demarcation. Internal tensions may therefore be released as one ascends
the ladder of boundary layers, so that a conflict between different theoretical views is framed as a conflict between disciplinary approaches and
this in turn as a conflict between science and non-science.[46] Both these
shifts are well exemplified by the following claims made by Robert Gallo
with regard to the HIV–Duesberg controversy:

> A discussion between us [Gallo and Duesberg] would make no
> sense. He is an organic chemist. I would never discuss with him
> the resonance of the electron spin in the molecule of an organic
> compound. Peter [Duesberg] does not understand the biology he
> is talking about. That's it. I have no intention to engage in a point-
> less discussion.[47]

> When I am asked to explain why these critics do not accept the
> scientific results we have achieved with HIV, I reply that there
> actually are people (I hope not many scientists) who do not believe
> the US placed a man on the moon. There is also, I am told, a
> Flat Earth Society which has evolved a complex rationale to explain
> away all the evidence that the earth is round.[48]

If one imagines this process figuratively, it is equivalent to the collating of
a three-dimensional space into a two-dimensional and then into a one-
dimensional space. The process ultimately reassesses both internal and
external consistency, as it conveys to the public an image of science as
consensual and reaffirms 'corporate solidarity by drawing orthodox members
of the institution together in the face of a common enemy'.[49] The comple-
tion of the process may be symbolized by the expulsion of internal deviants
(on whom is placed responsibility for the internal tensions) with their views,
methods and results reappraised as quackery or religious myths. Thus, in
the case of cold fusion the boundary between scientific orthodoxy and scientific heresy overwhelmed the more internal boundary layers at stake, while
in the Big Bang case the boundary between science and religion became
the predominant focus of the debate, overshadowing paradigm negotiation
on the Big Bang as well as disciplinary negotiation.

Members of a scientific community, especially those in 'marginal positions' or pursuing less conventional lines of research, may strongly resist this flattening process, in the awareness that unidimensional consensus can only be achieved at the cost of obscuring the internal debates and controversies in which they are involved.

During one of the many public debates taking place in the US about creationism, Richard Lewontin encouraged colleagues to confront this 'heresy' by publicly emboldening the evolutionary paradigm as representing a situation of complete agreement among researchers.

> It is time for students of the evolutionary process, especially those who have been misquoted and used by creationists, to state clearly that evolution is *fact*, not theory, and that what is at issue within biology are questions of details of the process and the relative importance of different mechanisms of evolution.[50]

Several distinguished scholars, including Stephen Jay Gould, reacted sharply to this call to arms:

> I am saddened by a trend I am just beginning to discern among my colleagues. I sense that some now wish to mute the healthy debate about a theory that has brought new life to evolutionary biology. It provides grist for creationists' mills, they say, even if only by distortion. Perhaps we should lie low and rally around the flag of strict Darwinism, at least for the moment – a kind of old-time religion on our part. We should borrow another metaphor and recognize that we too have to tread a straight and narrow path, surrounded by roads to perdition. For if we ever begin to suppress our search to understand nature, to quench our own intellectual excitement *in a misguided effort to present a unified front where it does not and should not exist, we are truly lost.*[51]

Collating the different boundary layers together cuts-out all the positions and actors that do not fit in this squared, condensed wall of frontstage consensus which is set to represent science. This unidimensional condensation often brings a single scientific result, representative of a single scientific discipline and a single, utterly visible, scientific speaker, to embody 'SCIENCE' in public. Thus COBE is not just a result purporting to provide evidence for a specific line of scientific work but is repeatedly translated as 'decisive proof of the Big Bang' and ultimately as representing science when science must publicly confront religion; Hawking is not just the proponent of a cosmological model, however important; he is cosmology and he is science. The same goes for Pasteur in the multiple debates surrounding his experiment, and also for the scientists officiating over the ritual excommunication of Pons and Fleischmann, who did not simply criticize a theory from their own point of view, but spoke on behalf of science and arranged for 'garbage'[52] to be relocated outside it. Such a glittering, harmonious box displayed in public can no longer include unevenness or disagreement, which have to be identified as something 'external'. At this stage of public negotiation, some sort of 'reciprocity of perspectives' assumption holds.[53] Members of the scientific team will be expected to adhere smoothly to such a neatly arranged picture. Failure to do so may be accommodated by arguing their being temporarily playing a different language game[54] from science, i.e. as 'joking' or as 'chatting with journalists'.[55] In the long run, their failure to comply must be accounted for as grounded on typically non-scientific, non-rational reasons: insanity, greed and so on.[56]

In this process of collation into a unidimensional distinction between science and non-science, an important role is usually played by a 'reflexive' demarcation rhetoric, that which is drawn between science and the public. Depending on specific needs and situations, actors and communicative performances may be placed inside or outside the boundaries of science, being classified as truly 'scientific' or as 'science for the public'.[57] The boundary also runs more subtly through public communication of science, demarcating popularization (i.e. appropriate scientific dissemination) from distorted spectacularization. Deviation may thus be strategically assigned to one or the other type. This is most evident when one compares two almost formally identical cases of deviation like cold fusion and the COBE case. In the former case, Pons and Fleischmann's initial press conference was criticized as an inappropriate public stunt which by-passed the scientific institutional control system; in the COBE case, although the Smoot team press conference took place prior to any official publication or peer review process, it was considered to be legitimately 'scientific' and timely arousing public attention and interest in cosmological research.

When the process of collating all of these boundary dimensions into one has been completed, deviation is reduced to popularization and the routine communication flow between science and the public is restored. This is what I mean by reflexive boundary work: through the turn to the public the very conditions for 'going public' and ultimately for turning to the public are negotiated.

The second axis

Clearly, as Gerson has also pointed out,[58] the negotiation and adjustment of boundaries between different lines of work within science as well as between science and non-science, is a continuous process that only in special situations needs to be conducted in public. When the boundaries are well structured and defined, the relative configurations of disciplinary fields and identities are tacitly assumed to be pre-given and generally unquestioned.

Only when these boundaries are threatened by specific marginal situations is it necessary to publicly reassess their solidity by repulsing the enemies as a source of impurity.

However, there are situations in which such boundaries have not only to be enforced or made more visible but rather truly constituted. In a recent essay, Andrew Abbott has explained how boundaries are not simply located around social entities, but are used to bring such entities into being by connecting 'oppositions and differences into a single whole that has a thing-ness quality'.[59] For instance, when a discipline must first establish itself, it has to define a distinct set of activities and bring together those scholars who are engaged in them, differentiate its activities from those of pre-existing disciplines and place itself in a historical perspective by identifying appropriate founders and forerunners;[60] in short, it must gain recognition as respectable and 'scientific'. These preconditions are usually fulfilled with participation by the public, which is then pushed 'outside' again, once it has granted its support and blessing to the new line of work. I provided various examples of this process with regard to the establishment of scientific disciplines, institutions and even of the scientific profession itself, in Chapter 2. Here I wish only to point out that it is also evinced by two of the case studies conducted here.

In the COBE case, it is possible to see the development of a discipline, cosmology, without an established status and still defining its position with regard to other disciplinary areas as it secures its 'scientific' quality, although addressing questions that are akin to those addressed by religion. In the case of Pasteur, a new line of work and a new paradigmatic approach to the study of diseases centred on laboratory experimentation was being established by yoking together different lines of scientific work.

I suggest that further insights into deviation processes and therefore into the role of public communication of science are gained if the two axes define a Cartesian space. The vertical dimension measures the size of the boundary at stake. At the lower end it has the minimum threshold of negotiation possible in public, that around the boundaries of a paradigm. At the top, it has the most general layer that can be at stake in the public communication of science: that between science and non-science. The horizontal dimension measures the intensity with which boundary negotiation can be carried out at each specific level. Again, this is a *continuum* with infinite possible situations, which for the sake of simplification can be described by setting its two extreme poles. On the left-hand pole we have those situations in which boundary stability is maximum; boundaries around science, around disciplines or around paradigms are clearly set and visible both to internal and to external actors. On the right-hand pole, we have the opposite situations; those characterized by maximum boundary instability. The boundaries around scientific enterprise as well as around disciplines and paradigms have to be constituted. The distinctiveness and thingness quality of a paradigmatic approach, of a line of work or even of the scientific enterprise as such are still to be established.

In this space one can therefore plot different configurations around a certain scientific issue as combinations of the two axes. A situation is described by the conjunction of three points in space identifying the stability of each boundary layer.

The simplest situation is that of alignment of the three points on the left part of the scheme. Boundary sensitivity is minimum everywhere. The boundaries around the paradigm are very stable; anomalies are discarded without fuss. Deviation is unlikely to take place: popularization is more than sufficient to convey a sense of this stability to participants and spectators. Only if we move to the centre of this bottom area does the situation begin to change slightly. The paradigm's consistency is questioned by alternative theories and unexpected results. Deviation may appear as an opportunity for dissenters. However, if the above (disciplinary, science/non-science) layers are still quite close to the left side in terms of stability, it will be relatively straightforward for the group committed to the preservation of the paradigm to bring the negotiation to those levels and discard the emerging views as coming from a discipline whose members are not entitled to speak on the issue. If the stability of this level is also shaking, another step must be taken to present such views as non-scientific. Turning to the public will then be sanctioned as a source of danger and pollution and the public stage will be used to excommunicate those responsible for it. The cold fusion case is located here. (See Figure 4.1.) However, the more we slide towards the right part of the scheme, the less stable the boundaries become.

Suppose there is a paradigm to be protected against growing criticism, but disciplinary ownership in terms of rights and competencies is still being defined. Suppose that around this issue science is still to some extent negotiating its position with regard to other social arenas (e.g. religion). Not only does the expulsion ritual becomes difficult to perform but deviation begins to represent an opportunity to the whole configuration and not just a threat to its stability. Through deviation, the status of the discipline within science and that of science within society can be further established: new territories and further recognition can be acquired. We are now around the middle of the scheme and this is where the line describing the COBE case can be placed. (See Figure 4.2.) If we move the central and bottom portion of the line again towards the right part of the scheme, we approximately identify the position of the Pasteur case. (See Figure 4.3.) Here a new paradigm is taking definitive shape together with a new line of work. The public stage may still entail dangers in terms of the appropriation and manipulation of the scientific ideas put forward; but it is definitely worth taking the risk because at this stage the open communication needed to bring different practitioners together will be facilitated. Although in this

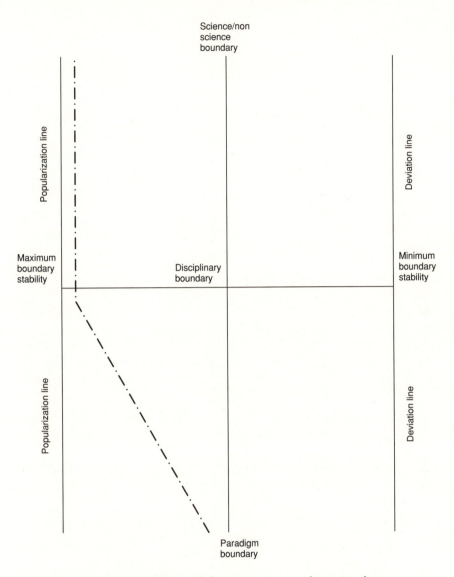

Figure 4.1 Visualization of the cold fusion case in two-dimensional space

case also the science/non-science boundary was clearly less structured (which allowed for the exchange not just between different scientific practitioners but also with outsiders such as farmers), we are not yet on the configuration line placed to the extreme right of the scheme. This is clearly a pattern difficult to observe empirically as it is characterized by utmost institutional fluidity: it is not clear what should be said about a certain issue, who is

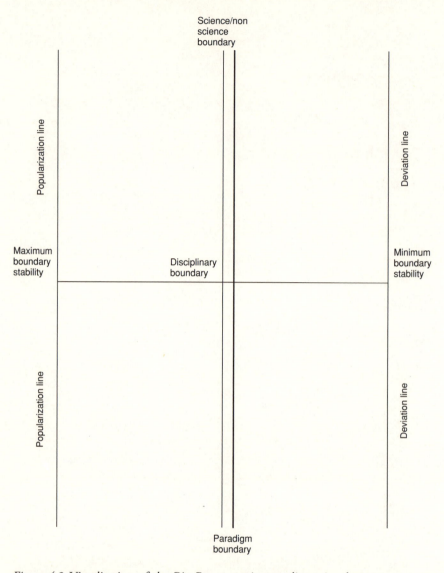

Figure 4.2 Visualization of the Big Bang case in two-dimensional space

entitled to say it and in which communicative forums the related communication should take place. Nor is it certain yet whether the issue is a
scientific one, whether the discipline under formation will be a scientific
discipline and how outsiders can be distinguished from insiders. The
boundary itself between science and non-science is ill-articulated. As I
suggested earlier, either one should go back in the history of science,

140

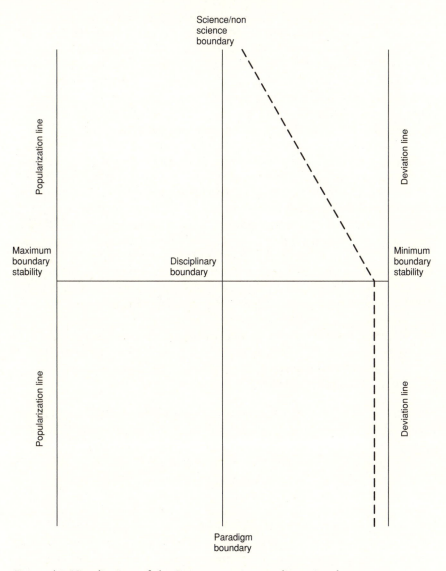

Figure 4.3 Visualization of the Pasteur case in two-dimensional space

analysing the role of the public in the process of scientific professionalization or one should be lucky enough to capture a sense of this configuration in the ongoing structuration of new sectors of activity which are not generated by the segmentation or intersection of pre-existing disciplines within a stable scientific frame. The formation of the latter takes place via the continuous interaction in informal contexts between scientific experts and

141

members of other categories such as technology users (as was the case of computer sciences until a few decades ago) or activists (as is the case with the environmental sciences). Deviation will not be the exception, but the rule. In the absence of refereed journals and university courses, a variety of non-institutionalized forums (e.g. magazines, newspapers, websites) at the public level not only provides additional space for the fostering of knowledge exchanges (as for more stable configurations) or public visibility but also the basic stage for communication to take place.

So far, in order not to complicate my treatment further, I have not explicitly mentioned either Mary Douglas's grid/group model for classifying societies and their related concerns for purity and order,[61] or Bloor's model which applies the same dimensions to scientific communities and their reaction to anomaly.[62] Although I am clearly indebted to both of them in general terms for the approach adopted here, my concern is quite different since it deals with the association between boundary negotiation and public communication of science and with the different forms assumed by this association in different situations. However, I shall partially repay my debt here, at least to Douglas, by citing a sentence from her which helps me to summarize the arguments of this chapter. She writes:

> Where the social system is well-articulated, I look for articulate powers vested in the points of authority; where the social system is ill-articulated, I look for inarticulate powers vested in those who are a source of disorder.[63]

Translated into the terms of my model, this would read: *Where the boundaries around a scientific issue are well articulated, deviation is unlikely to occur and public communication of science is likely to play a minor role in the process of making science; where boundaries are ill-articulated, deviation is likely to be present and public communication of science is likely to play an important role in the process of making science.*

This points in my direction, but it is not precisely what I want to say. My concern here is not just with the 'greater' or 'lesser' importance of deviation and science in public. Rather, I have tried to show that *different configurations of boundary stability are associated with the different uses of deviation and the roles played by deviation to the public.* These differences are both quantitative and qualitative. Figure 4.4 summarizes Figures 4.1–4.3.

Note that this helps us at least partially to overcome one of the main limitations faced by the continuity models in general. This limitation arises when these models seek to answer questions such as the following: why does turning to the public sometimes result in the reinforcement of a scientific fact and sometimes in its deconstruction?; is it just because backstage exposure is selectively applied to some facts and actors and not to others?; and why is this so?; are the ultimate explanatory factors – as many studies

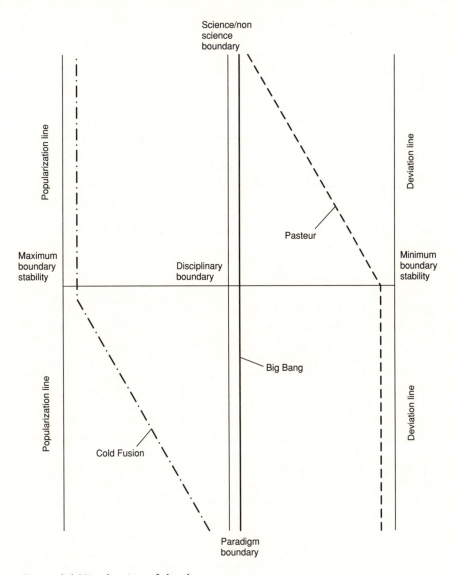

Figure 4.4 Visualization of the three cases

seem to argue more or less explicitly[64] – the greater power and public recognition enjoyed by some actors, their greater ability to persuade the public and bring it onto their side, enthusiastically echoing their claims and maliciously inspecting their adversaries' backstages? With regard to my present purposes, this manner of posing the questions is to some extent meaningless. *Mutatis mutandis,* trying to impose a predetermined outcome on

143

deviation is like trying to predict *a priori* the outcome of a scientific debate at the specialist level. It may work for popularization as a predictable, unidirectional and non-negotiable communication flow. But deviation introduces open negotiation at the public level that is shaped by a number of elements and forces. Moreover, like most scientific negotiations, this will rarely have a straightforward outcome in terms of 'success' and 'failure'. Consensus and dissent will be fringed across communication levels, positions will merge and compromises will be reached along the way. I have already commented on this. What I would add here is a tentative answer to the remaining part of the problem, which can be formulated as follows: is there a way to place situational constraints on the use of the public level to shape scientific debate? The model introduced above suggests that different configurations of boundary stability will orient to different uses of deviation, e.g. to more 'constructive' or to more 'destructive' uses. Which is not to deny an important role of power, reputation and rhetorical elements. Boundary configuration, so to speak, sets the scene for actors to carry out deviation and the related public negotiation.

With reference to Bloor's model, my approach does not regard the configuration as entirely defined by scientific actors. The degree of boundary precision at the different layers is also publicly negotiated, i.e. the public does not participate in boundary-work only when a marginal situation arises: it concurs in the definition of such situation as a marginal one to which boundary-work in public can be applied. This is clearly more visible the further we move up the ladder of boundary layers: although non-scientific actors may play a relatively minor role in evaluating the stability of an internal paradigm boundary compared with the experts involved, the closer we approach the negotiation of external boundaries around science the more substantial public participation is likely to be.[65] This also accounts for my use of such terms as 'configuration' instead of more sociologically established ones such as 'system' or 'community', which would instead emphasize actor membership and give the impression that the situation is first defined autonomously by the scientists and then made in public to be solved.

A major problem still remains, however. I have spoken of association and relation between boundary negotiation and deviation, deliberately failing to specify the causal direction of the link. Do demarcation problems (and in particular, certain configurations of demarcation problems in terms of the intensity and level at which boundary work is required) trigger alternative modalities of public communication of science or does the occurrence of such modalities (i.e. deviation processes) activate tensions at the different layers of scientific boundaries? Is the public mobilized when sharp tensions arise within science (or between science and society), or does public participation result in boundary negotiation? Needless to say, I cannot give a clear-cut answer to such legitimate questions.

Before approaching the problem of causal direction, however, I must discuss the extent to which my model can be conceived in terms of causality. When introducing marginal situations as *conditions* for deviation, I did not specify whether these conditions are necessary and/or sufficient conditions, nor can I hope to have clarified this point merely by citing evidence from three case studies, however deeply analysed. In inquiring further into the nature and articulation of such conditions, I have argued that they cannot be simply categorized in terms of presence/absence of 'pressure on the margins'. Rather, boundary instability may be sustained to a certain degree before it is publicly recognized as a marginal situation and deviated communication arises. Other types of conditions may help or hinder this recognition: e.g. the public's sensitivity to a certain scientific issue, the extent to which it can be incorporated into journalistic practices at the level of the general media (which are considerably different from those of popularization writers; for instance a scientific controversy will need some focusing event before it is covered), the visibility of the scientific actors and institutions sponsoring the issue and so on. Once the process is triggered, distinguishing causes and effects becomes even more difficult, as both elements reinforce each other: public discussion places pressure on the boundaries, and boundary negotiation demands to be carried out in public. Remember that deviation may expose backstages and add another line of tension – that between frontstages and backstages to the configurations. Similarly, the process declines when a condition of stability is (re)established and/or when the negotiation exceeds (in terms of time span, scheduling and carrying capacity) the limits of the public agenda. That this 'looping' process of mutual reinforcement occurs is confirmed by the fact that the boundary itself between deviation and popularization is also involved in the negotiation.

This is also the reason why one should refrain from characterizing deviation as a process that completely substitutes popularization under specific conditions, whose beginning and end can be precisely marked. Although separable for analytical purposes, these two communication modalities are to be understood as the extremes of a *continuum*, where any communicative situation and every single communicative performance carried out in public with regard to a scientific issue combines some degree of deviation with some degree of popularization. In routine situations, however, only a modicum of deviation will be incorporated into public communication of science because a continuous, implicit definition of boundaries can be achieved by means an institutionalized unilinear process of communication, the gatekeepers (e.g. scientific journalists) and stages of which are identified and emphasized by continuity models, i.e. popularization. There may be circumstances, however, in which it is not sufficient for scientists to follow this expository path because a more substantial and dramatic assessment, either as defence, extension or actual constitution of boundaries

145

is required. Stages and formal fulfilments are then set aside and researchers turn directly to the general public. Deviation takes the floor when these latent tensions around different layers of scientific boundaries interact with the needs of audiences and the exigencies of newswork, an interaction which finds concrete expression in specific newsworthy performances like press conferences or public experiments. This work is not meant to undervalue the second set of elements involved in the interaction. Thorough understanding of deviation processes would also clearly benefit from serious investigation of the media and journalistic practices relevant to public communication of science. It would then be possible to supplement my model with another axis identifying the different levels of public sensitivity to science issues.

I have focused primarily on the first element – namely on the conditions and forms of the deviation process in relation to the scientific debate – because its study could reveal an aspect of public communication of science completely neglected by the canonical account (i.e. the importance of the level of public communication of science in shaping the scientific debate) and insufficiently addressed by continuity models (which gave to this level a pre-eminently reinforcing, confirmatory role with regard to the debate being carried out at the specialist levels).

From this perspective, one notes with interest the ambivalence of scientists towards situations characterized by a high degree of deviation and, in general, towards their relationships with the public.[66] Just as deviation processes may represent an opportunity to overcome the timings and constraints of the popularization process, so they are often regarded with apprehension by specialist communities. When thrust into the public arena, a scientific issue loses at least some of the special status that it could still enjoy within popularization frames (like popularization magazines or science sections in newspapers). It may, for example, become subject, like any other issue, to processes of issue-linking or to timed 'life-cycles'[67] and scientific claims may eventually be assimilated into interest- and value-laden political claims. Moreover, its ongoing manipulation as well as its incorporation in the public arena is likely to be performed also by actors external to the scientific community (e.g. media actors).

This helps to explain the increasing efforts made by scientists to extend their control over the processes of communication with the public. Scientific institutions organize seminars on the subject, scientists write handbooks for other scientists on how to cope with the media and hands-on laboratory sessions are designed to have scientists teach journalists how to communicate science. Public relation offices and other devices[68] are set up, not to exclude the possibility of deviations (something rather difficult to achieve) but to extend the scientific community's control over the recognition of marginal situations and over the related activation of deviation processes so that it can resort to them *ad hoc* or, in turn, criticize them. To what extent such efforts may be – or have been so far – successful is uncertain. For example, it could be argued that as forms and rules of popularization have become established over time, its demarcation from deviation communication (still blurred in a case like Pasteur's) has been strengthened. This may make deviation processes less frequent, but at the same time more noteworthy, easily recognizable, and therefore richer in consequences.

A tension nevertheless exists within the scientific community between institutionalizing deviation by absorbing it (through the constitution of appropriate mechanisms) into ordinary expository practice (popularization) to prevent its 'uncontrolled abuse' and at the same time preserving it as a sort of 'emergency exit' for specific situations, as well as a potential source of scientific change. This tension should not necessarily be viewed as an obstacle to be overcome sooner or later. It is interesting to analyse how scientific researchers cope with and to some extent exploit such tension by balancing (rather often through deviated communication itself) the weight of the two communication styles depending on the different circumstances and purposes. As I have emphasized, the relative predominance of one of the two styles is not just to be seen as resulting from a certain configuration, it also conspires to define it. A considerable part of the scientists' discourse in the media is in fact not devoted to the presentation of theories and ideas. Instead, it tries to show how public communication of science should be accomplished, thereby seeking to recast either 'popularization' situations in a prevailing deviation frame (this was for instance the aim of Pons and Fleischmann and their supporters during the cold fusion controversy) or deviation situations (the aim of most high-energy physicists during the development of the same controversy) in a prevailing popularization frame.[69] Not just the public as such but the manifold ways in which public involvement is activated and negotiated are therefore a political resource available to scientists to include or exclude theories and actors from the scientific debate and ultimately shape such debate.

NOTES

PREFACE

1 I have obviously modelled these short accounts on real cases: the cold fusion controversy, Pasteur's public experiment on anthrax at Pouilly-le-Fort and Robert Willner's self-injection. However, one can easily understand that they could fit potentially many other cases of 'turning to the public', like for instance Feynman's public demonstration of the cause of the Shuttle accident (see Gieryn and Figert, 1990 and the short account given later); the huge publicity campaign organized by CERN to present the discovery of the W/Z⁰ bosons (for which Rubbia and Van der Meer later received the Nobel prize) before the official publication of the relative paper (Krige, 1993); or the COBE satellite story, begun with a press conference even more triumphal than the cold fusion one, with its claims about having observed the scientific equivalent of 'God' in the universe. Both the cold fusion and the Pasteur case will be presented later in detail. Concerning the Willner case: Robert Willner, a physician, held a press conference on 28 October 1994, at a North Carolina hotel, during which he took a needle, stuck it into a man infected by HIV virus, then jabbed his own finger with the needle (see Cohen, 1994). According to Willner, this public injection was meant to prove to the public that there is no connection between the HIV virus and the AIDS disease.

   Willner supports the views of Peter Duesberg, a Professor of Molecular Biology at the University of California, Berkeley, whose case will be recalled several times throughout this work. See Chapter 2, note 16.

1 INTRODUCTION

1 See, for instance, Ben-David (1971).
2 Shapin (1990: 1001).
3 Raichvarg and Jacques (1991: 39).
4 Raichvarg and Jacques (1991: 39). On the significant metaphor of science as cookery, see further, especially Chapter 3, The cold fusion case, and Chapter 4.
5 For a detailed description of the transition, in the second half of the nineteenth century, from the more restricted model of scientific communication of scientific reviews to the more informative and accessible science magazines, see Knight (1994).
6 Shapin (1984, 1990).

7 The term 'canonical account' was introduced by Shapin; others use expressions with equivalent meaning like 'dominant concern' (Dornan, 1990), 'dominant view' (Hilgartner, 1990), 'popularization model' (Väliverronen, 1993), 'diffusionist model' (Cooter and Pumfrey, 1994; Lewenstein, 1995a).
8 Quoted in Pais (1982: 309).
9 See for instance Ait el Hadji and Belisle (1985).
10 Cooter and Pumfrey (1994: 248).
11 The construction of an 'ideology' of scientific writing is most visible in the United States, where it can be historically situated between the two world wars (Dornan, 1988; Lewenstein, 1992b).
12 Burkett (1965), Krieghbaum (1967), Crowther (1970), Farrands (1993).
13 Dornan (1990).
14 On the recurrent equation 'public understanding of science'='public appreciation of science' see again Lewenstein (1992b). As a clear example of it, Farrands states: 'There is anti-intellectualism in the air and particularly, anti-science. The root cause of this is the popular ignorance of the scientific process itself . . . If the methods and limits of science and scientists were better understood the fears would remain, but they would, one hopes, be more rational.' (Farrands, 1993: 18).
15 See for example the wide range of articles about scientific journalism which appeared on the journal *Journalism Quarterly* from the 1970s through the 1980s, or some of the essays included in the volume edited by Friedman, Dunwoody and Rogers (1986).
16 See again Farrands (1993). Wynne (1993, 1995) shows how 'public ignorance of science' has been constructed by problematizing the public while leaving scientists unproblematic within the dominant frame of Public Understanding of Science studies.
17 Väliverronen (1993).
18 This adherence to an idealized-normative model of communication is confirmed by the fact that studies on scientific communication to the public have focused mainly on journalistic coverage, neglecting other possible sources of media representation of science like fiction (Dornan, 1990; rare notable exceptions are Hirsch, 1962; Basalla, 1976).
19 Leyens (1988).
20 Moscovici (1984: 29).
21 Moscovici (1984: 29).
22 Moscovici (1961, 1984). See also Farr (1993).
23 Apparently of a very similar nature are the 'amplification effects' identified by Kasperson and Stallen in the transmission of risk-related information. As the message passes through different intermediaries, it is combined with other messages, filtered and emphasized (Kasperson and Stallen, 1991).
24 Di Clemente *et al.* (1987).
25 Moscovici (1961: 35).
26 Cooter and Pumfrey (1994: 240).
27 Cooter and Pumfrey (1994: 249–50). See also Wynne (1987, 1992), Gieryn and Figert (1990).
28 I.e. common sense ideas guiding scientific elaboration. See Fleck (1979).
29 'If, for example, we deal with relativity, which is so popular that books about it can be sold like sandwiches in supermarkets, then we should separate from the theory the mathematical demonstrations which only a few can understand and even fewer can reproduce. In their place we find common paradigms and imaginary experiences which take place on trains or make reference to

watches, things anyone thinks to know and to be able to deal with.' (Moscovici and Hewstone, 1989: 523).

30 The same holds for value-laden judgements and moral elements, which are not just added in public presentations but often characterize scientific elaboration as such. See Mulkay (1979), Green (1985).

31 Jacobi (1987: 35).

32 Jacobi (1987: 36).

33 For an overview see again Cooter and Pumfrey (1994).

34 Cooter and Pumfrey (1994: 241).

35 Nor should we underestimate the influence of conceptualizations such as Schutz's, which views the relationships between science and common sense as two separate 'provinces of meaning'. A number of contributions by the post-Mertonian sociology of science have reacted to this idealized contraposition by substantially levelling scientific activity on common sense practices and thereby seeing no point in further addressing the problem of the relationships between specialized and lay knowledge. See Schutz (1956), Eliot (1974).

36 Bourdieu (1976).

37 According to a survey carried out by Jacobi, approximately 80 per cent of French university professors and researchers in the natural sciences have had direct experience as authors of popular science material (Jacobi, 1987). Hansen (1992a,1992b) has similarly shown that many science stories in the media are initiated by scientists' and research institutions' press offices.

38 Jacobi (1985, 1986, 1987), Jacobi and Schiele (1988), Verhaegen (1990), Bucchi (1996c).

39 Cloître and Shinn (1985, 1986), Jacobi (1987), Hilgartner (1990), Lievrouw (1990).

40 Hilgartner (1990).

41 Cloître and Shinn (1985).

42 Taylor (1991).

43 See also Bunders and Whitley (1985).

44 Fleck (1979).

45 Kuhn (1962).

46 On this aspect see also Hansen's survey of science articles in the British daily press (1992a).

47 Gamson (1988), Hilgartner and Bosk (1988), Lievrouw (1990), Hansen (1992b). The importance of 'sponsor activities' by scientists should also not be forgotten (Gamson, 1988; Aronson, 1982).

48 Balmer (1990).

49 Cloître and Shinn (1985: 55).

50 'Public' is clearly a more appropriate adjective for such level. However, as my analysis here develops in relation to the Cloître and Shinn model, I shall retain their term 'popular' (therefore using expressions such as 'public level' or 'popular level' interchangeably), although it could be easily criticized as misleading, in that it can mean not only 'common to all levels of society' (as is the case here) but also 'non-élite'. See Cooter and Pumfrey (1994: 252).

51 Kuhn (1962), Fleck (1979), Biezunski (1985), Clemens (1986, 1992).

52 'Even the simple communication of an item of knowledge can by no means be compared with the translocation of a rigid body in Euclidean space. Communication never occurs without a transformation, and indeed always involves a stylized remodeling, which intracollectively achieves corroboration

and which intercollectively yields fundamental alteration. Those who fail to grasp this point will never reach a positive epistemology' (Fleck, 1979: 111). See also Knorr-Cetina (1981).
53 Fleck (1979), Epstein (1995, 1996).
54 Cloître and Shinn (1986).
55 Phillips (1991). Similar findings also in Dubois (1986). Jacobi (1987) has studied the readership of popular science publications, which is largely made up of researchers and other categories variously involved in science (e.g. university students, high school teachers).
56 The geochemicist Ganapath thus recalls his involvement in the debate on the 'mass extinction' hypothesis, i.e. the hypothesis relating dinosaur extinction to the impact of the earth with asteroids: 'I became interested in this subject after reading in a local newspaper and a popular scientific weekly about the revival of the supernova hypothesis to explain findings by the Alvarez group' (quoted in Clemens, 1986: 428).
57 See Chapter 3, The cold fusion case.
58 See Chapter 3, A public explosion. Quoted from Miller (1994: 449).
59 For an analysis of politics in the media within such a perspective, see Rositi (1982).
60 Cloître and Shinn (1985), Whitley (1985) and Schiele (1985).
61 Latour and Woolgar (1979), Knorr-Cetina (1981), Collins (1985, 1987), Latour (1987). Collins employs attractive formulas to describe such process, such as 'distance leads enchantment' or 'the ship in a bottle' (i.e. the impossibility of recapturing the contextuality of scientific practice once it is fixed and 'packaged'). Collins (1985, 1987).
62 Whitley (1985: 13).
63 Namer (1982).
64 Peters (1994a, 1994b).
65 Curtis (1994).
66 Collins (1988) seems to include (though without using the word 'deviation') deviation cases in his general discussion of cases of 'core-set distortion' (i.e. alterations to the set of persons qualified to actively contribute to scientific debate). He discusses distortion by over-restrictiveness of the core set (i.e. when some researchers are pre-excluded from the debate for different reasons, an example being Lysenkoism in the former USSR) and by over-extension of the core-set (appeal to the laity in favour of one scientific part). It is not clear, though, why Collins labels both kinds of situation as 'pathological science'. Also, appeal to the public may only apparently result in an extension of the discussion frame: it may equally be exploited to exclude some actors from the debate. Duesberg's theories about AIDS become particularly unacceptable and 'crazy' when they reach the public level and their political consequences are drawn.
67 See Lehay and Mazur (1980).
68 Take again the professional image of Peter Duesberg. Regarded as an authoritative scientist (he is a member of the National Academy of the Sciences and a former recipient of the NIH Oustanding Investigator Grant) before he entered the public controversy about AIDS, he is now considered as a pretty much disreputable scientist who simply tries to impress the media. For a short account of Duesberg's story see Chapter 2, note 16. See also Cohen (1994), Fujimura and Chou (1994).
    Polywater is another example of deconstruction in public (Benguigui, 1993). Gieryn and Figert (1990) present a case (Feynman's reconstruction of the

Shuttle accident) of the use of science as an unquestionable authority in support of one's own argument. For the political uses of science see also Ezrahi (1990).
69 Good examples of 'black-boxed' common sense to back up scientific arguments are to be found in many of the public controversies provoked by Darwin's theory of evolution (e.g. Antonelli, 1986).
70 Cooter and Pumfrey (1994: 254).

2 WHEN SCIENTISTS TURN TO THE PUBLIC

1 According to Gieryn, boundary work is a rhetorical style for the pragmatic demarcation of science from non-science, performed locally by actors through 'the attribution of selected characteristics to the institution of science' (Gieryn, 1983: 782) when they 'contend for, legitimate or challenge the cognitive authority of science – and the credibility, prestige, power and material resources that attend such a privileged position' (Gieryn, 1995: 404).
2 Gieryn (1983). Phrenology developed in the late eighteenth century and the early nineteenth century following the work of Franz Joseph Gall. Phrenologists claimed a strong relationship between the form and size of certain areas of the brain and the mental/moral qualities of a man. For a number of years, they enjoyed a respectable 'scientific' reputation and great public popularity. Later, especially in Scotland, a broad debate on the status of phrenology was conducted in public, with anatomists strengthening the definition of science to exclude phrenology as 'non-scientific', e.g. by emphasizing the indifference of science to political and religious aspects that were instead part and parcel of the phrenological approach or by discrediting phrenology for its heavy reliance on popular consensus.
3 Webster (1979). In 1972 James Reston, journalist of the *New York Times*, was struck down by appendicitis during a visit to China. After surgery, complications arose which were only resolved by acupuncture treatment. Back in United States, he told his story in enthusiastic terms. His and other similar cases aroused considerable interest in acupuncture: research funds were provided, articles published in neurophysiology reviews, and a group of American researchers was sent to China. In the end, this threat to the prestige and authority of medical professions was averted by focusing solely on the practical value of acupuncture, thereby precluding its recognition as an alternative to neurophysiology. It was depicted as one of the many therapies available to a physician, of value only within the general frame of medicine. Later, the Federal and Medical State Boards decided that acupuncture could be practised only by physicians or under the supervision of a physician. See also Wolpe (1985).
4 Gieryn (1983). The physicist John Tyndall (1820–93) was appointed Superintendent of the Royal Institution in London after Michael Faraday. He 'used his visible position to promote a variety of ideological arguments to justify scientists' request for greater public support. He faced two impediments: the intellectual authority of Victorian religion and the practical achievements of Victorian engineering and mechanics.' (Gieryn, 1983: 784). Thus on the one hand, he argued that science was more 'practical' than religion while, on the other, he concluded that science was a much more theoretical and noble enterprise than mechanics.
5 La Vergata (1988), Gillispie (1960).

6 Quoted in Bayertz (1985: 216).
7 'In general, today's scientists are scarcely able to feel that their work may have a transcendent significance. This does not mean that they are not completely devoted to science, but rather that they are not capable of justifying it in public terms acceptable to themselves and to the non-scientific audience.' Shils (1976: 10–11). The transition from a more general, 'constitutive' type of demarcation strategy (aimimg at differentiating 'commodities of science from those of other forms of knowledge') to a more specific one ('protecting public investments in science by excluding as non-scientific a potential competitor for those resources') has also been pointed out by Gieryn (1985).
8 This shift of attitude is well exemplified in physics by the following quotation from Tyndall himself:

> I walked down Regent Street some time ago with a man of great gifts and acquirements, discussing with him various theological questions. I could not accept his views of the origin and destiny of the universe, nor was I prepared to enunciate any definite views of my own. He turned to me at length and said, 'You surely must have a theory of the universe'. That I should in one way or another have solved this mystery of mysteries seemed to my friend a matter of course. 'I have not even a theory of magnetism', was my reply. We ought to learn and wait and pause before closing up with the advances of those expounders of the ways of God to men, who offer us intellectual peace at the modest cost of intellectual life.
> 1871: 105

9 Knight (1993). The importance of the public in the institutionalization phase has also been studied in Shapin (1974).
10 Chapman (1994). These 'open doors' initiatives took place in the years 1835 and 1836 especially. Invited journalists included such famous names as Charles Dickens. As soon as recognition came, the Observatory closed its doors to public curiosity.
11 Chaisson (1994).
12 McAllister (1992).
13 During the last decades of the nineteenth century, an alleged 'end of physics' was discussed in textbooks, popular scientific writings and public speeches. Nuclear physics was interpreted as the last stage in the development of the discipline, which now had to compete with chemistry in order to move into new areas of inquiry (e.g. the study of molecules and atoms). Gavroglu (1994).
14 Bunders and Whitley (1985), Clemens (1992).
15 Fleck (1979), Kuhn (1962), Biezunski (1985), Clemens (1986). It is not unlikely that we may find several of these (and other, still unidentified) conditions combined in a single case. When Pons and Fleischmann turned to the public to announce their cold fusion discovery, they were not just reacting to competition by trying to ensure priority over their discovery. In the awareness of the difficulties awaiting them when they would have submitted their results to the scientific community (as outsiders to the field and as diverting from traditional approaches to the problem) they seemingly tried to bring the discussion into a broader context in which their results would appear more attractive (e.g. home-made, creative, cheap science against bureaucratic and expensive science).

16 Lessl (1988). The whole process is evidenced by the cold fusion affair. One of the parties involved managed to recast a conflict between different experimental and theoretical claims as a contrast between disciplinary fields (physics and chemistry), and later as a contrast between orthodox scientists and heretics. See Sullivan (1994). The marginalization of Peter Duesberg in the course of the controversy about HIV is another striking case. One of the world's leading experts on retroviruses, Duesberg is a member of the National Academy of Sciences and a recipient of an Oustanding Investigator Grant from the National Institutes of Health since 1985. He was considered a strong candidate for the Nobel Prize for his work on oncogenes and was generally recognized as a distinguished scientist by most of those involved in leading AIDS research, including Robert Gallo until 1987, the year when he published a paper in the Journal *Cancer Research* questioning the link between HIV and AIDS. He argued that HIV, a retrovirus, is not sufficiently active and infective to be responsible for AIDS. Duesberg has published several other works on this topic, citing epidemiological data to support his critique (e.g. data showing that not only are there HIV positive and AIDS free cases, but also AIDS cases in HIV-negative individuals). He has further argued that, given the non-viral nature of the disease (which to him is largely due to the diffusion of new, still insufficiently studied, drugs), remedies such as AZT do more harm than good to the patient. The interesting aspect in all this story is the vehemence with which orthodox researchers belonging to the HIV-AIDS paradigm and the scientific community in general have reacted to Duesberg's claims. His hypothesis has not so much been criticized or counteracted in scientific forums; rather, he has been publicly marginalized and denigrated as an 'irresponsible scientist', as propagating dangerous views and inducing dangerous behaviour, thus undermining all the efforts made through public campaigns to alert the public about the dangers of AIDS. As Gallo claimed: '[An acceptance of Duesberg's views] may lead to an irresponsible, carefree spread of the virus and progressive decline in the credibility of scientists, physicians and health care workers.'

Over the years, despite his reputation, Duesberg has been increasingly denied access to research funds and opportunities to express his views. In 1990, as a member of the National Academy of Sciences, he submitted a paper to the Academy Proceedings. Usually members of the Academy are entitled to publish their contributions without refereeing, but Duesberg was denied this privilege, something that had happened only once previously, to Linus Pauling in 1972. In 1993, John Maddox, the editor of *Nature*, refused to let Duesberg reply to a paper that had appeared criticizing his views in the journal. He later allowed Duesberg to submit a comment, but warned him that only 500 words would be published, whatever the length. Between 1993 and 1994, six of his applications for research grants – to investigate cancer, not AIDS – presented to the National Institutes of Health were rejected. Other subsequent applications for research on AIDS to the Interuniversity AIDS Research Programme run by the University of California and to the National Institute for Drug Abuse have been turned down, despite favourable comments by referees and letters of recommendation by the editor-in-chief of the journal *Science*, Daniel Koshland (Epstein, 1996; Maddox, 1993; Fujimura and Chou, 1994; Horton, 1996).

17 Collins, for instance, seems to take a surprisingly normative standpoint by describing 'over extensions of the core-set' (which seem akin to deviation processes, see Chapter 1, note 66) as 'pathological science'. Collins (1988).

18 Pinch and Collins (1984). Clearly, the identification of deviation with deviant science fails also to account for those cases in which deviance is not the dominant issue and researchers involved hardly fall within the category of 'marginal scientists', e.g. the Pasteur case, the COBE case or the CERN case, in which deviated communication was far from being sanctioned (the discovery that Rubbia and Van der Meer announced by press conference earned them a Nobel prize).

19 Great controversy ensued when zoologist/psychologist David Crews announced he had observed sexual postures in lizards which usually reproduce by parthenogenesis, a discovery widely publicized by several non-specialized publications including *Time*. For a description of this case see Collins and Pinch (1994).

20 Contributions like that of Lehay and Mazur are relevant here, since they suggest that the very representation of a scientific issue as a controversy in the media may have negative consequences on the credibility of the actors involved. Lehay and Mazur (1980).

21 One detects a trace here of what Cooter and Pumfrey call the 'cultural lag' idea, i.e. the longstanding anthropological temptation to collapse popular lore and ancient lore. Scientific knowledge at the popular level would be nothing but wreckage from former, 'old-fashioned' science. Cooter and Pumfrey (1994).

22 Barrow (1994). See Chapter 3, A public explosion.

23 Resorting to the public as a mechanism to head off controversies is discussed in for instance Martin and Richards (1995).

24 The original formulation of the principle of symmetry as part of the 'strong programme in the sociology of knowledge' is to be found in Bloor (1976).

25 Big bang models are again a beautiful example from this point of view. During the 1950s and the early 1960s, the popular press was a crucial arena for the acceptance and stabilization of such models as the standard explanation of the origin of the universe while they were still debated among the specialists. In the last years, the public level has contributed to shield the authority of Big Bang models from critiques growing at the intraspecialist and interspecialist levels. See later, Chapter 3, A public explosion. I am here indebted to Craig McConnell for important information and interesting discussions on the topic.

26 Cold fusion research has not disappeared right after Pons and Fleischmann's 'excommunication': researchers still work on similar experiments and some results are reported from time to time, although with less emphasis and most often carefully avoiding to mention explicitly the 'dangerous' label of cold fusion. A journal exclusively devoted to cold fusion research is still published in the US. See Chapter 3, The cold fusion case, and Bucchi (1996b).

27 Peters (1994a).

28 Clemens (1986, 1992).

29 This is the term used by Raup (1991).

30 'If that proves indeed to be the case, the tenor of much public argument about the morality of homosexuality would be transformed – or should be. How could Christians, for example, continue to define homosexual behaviour as sinful if it were known to stem from some hard-wired neural structure.' (Maddox, 1991: 13).

31 Peters (1994a).

32 Berridge (1992).

33 Only recently, several years later, have the general media felt it necessary to reopen the problem of AIDS aetiology. In terms of Peters' model, it is interesting to notice how the shifting of the issue from a 'popularization frame' to a 'controversy frame' was achieved by passing through the 'scandal frame' (Peters, 1994a).

34 Martin and Richards (1995).

35 Wynne points out how even actor network theory has from this point of view inclined 'to overstate the correspondence of interests and identities with the dominant networks to which they have been ostensibly enrolled. There is no recognition of the underlying ambivalence that may be harboured beneath the actor's public alignment and – according to the rhetoric – complete identification with the network macro-actor.' (Wynne, 1993: 331).

36 See Lewenstein *et al.* (1991b), Peters (1994a).

37 Lewenstein (1995a).

38 Lewenstein (1995a).

39 See for instance Jacobi (1985, 1987).

40 Schutz (1956).

41 Moscovici (1961: 63).

42 Weinrich (1976).

43 Vosniadou and Ortony (1989).

44 Rossi (1984) underlines the role of analogy in the historical passage from the study of directly observable entities to the study of non-observable entities.

45 Black (1962).

46 Mazzolini (1988) shows that it is not indifferent which of the two terms is employed as a metaphorical source and which is instead the target of the metaphorical description.

47 Boyd (1979).

48 Boyd (1979: 358, italics original).

49 Keller gives other good examples of this kind of metaphor in her analysis of the establishment and transformation of a discourse of 'gene action' in twentieth-century biology. ' . . . The notion of genetical information that Watson and Crick involved was not literal but metaphorical. But it was extremely powerful. Although it permitted no quantitative measure, it authorized the expectation . . . that biological information does not increase in the course of development: it is already fully contained in the genome' (Keller, 1995: 19).

50 Clearly, DNA is not a metaphor. Boyd simply uses it to elucidate the notion of epistemic access. Probably a label like 'gene' would have served as a better example of both metaphor and of differentiated access by different publics.

51 Boyd (1979: 383–4).

52 Boyd (1979: 389).

53 Hesse (1966: 157).

54 Edge (1988: 264).

55 Eco (1980).

56 1 From genus to species (e.g. 'mortals' for 'men'); 2 from species to genus (e.g. 'a thousand' for 'many'); 3 involving three elements (e.g. 'the mountain's tooth', where both the mountain and the teeth share a common quality). See Eco (1980).

57 Holton (1986).

58 Holton (1986: 248).

59 'La vulgarisation en outre peut concrétiser, sous le forme d'images, les analogies et les métaphores qu'aujourd'hui encore la communauté scientifique mobilise à des fins heuristiques.' (Jacobi, 1985: 863).

NOTES

60 On Bohr's model see Petruccioli (1988).
61 Schlanger (1971).
62 The possibility of a reversal process should not be underestimated. Cloître (1986), for instance, documents the appropriation by specialists of a metaphor ('the ant in the labyrinth') originally created to explain the brownian motion of particles in popularization contexts.
63 Holton (1986).
64 Hesse (1966).
65 Weinrich (1976).
66 Weinrich (1976).
67 Hesse (1966: 160).
68 Quoted in Holton (1986: 250). Confirmation of this point is provided by the fact that Holton calls the already mentioned relativistic paradox of the twins a metaphor.
69 See for instance Jacobi (1986).
70 The 'paradox of the twins' was introduced in 1911 by Paul Langevin, a French scientist who played a major role in supporting and disseminating Einstein's ideas. The paradox illustrates the difference that occurs in the time dimension between two systems when one of them is moving at a speed close to that of light, by considering the case of two twins. While one boards a spacecraft moving at almost the speed of light, the other remains on earth. When, after some years, the first returns from his voyage, he will find that his twin is much older than he is.
71 Russell's paradox of classes states that there can be no class (as a whole) of those classes that (as a whole) do not belong to themselves.
72 Yourgrau (quoted in Ferrari, 1977) disagrees on this point, restricting the status of paradox to 'deviations of a formal reasoning that contrasts with formal categories' (and not with common sense, which he holds to be informal) and thereby excluding non-logical paradoxes such as the anomalies in quantum mechanics. A critique of this position is to be found in Ferrari (1977).
73 Encyclopedia of Philosophy (1967). A more general definition of paradox is to be found in Ford and Backoff (1988: 89) as 'some "thing" that is constructed by individuals as soon as opposed tendencies are brought to a recognisable proximity through reflection or interaction'.
74 With regard to the resolution of these and other similar paradoxes, see Sainsbury (1987).
75 The 'barber' version of Russell's paradox is the following: in a small village there is a barber who shaves all the people who do not shave themselves. Can the barber shave himself? If he does, then he belongs to the group of people who shave themselves and therefore cannot be shaved by the barber. If he does not shave himself, however, he is one of those who should be shaved by the barber. See again Sainsbury (1987).
76 Consider the large body of research prompted by the wave–particle duality of light, or the debate about the EPR paradox.
77 As Laudan observes, 'Unsolved problems generally count as genuine problems only when they are no longer unsolved.' (Laudan, 1977: 18). Introducing the twins paradox, Klein (1991: 125) writes, 'Although created in a scientific context, it talks to our imagination ... finally, it has great didactic value as it helps to understand the axioms and the consequences of the astonishing special theory of relativity, that are both far away from the habits of our everyday experience ... paradoxes and pedagogy go always hand in hand.'

78 The so called EPR (Einstein–Podolski–Rosen) paradox was introduced by the three authors to question the completeness of quantum mechanics. A theoretical experiment is presented which makes it possible to know both the impulse and the position of a particle without physically interfering in the system through measurement, a possibility ruled out by the orthodox (Copenhagen) interpretation of quantum mechanics (Einstein–Podolsky–Rosen, 1935, see Klein, 1991).

79 On the different status of certain paradoxical statements for different subjects, see also Sorensen (1988).

80 See Chapter 1.

81 Krippendorff (1984).

82 Rowan (1991). See also Rowan (1988).

83 Ford and Backoff (1988: 92).

84 Star and Griesemer (1989).

85 Star and Griesemer (1989: 393).

86 Jacobi uses the expression 'termes-pivot' for those linguistic elements that are common both to specialist and to popular discourse (Jacobi and Schiele, 1988).

87 Nelkin and Lindee (1995).

88 See Bucchi (1997).

3 CASE STUDIES

1 Kuhn (1962).

2 Shapin (1984).

3 See for instance the books by Close (1991), Huizenga (1992) and Taubes (1993), the aggressive editorials written by *Nature* editor John Maddox or the periodical accounts issued by CERN physicist Douglas R.O. Morrison in his *Cold fusion newsletter* sent via e-mail to scientists and non-scientists throughout 1989.

4 For the moment, it suffices to note that cold fusion cannot be defined as a case of 'fraud in science' (as some would seem to imply by referring to pathological processes) since there was no deliberate falsification (Wible, 1992; see also Kohn, 1986). If, instead, the pathological element is to be located in competition among scientists, the reference is to those works highlighting the importance of competition mechanisms in structuring the scientific arena (Merton, 1957; Price, 1963; Bourdieu, 1976). The charge of plagiarism brought against Pons and Fleischmann is one of the kinds of reaction that Merton regards as typical in cases of competition for priority and multiple discoverers.

5 One of the reporters who dealt most extensively with the issue, Jerry Bishop of the *Wall Street Journal*, received the 1989 annual prize for scientific writing awarded by the American Institute of Physics for the quality and accuracy of his articles on the cold fusion story.

6 See Gieryn (1992), Sullivan (1994). The same term 'cold fusion', the dominant linguistic convention used by both specialists and non-specialists to refer to the phenomenon, did not originate in the official publication by Pons and Fleischmann (titled 'Electrochemically induced nuclear fusion of deuterium'), but has gradually arisen from subsequent public presentations and discussions of experiments (in the Italian press it appeared towards the early days of April: previously the labels used were 'test-tube nuclear fusion' or 'laboratory nuclear fusion').

7 This Archive was established in 1989 by Bruce Lewenstein of Cornell University and Thomas F. Gieryn of Indiana University with the help of other American and international scholars. It gathers a wide range of materials related to Cold Fusion: media clips, e-mail messages, correspondence, paper preprints, faxes, etc. On the organization of the Archive, see Lewenstein (1991).

8 A detailed analysis of this material is to be found in Bucchi (1996b).

9 'There are those who feel compelled, either for money or fame, to ballyhoo discoveries before anyone can reasonably judge their merits. Superconductors, AIDS treatments and new energy sources bring behind them patent lawyers and venture capitalists, to whom breaking the press embargo of an academic journal probably seems a negligible misdemeanor' (Maddox, 1989a: 361–2).

10 *Frigidaire* was a comic-underground Italian magazine, *Seagreen* an environmentalist magazine.

11 Lewenstein, 1992d: 158.

12 Lewenstein, 1992a: 67.

13 With regard to cold fusion, this attitude has been best expressed by the articles published by John Maddox in *Nature*.

14 Shinn and Whitley (1985), Hilgartner (1990), Dornan (1990), Lewenstein (1995a, 1995b).

15 Beside the works already cited, see in particular Collins (1987), Phillips (1991) and obviously Fleck (1979).

16 See Jacobi (1985), Green (1985), Martin and Richards (1995).

17 Lewenstein (1992a).

18 *Cold Fusion*, TV documentary produced and directed for the programme *Horizon* by James Burge. First broadcast on 26 March 1990 by BBC2 at 7.11 pm.

19 'We looked at them [the videotapes of the TV announcement] to find out what the readings on their thermistors were, where the electrodes where, and how they were doing their calorimetry', said Nathan Lewis, professor of Electrochemistry at Caltech. Michael Sailor, a Caltech postdoctoral student, explained 'We used photographs from the *L.A. Times* of Pons holding the cell, and you could see pretty well how it was made' (Lewenstein, 1992a: 143).

20 See note 18.

21 Martin Schloh, in the *Cold Fusion* documentary, see note 18. Again in late April, Ulysses Montgomery, director of the Engineering Research Institute of the University of the District of Columbia, wrote to Harold Farth of the University of Princeton: 'Dear Dr Farth, we recently read about the results you had with the "Tabletop Fusion test" in the 19 April 1989, issue of the *Washington Post*.' Letter dated 24 April 1989, Cornell Cold Fusion Archive.

22 It is not possible here to examine the role played by new communication technologies (fax, e-mail) in the controversy. Such analysis has been partially carried out by Lewenstein (1992c, 1995c). It is of interest, however, to recall two of the main consequences that he attributes to such innovations. The first is information instability, which I have mentioned with regard to the mass media as well. The second is the inequality in the opportunity to access information distributed via such channels, that he attributes to personal ties among colleagues.

23 Particularly significant in this sense is the role of Jones, initially involved in a priority dispute with Pons and Fleischmann (and therefore the advocate of experimental results very similar to theirs) but later presenting himself as a harsh opponent of such results.

24 Lewenstein (1992a)
25 Lewenstein (1992d: 143).
26 Cornell Cold Fusion Archive, document dated 22 May 1989.
27 Note the reference to a court trial. This was to become one of the frames through which the controversy was interpreted.
28 *Panorama* and *L'Espresso* are the most widely circulating weekly magazines in Italy.
29 Belloni (1989: 161).
30 Lewenstein (1992d).
31 *L'Unità*, 26 March 1989.
32 Source: newspaper abstracts on line (from Lewenstein, 1992d: 155).
33 This finding is consistent with other surveys of science articles in the Italian media, see Bianca *et al.* (1986).
34 Jacobi and Schiele (1989). A more articulated presentation of such rhetorical strategies is in Mulkay (1985).
35 Metaphors were employed equally as frequently in articles signed by journalists as in those signed by researchers.
36 A list of metaphors found in cold fusion articles is given in Appendix 3.B.
37 Curtis identifies the 'detective story' as one of the main narrative models of popular science (Curtis, 1994). See later, Chapter 4, note 18.
38 For those not familiar with the vagaries of Italian football: Sacchi and Trapattoni are two coaches who to the public embody two opposed theoretical approaches to football strategy, one typically offensive, the other mainly defensive.
39 Whitley (1984), McAllister (1992).
40 On the general delegitimating effect of public scientific controversies see Lehay and Mazur (1980).
41 Lewenstein (1992d).
42 *La Repubblica*, 24 March 1989.
43 See for instance *Il Corriere della Sera*, 24 March 1989. 'Paranormal science' is also the title of a chapter in Belloni's instant book about cold fusion (1989).
44 Garfinkel (1956: 421–2).
45 Garfinkel (1956: 421).
46 'The preferences must not be for event A over event B, but for event of type A over event of type B.' (Garfinkel, 1956: 422).
47 'Ideally, the witnesses should not be able to contemplate the features of the denounced person without reference to the counterconception, as the profanity of an occurrence or a desire or a character trait, for example, is clarified by the reference it bears to its opposite, the sacred'. (Garfinkel, 1956: 422–3).
48 Merton (1973).
49 Prelli (1989). See also Barnes and Dolby (1970).
50 See also Luhmann (1990: 626).
51 Moshe Gai, physicist at Yale University, from the documentary *Confusion in a jar*, first broadcast on 30 April 1991 on NOVA science series, PBS. Quoted in Sullivan (1994: 299).
52 Draft of a letter to Mary L. Good, chair of the National Science Board, 25 October 1989, Cornell Cold Fusion Archive.
53 Morrison (1989).
54 Jones *et al.* (1989b: 1, my emphasis). This paper was presented by Jones at Erice on 12 April 1989.
55 Jones, letter to Bruce Lewenstein dated 16 January 1992, Cornell Cold Fusion Archive.

56 'Science by press conference' was one of the disparaging expressions most frequently employed to identify this pattern of communication with the public.

57 Taylor (1991: 406).

58 Mallove (1991: 124).

59 Goodstein (1994: 57).

60 La Follette (1990: 2).

61 Chubin and Hackett (1990: 135).

62 'When something is firmly classed as anomalous, the outline of the set in which it is not a member is clarified' (Douglas, 1966: 38).

63 Sullivan (1994). For delegitimation rituals in science see also Gieryn and Figert (1986). On the general characteristics of degradation ceremonies see Garfinkel (1956).

64 The voice-over during the documentary *Confusion in a jar* (first broadcast on 30 April 1991 on NOVA science series, PBS) claimed that this sentence appeared on a bumper sticker. Quoted in Sullivan (1994: 290). Several newspapers referred to Koonin, Lewis and other strong critics of cold fusion as 'the holy Inquisitors'. See *La Repubblica*, 27 April 1989.

65 *Sette* (*Il Corriere della Sera* weekly supplement), 28 September 1995.

66 Douglas (1966: 39).

67 *L'Espresso*, 9 April 1989: 11.

68 John Maddox, from the documentary *Confusion in a jar*, first aired on 30 April 1991 on NOVA science series, PBS. Quoted in Sullivan (1994: 298, my emphasis).

69 Caporetto was one of the most tragic defeats ever suffered by the Italian army. It took place in October 1917, during World War I, and gave rise to a wide debate on who was responsible for the defeat. Many members of the army were charged with cowardice.

70 Mallove (1991: 190).

71 On the importance of caricatures and other forms of humour for the study of science, see Rudwick (1975). Some sixty cartoons about cold fusion are kept in the Cornell Cold Fusion Archive. A general analysis of their features is in Lewenstein *et al.* (1991a).

72 Freud (1960: 248).

73 Freud (1960: 250). Garfinkel points out 'the irony between what the denounced appeared to be and what he is seen now really to be' (Garfinkel, 1956: 422). Deconstruction by means of irony is considered by Woolgar (1983) to be also typical of the standard sociology of science when it claims itself able to unveil the actual practices hidden behind scientists' accounts of their work. Unfortunately, quite a few of the sociological studies deal with humour and in particular, with humour and science. Some exceptions are Mulkay and Gilbert (1982), Mulkay (1988). On humour as a tool in scientific debates, see Rudwick (1975).

74 *La Repubblica*, 4 May 1989.

75 Quoted in Mallove (1991: 245).

76 Lewenstein (1992d: 153).

77 Goffman (1959), Pinch and Collins (1984).

78 Pinch (1992: 504).

79 Goffman (1974: 359–366).

80 As Freud put it with regard to comic comparison, 'when an unfamiliar thing that is hard to take in, a thing that is abstract and in fact sublime in an intellectual sense, is alleged to tally with something familiar and inferior, in

imagining which there is a complete absence of any expenditure on abstraction, then that abstract thing is itself unmasked as something equally inferior. The comic of comparison is thus reduced to a case of degradation' (Freud, 1960: 261).

81 Pinch (1984: 522).
82 See again Rudwick's study of De la Beche's humorous sketches depicted against Lyell (Rudwick, 1975). I have analysed cookery as a commonsensical counterpart of science, and the two-way metaphor of science as cookery in Bucchi (1996d).
83 Sullivan (1994: 301).
84 A. Krumhnsl, letter to Mary L. Good, chair of the National Science Board, 25 October 1989, Cornell Cold Fusion Archive.
85 Eric Bloch, Letter to James A. Krumhnsl, 5 November 1989, Cornell Cold Fusion Archive.
86 Toumey (1996: 128).
87 Pinch (1992).
88 Taped interview, Cornell Cold Fusion Archive.
89 A similar conclusion has been reached by Lewenstein (1992c, 1995c) with regard to the importance of new electronic media for communication among scientists during the affair. Greater dependency on personal contacts and peer networks was to be observed. See note 22.
90 Gieryn and Figert (1986: 69). As a senior researcher from the Lawrence Livermore Laboratory complained during the Los Angeles meeting, 'For science's sake, please: this story harms us all.' (*Il Corriere della Sera*, 11 May 1989).
91 'A polluting person is always in the wrong. He has developed some wrong condition or simply crossed some line which should not have been crossed and this displacement unleashes danger for someone' (Douglas, 1966: 113).
92 Sullivan (1994).
93 *Cold Fusion*, TV documentary produced and directed for the programme *Horizon* by James Burge. First broadcast on 26 March 1990 by BBC2 at 7.11 pm.
94 'Indeed, it was the "circus" aspects of cold fusion that became most prominent in the media frame of meaning for Cold Fusion' (Lewenstein, 1992d: 157).
95 Gieryn and Figert (1990: 73).
96 Cornell Cold Fusion Archive, press release.
97 Moscovici (1961).
98 Mallove (1991: 189)
99 *Fusion Technology, Infinite Energy, Cold Fusion Times* and the newsletter *Fusion Facts*.
100 Lewenstein likewise talks about different 'frames of meaning' that would have been available throughout the controversy, intersecting different audiences at different times. (Lewenstein, 1992d).
101 See the section on the Pasteur case.
102 Toumey (1996: 131).
103 See page 59.
104 Storms (1994: 49), quoted in Toumey (1996: 130).
105 Taku Ishida, Study of the anomalous nuclear effects in solid deuterium systems, University Thesis, February 1992. Cornell Cold Fusion Archive.
106 31 March 1990, quoted in Mallove (1991: 210).
107 The Italian daily press, for instance, showed scant interest: *Il Corriere della Sera* featured only two articles by its science correspondent, one of them devoted to an alleged Italian precursor of the discovery, the Italian astronomer

Francesco Melchiorri, who had seemingly obtained a similar result although with less precision in 1981. See *Il Corriere della Sera*, 25 April 1992.

108 The book was published one year later (Smoot and Davidson, 1993). Two other books were published almost simultaneously on the COBE story: Chown (1993) and Rowan Robinson (1993).

109 Quoted in S. Miller (1994: 449).

110 Hawking wrote an article for the *Daily Mail* of 24 April.

111 However, note that just like Pons and Fleischmann, Smoot and colleagues held a press conference without an official publication of their final results to hand, immediately after a short presentation delivered at the American Astronomical Society meeting in Washington.

112 S. Miller (1994).

113 This short account of cosmological research relevant to the COBE issue is based on a number of works by scientists and historians of science. Among them: Hawking (1988), Boslough (1985, 1992), Barrow (1994), Davies (1995).

114 Eddington (1931) quoted in Bellone (1988: 834).

115 Quoted in Smoot and Davidson (1993: 234).

116 Quoted in Smoot and Davidson (1993: 235).

117 Smoot and Davidson (1993: 242).

118 Boslough (1992: 11).

119 Hawking (1988: 67).

120 Maddox (1989b: 425).

121 S. Miller (1994: 446).

122 Maddox (1995: 99).

123 Quoted in Powell (1995: 19).

124 Ostriker and Steinhardt (1995).

125 See for instance Linde (1995).

126 Barrow (1994)

127 Quoted in Powell (1995: 19).

128 Boslough (1992).

129 Barrow (1994: 42).

130 McConnell (1998).

131 'Hoyle's idea of a static universe never caught on with the public. His name for it, the steady state universe, may have been too mundane. In any event, the 'big bang' stuck, with Hoyle opposing the very notion of it from the day he dreamed it up' (Boslough, 1992: 39).

132 Quoted in Boslough (1992: 55).

133 Pius XII, in Pontificia Academia Scientiarum (1993). Quoted in Lerner (1991: 385).

134 Jaki (1989).

135 Lerner (1991: 54).

136 See for instance Smoot and Davidson (1993: 246–7), where media hostility is clearly part of a discursive strategy designed to present the COBE discovery as a major breakthrough providentially rescuing the reputations of both Big Bang and cosmology reputations at large. In fact, most of their cited examples of criticisms of the Big Bang model (articles, headlines) are drawn from the specialist and interspecialist literature (e.g. *Astronomy, Science*). In terms of Brannigan's (1981) folk theories of discovery, Smoot and his colleagues and supporters constantly sought to balance the discourse of genius (i.e. discovery as an act of individual creativity) with that of cultural maturation (i.e. discovery as a natural product of a cumulative research tradition). See also Chapter 4, p. 128.

137 Criticism, instead, was (and still is at the time of writing) located mainly at the specialist and interspecialist levels (see note 131).

138 *Daily Telegraph* (27 February 1992).

139 Quoted in S. Miller (1994: 446).

140 A number of the metaphors used – by insiders as well – to describe the debate on Big Bang were borrowed from military jargon. Smoot and Davidson described their most distinguished critics (e.g. Jayant Narliker, Geoffrey Burbidge) as 'veteran foes of the Big Bang'. Other comments variously emphasized the conflict between supporters and critics as a fight with no quarter. Swedish physicist Hannes Alfvén used to refer to the Big Bang theorists as 'the Big Bang mafia' (Svante Lindquist, personal communication).

141 See Chapter 1 or the analysis of the Pasteur case.

142 Several letters written to newspapers give examples of this selective appropriation of the COBE results and Big Bang theory within a religious framework. 'The second law of thermodynamics and Big Bang cosmology point more toward a universe that evolved from purpose than to one originated by chance out of chaos without the intervention of some "outside creative force"' (*Daily Telegraph*, 30 March 1992). 'The conclusion that there must be a supernatural lawgiver is confirmed by our improving understanding of the universe' (*Daily Telegraph*, 30 March 1992).

143 Lerner (1991: 54).

144 Hawking (1988: 137). 'Toute hypothese scientifique sur l'origine du monde', explained the pope, 'comme celle d'un atome primitif d'où deriverait l'ensemble de l'univers physique, laisse ouvert le problème concernant le commencement de l'univers. La science ne peut par elle-meme résoudre une telle question: il y faut ce savoir de l'homme qui s'élève au-dessus de la physique et de l'astrophysique et que l'on appelle la métaphysique; il y faut surtout le savoir qui vient de la révélation de Dieu' (Pontificia Academia Scientiarum, 1993: 178).

145 'In fact, we might paraphrase the first three verses of Genesis as follows to make them fit the scientific opinion of the beginning of the universe: "To begin with, fifteen billion years ago, the Universe consisted of a structureless cosmic egg which exploded in a vast outpouring of energy"' (Asimov, 1981: 24).

146 Regge (1981: 71).

147 *New York Times*, 28 February 1989, quoted in Jaki (1989: 82).

148 Boslough (1992: 88).

149 Regge (1981: 75).

150 *Daily Telegraph*, 2 March 1992.

151 See his communication 'Sur le maladies virulentes et en particulier sur la maladie qu'on appelle cholera des poules', given on 9 February 1880 (*Oeuvres Completes*, henceforth OC, VI: 293–4).

152 See OC, VI: 335.

153 Vallery-Radot (1900).

154 Vallery-Radot (1900).

155 OC (VI: 347 ff.)

156 Cadeddu (1991), Geison (1995).

157 In the last ten years, the works by Cadeddu and Geison have shed new light on the procedure used by Pasteur and his assistants to attenuate the virus. While in all his public accounts of the experiment he gave the impression that he had used his old method of attenuation through exposure to

oxygen, it is now clear that a few days before the experiment he decided to use potassium bichromate (Cadeddu, 1987, 1991; Geison, 1995). *The Times* reporter generically describes the method as 'chemical action', which can probably be interpreted in both senses.

158 One notes that an identical detailed list of the witnesses was provided by Pasteur in his official communication on the experiment to the Académie de Sciences (OC, vol. VI: 346–51). As the newspaper article was published almost one month before his official report, one wonders whether Pasteur was to any extent influenced by it.

159 Again, the article reproduces almost word-for-word the communication that Pasteur had sent to the Académie on 28 February.

160 'Discussion sur la vaccination charbonneuse', in Bulletin de l'Académie de médecine, séance du 14 juin 1881; in OC, vol. VI: 355–7. See also Cadeddu (1991: 244–5).

161 This appeal to the old ancestors of immunization seems to be another instance of a multipurpose rhetorical resource. It is in fact employed both to question the originality and priority (and therefore the prestige) of an achievement (as is the case here with Colin's), but also to confirm its value. See Pasteur's 'Sur les maladies virulentes . . .' especially pp. 293–4 (OC, VI), or Bouley's speech to the Académie in which he defended Pasteur's use of the word 'vaccination' (on the basis of which Peter was claiming a prior discovery by Raspail) as 'l'hommage rendu par un homme de génie a un homme de génie, son predecesseur [Jenner]' (*Revue Scientifique*, 7 April 1883: 441).

162 An entire essay would be required for thorough analysis of the religious metaphors employed to describe and comment on Pasteur's discovery. Newspaper articles, reports in the various magazines as well as Pasteur's own writings are filled with 'prophecies', 'conversions' and 'faith'. Biographers mention his first words to the enthusiastic public that welcomed him at the train station on the final day of the experiment: 'Et alors, hommes de peu de foi!' (Nicolle, 1932, quoted in Verona, 1972: 66).

163 See preceding note.

164 Pasteur had thanked Toussaint for providing the infected blood with which he began his experiment on anthrax. However, Pasteur was always very careful to distinguish his method from Toussaint's. This was due partly to their different views on immunization, biological for Pasteur (the living organism as a 'milieu de culture', becomes unsuitable for new germ development after first infection), chemical (at least initially) for Toussaint (anthrax bacilli are killed in the preparation of vaccine) (Cadeddu, 1991; Geison 1995). Geison also relates Pasteur's reticence about the use of chemical attenuation in the Pouilly-le-Fort's trial to the competition between Pasteur and Toussaint. By admitting the use of a chemical method on his part, Pasteur would have implicitly acknowledged Toussaint's priority.

165 Latour (1984).

166 'These theories, conceived in the laboratory, discussed before the Academy of Medicine, and being warmly combatted, required to be tested by practical experiments . . .' (*The Times*, 3 June 1881: 4).

167 Cadeddu (1991).

168 'Pure blood and a healthy life will banish all diseases', was the conclusion of Dr W. B. Richardson at the Brighton Health Congress (quoted in the article 'Vaccination vs. Sanitation', *The Vaccination Inquirer*, April 1882: 108).

169 1876, quoted in Debré (1994: 283).

170 I am using here the term 'immunization' to refer to the experiments and discoveries of Pasteur with regard to vaccination against contagious diseases (such as chicken cholera and anthrax) by inoculation of the same attenuated virus. Although Pasteur himself uses the term 'immunity' among other linguistic labels (such as 'virus-vaccines'), it is important to remember that there was not yet an immunological theory at the time, into which his experiments could have been framed. See Silverstein (1989), Moulin (1991, 1992). Moulin's analysis is significant because it shows how Pasteur managed to make his results understandable by extending the concept of vaccination, originally introduced by Jenner for cowpox alone. It is not clear, however, why she considers 'vaccine' to be metaphor. If it was extended from an individual case to cover an entire family of processes, one should probably more appropriately speak of metonymy.

171 Bercé (1984), Darmon (1986).

172 See his letter to the French Minister of Agriculture on 17 September 1878 (OC VI: 225 ff.).

173 Pasteur only occasionally contributed articles of his own to non-specialist publications; however, he always carefully vetted articles regarding himself (Bensaude-Vincent, 1991).

174 Butcher (1896: 296). The same article also describes the discovery of Tuberculinum by Drysdale as having anticipated 'the remedy discovered by Koch' by ten years.

175 Presidential Address (1904). The affinity between the law of similars and vaccination was not clear only to homeopaths and their adversaries, however. George Bernard Shaw wrote, 'It would be difficult to cite any proposition less obnoxious to science than that advanced by Hahnemann: to wit, that drugs which in large doses produce certain symptoms, counteract them in very small doses, just as in more modern practice it is found that a sufficiently small inoculation with typhoid rallies our powers to resist the disease' (Shaw, 1906: 34).

176 Hermann (1880).

177 Nicholls (1988). On the incorporation of homeopathy into regular medical practice see also Tamaccio (1990) and Fye (1990).

178 See Tamaccio (1990).

179 Westacott (1949), French (1975), Bryant (1977), Stevenson (1977), Ritvo (1987) and the essays in Rupke (1987a). On anti-visectionism in France, see Elliott (1987) and Lalouette (1990).

180 On Darwin's active involvement in the debate and on his efforts to have a Bill passed in Parliament that would not have imposed too many constraints on physiological experimentation, see French (1975).

181 See French (1975).

182 French (1975).

183 The Congress did not allow women to register as delegates in order to forestall anti-vivisectionist proclamations; the movement was in fact driven largely by the enthusiasm of its female activists (Bynum, 1994). On women and anti-visection see also Elston (1987).

184 French (1975: 313).

185 It is probably no coincidence that one of the peaks in the discussion of vivisection in the specialist and popular press was instead reached in 1882, after Pouilly-le-Fort and the Medical Congress (Rupke, 1987b).

186 French (1975).

187 Garth Wilkinson (1886, quoted in Westacott, 1949: 178). See also Ritvo (1987). Anna Kingsford was probably the key accuser of Pasteur. She gave a portrait of the vivisector that seems very much inspired by the French scientist: 'He finds it easier to propagate and multiply the disease than to discover the secret of health. Seeking for the germs of life, he invents only new methods of deaths, and pays with his soul the price of these poor gains' (1882, quoted in Westacott, 1949: 157). It is interesting to note that criticisms of Pasteur for his experiments on animals were soon extended to his other works and discoveries. For instance, Edward Berdoe questioned the value of his work on fermentation, attributing priority to Schwann (Berdoe, 1903).

188 French (1975: 276).

189 Quoted in Westacott (1949: 471).

190 Quoted in Westacott (1949: 474).

191 Quoted in Westacott (1949: 475, italics mine).

192 Dudgeon (1882).

193 Among the pamphlets on behalf of vaccination: McVail (1887, 1919), Sharp (1889), British Medical Association (1902a and b). Among those against: Taylor (1881), Garth Wilkinson (1881), Siljestrom (1883), Tebb (1899), Milnes (1902), Lupton (1914). For the history of the anti-vaccination movement see also Darmon (1986).

194 The weakness of both anti-vivisectionist and anti-vaccination movements in France, compared with those in England, can be at least partially linked to the important differences in relations between science and the public in the two countries during the second half of the nineteenth century as traced by Sheets-Pyenson (1985). Whereas in England a vigorous circle of amateur scientists fostered a high level of public participation in discussion of scientific issues, in France the role of popular audiences was generally restricted to that of 'passive onlookers'. Official reports on the activities of academies such as the Académie de Science and the Académie de Médecine (representing the 'intellectual aristocracy' as stated by Louis Figuier) typically dominated this élitist scenario of popular scientific communication. A clear example of this is given by the impressively detailed accounts of Pouilly-le-Fort in the magazine *La Revue Scientifique*, which reported even the number of drops used by Pasteur (*Revue Scientifique*, 25 June 1881: 801).

195 Among other things, Pasteur was accused of eagerly profiting from the sale of his vaccines and of obtaining research funds only due to his political connections. Several articles from French journals like *La Semaine Française* were quoted, in which veterinarians complained about the difficulty of obtaining the vaccine and about its cost. Great publicity was given to an unsuccessful inoculation with the vaccine in Hungary.

196 Darmon (1986).

197 Dr William J. Collins, MD, B.S., B.Sc., became one of the key actors in the anti-vaccination crusade in 1863, when he declared his opposition after twenty years of service as a public vaccinator.

198 Differences clearly emerged, for instance, between the anti-vivisection and the anti-vaccination movements, the former being a more aristocratic and London-based movement while the latter enjoyed wider support among the working classes and in the provinces (French, 1975).

199 French (1975).

200 Animal experimentation and inoculations 'ruptured the causal connections between sin and disease in ways which many Victorians found profoundly disturbing . . . the new medical science was eliminating both vitalist concepts

from physiology, and links between physical health and moral order that were the foundation of sanitarian beliefs' (Elston, 1987: 274–5). Disease, as French brilliantly resumes, was the 'divinely ordained consequence of sin and folly, and was to be borne as such' (French, 1975: 306). See also Shyrock (1930).

201 French (1975).

202 In a French pamphlet against vaccination, Dr Cartier listed the three main social problems of his time: 'vaccination, vivisection and prostitution' (1880, quoted in Darmon, 1986).

203 Dr Charles Creighton and Prof. Edgar Crookshank (former Prof. of Comparative Pathology at King's College, London) were two among the most notable opposers of vaccination within the circle of official medical science. Creighton was the author of the entry 'vaccination' in the IXth edition of the *Encyclopedia Britannica*, in which he raised doubts on the method that fuelled a reprise of the debate.

204 Swan (1936: 77).

205 Collins (1988).

206 Collins (1985, 1987), Knorr-Cetina (1981), Latour and Woolgar (1979).

207 Bensaude-Vincent (1991) has shown how the attitude towards Pasteur became increasingly positive over the years. Whereas in 1867, at the time of the controversy with Pouchet over spontaneous generation, he still embodied the presumptousness of academia against the genuinneess of common sense, but by 1885 he was generally regarded as the epitome of scientific achievement and national prestige.

208 Latour (1983, 1984).

209 See Bynum (1994). Rupke observes that 'The scientific aspirations of medicine were the leading theme of the International Medical Congress of London' (1987: 7). On that occasion Pasteur introduced the term 'microbiology'. Claire Salomon-Bayet has spoken of a 'pasteurization of medicine' (Salomon-Bayet, 1986).

210 Cunningham and Williams (1992), Valentino (1994).

211 On Pasteur as a representative of this 'scientific mentality' in medicine see also Geison (1990). Vallery-Radot (1931) emphasizes the role of Pasteur in the scientific revolution that was taking place in medicine.

212 I have already tried to avert the simplistic impression that Pasteur mobilized popular ideas and public interests against his 'scientific enemies'. Public and lay knowledge should rather be seen as a reservoir on which different actors could draw. Cobbe's criticism of Pasteur (see above) made obvious appeal to the old fear of 'animalization', i.e. the idea that through inoculation – especially inoculation of animal vaccine – humans would assume animal traits (Bercé, 1984).

213 Collins (1988).

214 This was the case in his campaign against spontaneous generation, which he presented as a 'German theory' (Cadeddu, 1991). He paraded his accomplishments as embodying France's glory and nationalism on innumerable occasions. See for instance his letter to Napoleon III, where he underlines 'la nécessité de maintenir la supériorité scientifique française vis-à-vis des efforts des nations rivales' (OC, VI: 10–11), or his reply to Peter who had mentioned the criticisms of German and Italian scholars against his 'mèdications microbicides': 'Vous me permettez cependant de vous fair remarquer que, pour tenter vainement de combattre la découverte de l'atténuation des virus et des travaux de mon laboratoire, vous avez été cherché des armes étrangères … mon patriotisme à moi, Monsieur, est de telle nature que je

ne me consolerais pas que la grande découverte de l'atténuation de virus-vaccins ne fut pas une decouverte française!' (quoted in Debré, 1994: 437). Other examples in Bensaude-Vincent (1991).

215 On the relation between medical and alternative practices see Brown (1987), Saks (1992), Gevitz (1993).

216 'The movements [against vaccination and vivisection] struggled against professional solidarity, political expediency and bourgeois morality to bring issues of health and medical practice out of the hospital, the clinic – and dark corners of the Victorian psyche – on to public platforms, into editorial columns, where the voice of the community could be heard' (French, 1975).

217 (Shaw, 1906: 58). Pasteur himself resorted to these two different strategies. For instance, when writing to the Director of the *Journal des Brasseurs* to complain about criticism of his experiments that had appeared in the journal, he declared that a baker is not entitled to discuss scientific matters, 'Chacun sera ainsi dans son rôle', (Corr. vol. II: 576). On another occasion, instead, he argued that his germ theory was also corroborated by traditional folk practices: 'Lorsque Jenner démontra l'efficacité de la vaccine, le peuple des campagnes où il exerçait savait que la picote des vaches, ou cow-pox, préservait de la variole' (OC, VI: 293–4).

218 The use of terms like 'success' and 'failure' for a scientific theory has been criticized as misleading, insofar as different levels of communication may have different fortunes for a particular idea (even within the same level it may be difficult to say whether a theory is successful or not – see Chapter 2). Although from a certain point of view this defence and extension of scientific boundaries was generally profitable, in this as in most cases such boundary definition was not achieved once and for all. I have already mentioned the incorporation of homeopathic principles, acknowledged by the same regular practitioners. Concessions had to be made to the anti-vivisectionists as well, especially in terms of legislation. As the number of pamphlets and articles prove, anti-vaccinationism did not vanish after 1881 but continued throughout the following century (see for instance Peebles (1914) with more than 3,000 copies sold, and Swan (1936)). Formal and informal movements against vaccination still occasionally resurface today. 'A scientific community comes into being as a relatively independent entity not simply as a result of its own technical efforts or some self-definition of purpose, but via the continual negotiation of external and internal relations upon which a permanent sense of community remains ultimately dependent' (Bryant, 1977: 82–3).

219 Latour (1984), Callon (1986, 1988), Callon and Law (1982).

220 Pasteur's results were not the final link in this virtually infinite chain of legitimation. It is clear that he and Pouilly-le-Fort do not stand for themselves alone but represent science and its achievements. A clear example of this is provided by those who skilfully connect Pasteur's work with other already well-known scientists such as Darwin. 'Among the great men who have rendered the present century illustrious by the advances they have made in our knowledge of life, none stands out more conspicuously than Charles Darwin ... The one great end and aim of all life is to live, but it by no means follows that it is necessary to let live, for the latter may be quite inconsistent with the former, and the life of one species is often dependent on the death of another. ... So, also, do the low forms of life, of which we speak as germs, destroy man when they have gained entrance into his system, as it is by his loss alone they can live and propagate their kind' (Greenwood, 1886: 12–13).

221 Even the germ, the chief non-human actor in the process of enrolment and translation of interests as described by Latour (1984), was eventually available for use by the opponents of vaccination. In 1890, the magazine *Vanity Fair* published an article signed by 'A bacillus', in which the author explained the benefits of vaccination for germs. 'We find by experience that when we have been introduced in this way there will always be a basis for us sooner or later' (pp.176–7).

222 Wynne (1993).

223 'We are here reminded of the homoeopathic law of cure, that of "like cures like", though what a contrast is presented to Hahnemann's scientific precision in allowing for individual idiosyncracies, for whereas he submitted his drugs to Nature's laboratory, the stomach, according to the Pasteurian system, on the contrary, an introduction is made directly into the blood, regardless of Nature's precaution (..) It has indeed become the fashion for privy humanity to consider itself wiser than – choose the name you will – Nature or Providence' (Hume, 1923: 243).

224 See William Collins' two articles of 1882 in *The Vaccination Inquirer* (April: 5–6; June: 47), in which he explains how 'the second proposition of Pasteur, founded upon the sand of vaccination, is beginning to fall, while the first, established on the rock of sanitation, as yet remains impregnable'.

225 It is interesting to observe how arguments within the public arena showed a great degree of what Wynne calls 'reflexivity', i.e. a problematization of knowledge and of the prior commitments framing it (Wynne, 1993). Those participating in the debate often presented their critiques at a 'sociological' level by discussing the reasons for scientists to support certain beliefs. In his 'Essai historique sur l'origine et la propagation du dogme de la vaccine', for instance, Dudgeon claimed that the spread of vaccination was part of a strategy by political élites to divert attention from republican movements (Dudgeon, 1880, quoted in Darmon, 1986) while Constable (1873) had earlier attributed the spread of vaccination to the strong economic interests of practitioners.

226 As we have seen, the same people were often engaged in different movements and debates at once. Perhaps it should also be emphasized that debates rarely took the form of a clash between science and the public or between science and anti-science, going through the different layers of audiences. Quite a number of medical doctors, for instance, took an active part in the anti-vivisectionist and anti-vaccinationist campaign, trying to preserve 'the humanitarian values of medicine, which were about to be jettisoned in the wake of the experimental approach' (French, 1975). The famous biologist Alfred Russel Wallace expressed on several occasions his aversion to vaccination. On the relation between Wallace's theory of evolution and his anti-vaccination commitment see Scarpelli (1992).

227 'Les épidémies sont les champs de bataille de médecin. Dès que, sur un point du globe, en sévit une, dès que la rumeur des populations effrayées annonce son approche, il doit se preparer à la combattre avec toutes ses armes' (Jal, 1873: 3).

228 'Secondo un geniale concetto di Eugène Melchior de Vogüé in base alla dottrina e al metodo di Pasteur, non-si vincono i pericoli del socialismo se non-inoculando nell'organismo sociale e di stato, che la nuova scuola vorrebbe sconvolgere e distruggere, un germe tolto alla sua stessa dottrina, un virus attenuato e purificato, cioé un elemento, un senso più attivo ed intenso di solidarietà sociale e carità sociale' (1896, quoted in Ullrich, 1979, vol. I: 74).

229 It should be noticed that Pasteur's discoveries could brilliantly integrate with a longstanding tradition in the use of immunization metaphors in political discourse. Napoleon wrote to his brother Giuseppe in 1804, who was worried about the turmoils in Naples: 'A tout peuple conquis, il faut une révolte, et je regarderai une révolte comme un père de famille voit une petite vérole à ses enfants; pourvu qu'elle n' affaiblisse pas le malade, c'est une crise salutaire' (quoted in Bercé, 1984).
230 Pasteur, Corr. III: 266, 7 December 1881; italics original.
231 OC, VI: 347; italics mine.

4 LINES AND TENSIONS

1 Goffman (1959: 106–40).
2 Goffman (1959: 112).
3 Goffman (1959: 111).
4 The analogy between science and cookery is not fortuitous. Just as happens in cookery with a meal, the preparation of a scientific result is usually obscured by its final product and concealed from the eyes of those who will 'consume' it. As the former process is much more familiar to the public, a quite common strategy to denigrate a scientific object or performer is to reveal the similarities between the two, thereby debasing science to cookery. Scientists may be accused of having 'cooked' their results or of having assembled their result from leftovers. See the classic study by Rudwick on the De La Beche-Lyell controversy (Rudwick, 1975). Some examples from the Cold Fusion saga are in Chapter 3. On the double edged metaphor of science as cookery, see Bucchi (1996d).
5 Latour and Woolgar (1979) describe this process as the 'removal of modalities', i.e. of all those 'qualifying phrases or other markers of temporal or local reference (e.g. 'I believe this experiment shows that . . . ')' (Lynch, 1993: 93). See also Latour (1987), Woolgar (1988).
6 Grmek (1976: 41)
7 Mulkay *et al.* (1983), Gilbert and Mulkay (1980, 1984). See also Gilbert (1976), Gusfield (1976), Latour and Woolgar (1979), Bazerman (1988).
8 Gilbert (1976: 285).
9 See Collins (1988).
10 Pinch and Collins have given an example of this by describing the role of the public dimension in deconstructing paranormal claims (1984). See also Pinch (1992).
11 Goffman (1959: 112).
12 Maddox (1988).
13 Pinch and Collins (1984). The Italian committee for the investigation of the paranormal, CICAP (Comitato Italiano per il Controllo delle Affermazioni sul Paranormale) comprises several recognized scientists such as astrophysicist Margherita Hack, and the most popular scientific journalist in Italy, Piero Angela. CICAP (1996).
14 Popular science articles, for instance, are much more frequently accompanied by pictures of the scientists involved in a story than are ones in specialist publications (Jacobi and Schiele, 1989).
15 *Guardian*, 1 May 1992. The Big Bang is often also employed as a metaphor to describe Hawking's life story: 'Prof. Hawking's Big Bang came in 1988' (*Daily Telegraph*, 27 February 1992); 'The Hawking industry is expanding like the inflationary universe whose earliest ripples were captured recently by

the COBE satellite' (*Guardian*, 7 May 1992). The same synoptical process is applied to COBE and Smoot: 'George F. Smoot is the 47-year-old Californian astrophysicist who looked back 15 billion years for the birth of the galaxies and then – on 23 April – found that he himself had become a star' (*Guardian*, 12 May 1992).

16 'This tall American [. . .] beside being one of the greatest astrophysicists he is also modest, charming, funny and very nice. Worse still, he is handsome. It is almost too much to bear' (*The Independent*, 13 May 1992).

17 *La Repubblica*, 1 April 1989.

18 Brannigan (1981) has identified two main 'folk theories' of scientific discovery in scientists' accounts, that of 'cultural maturation' and that of 'genius'. Both are meant to preserve the principles of 'mundaneity' and 'reciprocity of perspectives': i.e. the assumption that reality is objective and is therefore perceived by every actor in exactly the same way. These folk theories justify the discovery process in the face of such principles, by arguing that discovery is either a product of inevitable collective knowledge growth ('cultural maturation') or a product of an 'exceptional individual' ('genius'). The first argument 'anonymizes the question of how a discovery arises. Discovery appears in a Durkheimian fashion, as though it were not particularly the object of human, individual agency' while the second provides the 'special circumstances under which the reciprocity of perspectives can be deemed accountably irrelevant' (Brannigan, 1981: 157; see also Mulkay, 1985). On the more personalized, 'heroic' narrative of science – and in particular of scientific discovery- prevailing at the public level, see Jacobi (1993), Jacobi and Schiele (1989). Consider the following account of the COBE discovery given by Smoot himself to the press: 'It was like waiting for a hostage in the family to be released. I had to train myself not to believe it' (*The Independent*, 13 May 1992). Curtis (1994) finds 'crime novel' storytelling employed in popular scientific magazines, with the scientist portrayed as a detective trying to uncover the puzzling mysteries of nature. See also Chapter 3, The Cold Fusion Case and Silverstone (1985).

19 Woolgar (1988: 61).

20 Curtis mentions the report of an AAAS Committee which 'admitted that debate may regrettably surface from time to time within the scientific community, but advised that it is best kept out of the press, since debate can only "confuse the public"'. Quoted in Curtis (1994: 459 note 143).

21 Goffman (1959: 112).

22 Collins (1988).

23 Goffman refers to similar processes when he deals with 'benign frame breaks clearly engineered in the interests of entertainment', e.g. the little winks and complicities between the performer and the public that ultimately reinforce the credibility of a performance (Goffman, 1974: 439).

24 Goffman (1959: 134 ff.).

25 Goffman (1959: 135).

26 Goffman (1959: 136).

27 See note 18.

28 See how Isaac Asimov recalls his concern that members of his university might come across his early science fiction (Asimov, 1972).

29 Scientists have nevertheless developed sophisticated discursive strategies to curb to some extent these tensions when simultaneously addressing their colleagues and the general public. 'Serendipity' is one such strategy with regard to discovery accounts. The 'genius' and the 'cultural maturation'

repertoires are made compatible by presenting the discovery as both naturally emerging from the development of a knowledge body and engendered
by a special quality of its author. Through hard work and reflection, he has
prepared himself to 'receive' a discovery that however comes unexpectedly
when he is not actively engaged in research. The case studies presented in
this work offer several examples of this accommodating, 'serendipity' repertoire. Consider Pasteur when he accounts for the uncertainty that he faced
in organising his public experiment: 'Le hasard, d'ailleur, favorise les esprits
préparés, et c'est dans ce [sens], je crois, qu'il faut entendre la parole inspirée
du poète: audentes fortuna iuvat' (OC, VI: 347 ff.).

30 A good example of how the 'public' exposure of a given performance can be
reconstructed through different accounts over time is in Wofe (1993). In
1846, in Boston, one of the first operations under anesthesia was performed.
A painting by Robert Hinckley portrays the operation and its witnesses.
However, the picture was painted almost forty years after the operation.
Hinckley mixed the witnesses to that operation with those to others by the
same surgeon because various dignitaries wanted to be visually included among
the witnesses now that the operation was generally recognized as a complete
'success' and a milestone in medical history.

31 Cohen (1994: 1642). With regard to the AIDS controversy, it is worth noting
that a much simpler performance, the kiss given by immunologist Ferdinando
Aiuti (one of the paladins of AIDS orthodoxy in Italy) to an HIV-positive
girl during a public AIDS rally to prove that the virus is not transmitted
through saliva, was widely circulated by daily press pictures and unques-
tioningly given proof-like status.

32 Gieryn and Figert (1990). On 11 February, 1986, the physicist and former
Nobel prize winner Richard Feynman, a member of the Presidential
Commission investigating the Challenger explosion of January of that year,
claimed before journalists that he could show the cause of the accident. He
took a piece of the O-ring seal designed to prevent hot gas escaping from
the joint connecting the individual rocket segments, put the rubber piece
into ice water, then squeezed it with a clamp and showed that the piece failed
to revert to its original shape. The material's poor reaction at low temperature (such as that recorded on the morning of the launch) had caused the
Challenger explosion.

33 Latour (1984), Callon (1986).

34 Majone (1989) makes this argument with regard to policy making: policy
makers may produce decisions in response to certain demands from this audience but this audience might have changed by the time the policy making
process is completed.

35 Gerson (1983).

36 Beside examples from the Big Bang case analysis, see for instance the promo-
tion campaign the recently published book by Robert Osserman, *Poetry of
the universe*, allegedly able to unify 'science and art, whose practitioners speak
different languages but whose lights are eventually inseparable. This book
proves that mathematics is not a cool and dry field of knowledge.' From the
leaflet advertising the science book series *La lente di Galileo*, published in
Italy by Longanesi.

37 Peters (1995).

38 Gerson (1983).

39 Gerson (1983: 367).

40 Epstein (1995, 1996).

173

41 Fleck (1979), Gerson (1983).
42 Holmquest (1990: 238).
43 Star and Griesemer (1989).
44 See for instance Law (1987).
45 Di Trocchio (1993: 56).
46 Randall Collins describes a similar tendency to transform the factional lines of a debate crosscutting groups of experts and lay actors into simple ideological dichotomies (through what he names 'the rhetoric of ideological mobilization'). R. Collins (1993: 308).
47 Interview in Farber (1988: 52).
48 Gallo (1991: 297).
49 Lessl (1988: 31), Douglas (1966).
50 Quoted in Lessl (1988: 28).
51 Quoted in Lessl (1988: 28, my emphasis).
52 Cold fusion was referred to as a 'dirty story'. Polywater was described as 'nothing but dirty water' and those criticizing it as an 'impurity lobby' (Franks, 1981).
53 Schutz (1956), Pollner (1974), Brannigan (1981).
54 Bloor (1983).
55 Cold fusion supporters were often described as joking or playing the game of 'science by press conference'.
56 See the frequent accusations that Pons and Fleischmann were out to made themselves rich, or the definition of Duesberg as insane. 'No scientist working on AIDS, *in possession of his mental powers*, doubts that AIDS has a sole cause, and that's it. I have said that in 1983, and at the beginning of 1984, I have said it in public' (Robert Gallo, interviewed by Anthony Liversidge, in Farber, 1988: 52, my emphasis). On the need to preserve an assumption of 'reciprocity of perspectives' or a 'scientific mundaneity' principle in public, the following quotation is revealing: 'I do not have any intention to reply to him [Duesberg], that's ridiculous! If I see a truck bumping into a man and the man falling down, and somebody asks me "Do you have the proof that it was beacuse of the truck?", well that's a very similar situation. Bullshit!' (Gallo in Farber: 1988: 52). The researcher must be blind or crazy not to agree with his colleagues!

As Pollner explains, 'a disjuncture is compelling grounds for believing that one or another of the conditions otherwise thought to obtain in the anticipation of unanimity, did not. For example, a mundane solution may be generated by reviewing whether or not the other had the capacity for veridical experience. Thus, "hallucination", "paranoia", "bias", "blindness", "deafness", "false consciousness" etc., in so far as they are understood as indicating a faulted or inadequate method of observing the world serve as candidate explanation of disjunctures' (Pollner, 1974: 48). See also this chapter, note 18.
57 Hilgartner (1990). A second paper by Duesberg was rejected by the *Proceedings of the National Academy of the Sciences* on the ground that it contained references to both academic and non-academic journals (those in which Duesberg had published his contributions after being denied publication by many scholarly journals). A Project Inform report later called him 'a propagandist, not a reasoning scientist'. A journalist of the *Los Angeles Times* accused him of formulating hypotheses that appealed to non-scientific audiences: 'Many of Duesberg's arguments have the ring of common sense' (Epstein, 1996).
58 Gerson (1983).
59 Abbott (1995).

60 Gerson (1983).
61 Douglas (1966).
62 Bloor (1983).
63 Douglas (1966: 99).
64 See for instance Latour (1987).
65 Gieryn and Figert (1990).
66 Rip (1986) finds a 'dual repertoire' in statements made by scientists within
    the public arena. As brilliantly summed up by Jerry Ravetz's aphorism ('Science
    takes the credit for penicillin, while society takes the credit for the bomb'),
    scientists at times emphasize their involvement in (and care for) public prob-
    lems, at other times they stress their need for independence and self-regulation.
    The idea that what is chiefly conveyed through public communication of
    science is this 'formal level' of scientific features and relationships (rather than
    true intellectual content) is also found in Wynne (1991).
67 See for instance Gamson and Modigliani (1987).
68 Gastel (1983), Goldstein (1986), N. Miller (1986) are examples of publica-
    tions teaching scientists how to confront 'media aggression'. The *New England
    Journal of Medicine* recommends to researchers: 'If you feel trapped, obfus-
    cate; it will get cut if it's too technical', quoted in Nelkin (1994: 25). The
    European Union, together with several national research institutions, is
    funding EICOS (European Initiative for Communicators of Science), a centre
    seeking to improve journalists' understanding of science through hands-on
    laboratory seminars. In the United States, and more recently, in Europe, a
    Media Resource Service has been created to assist journalists in locating reli-
    able scientific sources for interview. Finally, it has been proposed several times
    to create a Scientific Court where experts should reach a consensus on 'what
    is known' and therefore present it to the media and to public policy.
    Kantrowicz (1967), Rip (1986).
69 Another interesting case in this sense is reported by Dornan (1990). In 1975,
    while the risks of Recombinant DNA research were heavily discussed at the
    public level, a conference was held in Asilomar. Media participation was
    restricted by the scientists restricting the conference to only sixteen invited
    journalists who were permitted to write their articles only after the end of
    the proceedings and allowed to use only still cameras (no television coverage
    was therefore possible).

REFERENCES

Abbott, Andrew (1995) 'Things of boundaries', *Social Research*, 62, 4: 857–82.

Ait El Hadji, Smail and Belisle, Claire (eds) (1985) 'Elements pour une analyse de le répresentations', in S. Ait El Hadji and C. Belisle, *Vulgariser: un defi ou un mythe?*, Paris: Cronique Sociale.

Antonelli, Quinto (1986) *Fede e lavoro*, Trento: Coop. libraria universitaria.

Aronson, Naomi (1982) 'Nutrition as a social problem: a case study of entrepreneurial strategy in science', *Social Problems*, 29, 5: 474–87.

Asimov, Isaac (1972) *The early Asimov*, New York: Ballantine Books.

——, (1981) *In the beginning . . .* , New York: Crown.

Balmer, Brian (1990) 'Scientism, science and scientists', unpublished research paper. Science Policy Research Unit, University of Sussex.

Barnes, Barry and Dolby, R.G.A. (1970) 'The scientific ethos: a deviant viewpoint', *European Journal of Sociology*, 11: 3–25.

Barrow, John (1994) *The origins of the universe*, London: Orion.

Basalla, George (1976) 'Pop science: the depiction of science in popular culture', in Gerald J. Holton and Willam A. Blanpied (eds), *Science and its public: The changing relationship*, Dordrecht: Reidel: 261–78.

Bazerman, Charles (1988) *Shaping written knowledge: The genre and activity of the expository article in science*, Madison: The University of Wisconsin Press.

Bayertz, Kurt (1985) 'Spreading the spirit of science: Social determinants of the popularization of science in nineteenth century Germany', in T. Shinn and R. Whitley, *Expository science*: 209–27, infra.

Bellone, Enrico (1988) 'Le stelle e la loro storia', in Paolo Rossi (ed.), *Storia della scienza moderna e contemporanea*, Torino: UTET.

Belloni, Lanfranco (1989) *La vera storia della fusione fredda*, Milano: Rizzoli.

Ben-David, Joseph (1971) *The scientist's role in society. A comparative study*, Englewood Cliffs: Prentice Hall.

Benguigui, Georges (1993) 'Polywater, sociology of an artifact', *Social Science Information*, 32, 4: 643–67.

Bensaude-Vincent, Bernadette (1991) 'Louis Pasteur face à la presse scientifique', in Michel Morange (ed.), *L'Institut Pasteur. Contributions à son histoire*, Paris: La decouverte.

Bercé, Yves-Marie (1984) *Le chaudron et la lancette*, Paris: Presses de la Renaissance.

Berdoe, Edward (1903) *A chatechism of vivisection*, London: Sommerschein & Co.

Berridge, Virginia (1992) 'Aids, the media and health policy', in Peter Aggleton *et al.* (eds), *AIDS: right, risk and reason*, London: Falmer Press.

Bettetini, Gianfranco and Grasso, Aldo (1988) *Lo specchio sporco della televisione*, Torino: Fondazione Agnelli.

Bianca, Mariano, Rigutti, Mario and Santaniello, Maria Antonia (1986) (eds), *Divulgazione scientifica e didattica delle scienze: Atti del Convegno del Comitato di Coordinamento dell'Associazione Scientifica Italiana*, Firenze: Le Monnier.

Biezunski, Michel (1985) 'Popularization and scientific controversy', in T. Shinn and R. Whitley (eds), *Expository Science*: 183–93, infra.

Black, Max (1962) *Models and metaphors*, Ithaca: Cornell University Press.

Bloor, David (1976) *Knowledge and social imagery*, London: Routledge & Kegan Paul.

——, (1983) *Wittgenstein: A social theory of knowledge*, New York: Columbia University Press.

Boslough, John (1985) *Stephen Hawking's universe*, New York: William Morrow.

——, (1992) *Masters of time*, Reading: W. Patrick.

Bourdieu, Pierre (1976) 'Le champ scientifique', *Actes de la Recherche en Sciences Sociales*, 2, 3: 88–140.

Boyd, Richard (1979) 'Metaphor and theory change: what is Metaphor a metaphor for?', in Andrew Ortony (ed.), *Metaphor and thought*. Cambridge: Cambridge University Press.

Brannigan, Augustine G. (1981) *The social basis of scientific discoveries*, Cambridge, Cambridge University Press.

British Medical Association (1902a) *Vaccination, facts and problems*, London: BMA.

——, (1902b) *Facts about small-pox and vaccination and the lesson of one hundred years of vaccination in Europe*, London: BMA.

Brown, P.S. (1987) 'Social context and medical theory in the demarcation of 19th century boundaries', in William F. Bynum and Roy Porter (eds), *Medical Fringe and Medical Orthodoxy*, London: Croom Helm.

Bryant, Ian (1977) 'Vivisection: a chapter in the sociology of Victorian science', *Ethics in Science and Medicine*, 4: 75–86.

Bucchi, Massimiano (1996a) 'When scientists turn to the public: Alternative routes in science communication', *Public Understanding of Science*, 5: 375–94.

——, (1996b) 'La scienza e i mass media: la "fusione fredda" nei quotidiani italiani', *Nuncius*, 2: 581–611.

——, (1996c) 'Metafore e paradossi nella comunicazione della scienza', *Sociologia e Ricerca Sociale*, 51: 32–45.

——, (1996d) 'Surely you are cooking, Monsieur Latour! Science, cookery, and a double-edged metaphor', paper presented to the University of Padua, seminar on Science and the Media, 16 December.

——, (1997) 'Images of science in the classroom: scientific wallcharts', *British Journal of the History of Science*, special issue on 'The Visual Culture of Art and Science', in press.

Bunders, Joske and Whitley, Richard (1985) 'Popularization within the sciences', in T. Shinn and R. Whitley, *Expository Science*: 61–77, infra.

Bungarten, Theo (ed.) (1986) *Wissenschaftssprache und Gesellschaft*, Hamburg: Akademion.

Burkett, David Warren (1965) *Writing science news for the mass media*, Houston: Gulf.

Butcher, W. Deane (1896) 'The recent discoveries of Koch and Pasteur as illustrating the law of similars', *Annals and Transactions of the British Homeopathic Society*, 12.

Bynum, William F. (1994) *Science and the practice of medicine in the Nineteenth century*, Cambridge: Cambridge University Press.

Cadeddu, Antonio (1987) 'Pasteur et la vaccination contre le charbon: una analyse historique et critique', *History and Philosophy of the Life Sciences*, 9: 255–76.

——, (1991) *Dal mito alla storia: Biologia e medicina in Pasteur*, Milano: Angeli.

Callon, Michel (1986) 'Some elements of a sociology of translation: Domestication of the scallops and the fishermen', in John Law (ed.), *Power, action and belief: A new sociology of knowledge?*, London: Routledge & Kegan Paul.

——, (1988) *La science et ses reseaux*, Paris: La Decouverte.

Callon, Michel and Law, John (1982) 'On interests and their transformations: Enrolment and counterenrolment', *Social Studies of Science*, 12: 615–25.

Casadei, Federica (1991) 'Il lessico nelle strategie di presentazione dell'informazione scientifica', intervento al Colloquio sulle strategie linguistiche dell' informazione scientifica, Roma, 7–8 December.

Chaisson, Eric J. (1994) *The Hubble wars*, New York: Harper.

Chapman, Allan (1994) 'The Observatory observed: Charles Dickens, Greenwich and the astronomical public', paper presented at the Royal Institution Conference on 'Science and its Publics in Britain, 1851–1914', London, 21–23 September.

Chown, Marcus (1993) *Afterglow of creation: From the fireball to the discovery of cosmos*, London: Arrow.

Chubin, Daryl and Hackett, Edward J. (1990) *Peerless science. Peer review and US science policy*, Albany: State University of New York Press.

CICAP (1996) *Non ci casco!*, Roma: Stampa Alternativa.

Clemens, Elisabeth (1986) 'Of asteroids and dinosaurs: The role of the press in shaping the scientific debate', *Social Studies of Science*, 16: 421–56.

——, (1992) 'The impact hypothesis and popular science: conditions and consequences of interdisciplinary debate', in William Glen (ed.), *The mass-extinction debates: How science works in a crisis*, Stanford: Stanford University Press.

Cloître, Michel and Shinn, Terry (1985) 'Expository practice: social, cognitive and epistemological linkages', in T. Shinn and R. Whitley (eds), *Expository science*: 31–60, infra.

——, (1986) 'Enclavement et diffusion du savoir', *Social Science Information*, 25, 1: 161–87.

Close, Frank (1991) *Too hot to handle: The race for cold fusion*, London: Allen.

Cohen, Jon (1994) 'The Duesberg Phenomenon', *Science*, 266: 1642–9.

Collins, Harry M. (1982) 'The replication of experiments in physics', in Barry Barnes and David Edge, *Science in context*, Milton Keynes: The Open University Press.

——, (1985) *Changing order*, Chicago: The University of Chicago Press.

——, (1987) 'Certainty and the public understanding of science: Science on television', *Social Studies of Science*, 17: 689–713.

——, (1988) 'Public experiments and displays of vituosity: the core-set revisited', *Social Studies of Science*, 18: 725–48.

Collins, Harry M. and Pinch, Trevor (1994) *The Golem: What everyone should know about science*, Cambridge: Cambridge University Press.

Collins, Randall (1993) 'Ethical controversies of science and society: a relation between two spheres of social conflict', in Thomas Brante *et al.* (eds) *Controversial science: from content to contention*, Albany: State University of New York Press.

Constable, H. Strickland (1873) *Doctors, vaccination and utilitarianism*, London: Simpkin Marshall & Co.

Cooter, Roger and Pumfrey, Stephen (1994) 'Science in popular culture', *History of Science*, 32, 3: 237–67.

Cozzens, Susan (1990) 'Autonomy and power in science', in Susan Cozzens and Thomas F. Gieryn (eds) *Theories of science in society*, Bloomington: Indiana University Press.

Crowther, James Gerald (1970) *Fifty years with science*, London: Barrie & Jenkins.

Cunningham, Andrew and Williams, Perry (1992) (eds) *The laboratory revolution in medicine*, Cambridge: Cambridge University Press.

Curtis, Ron (1994) 'Narrative form and normative force: Baconian story-telling in Popular Science', *Social Studies of Science*, 24: 419–61.

Darmon, Pierre (1986) *La longue traque de la variole*, Paris: Perrin.

Davies, Paul (1995) *About time*, London: Orion.

Debré, Patrice (1994) *Louis Pasteur*, Paris: Flammarion.

Delisle, Marc Andrè (1977) 'Social functions of popularisation', *Communication et Information*, II: 209–26.

Di Clemente, R.J. *et al.* (1987) 'The association of gender, ethnicity and length of residence in the Bay Area to adolescents' knowledge and attitudes about Aids', *Journal of Applied Social Psychology*, 17, 3.

Dolby, R.G.A. (1982) 'On the autonomy of pure science: The construction and maintenance of barriers between scientific establishments and popular culture', in Norbert Elias, Herminio Martins and Richard Whitley (eds), *Scientific establishments and hierarchies*, Dordrecht: Reidel.

Dornan, Cristopher (1988) 'The problem of science and the media', *Journal of Communication Inquiry*, 12, 2: 53–70.

——, (1990) 'Some problems in conceptualizing the issue of science and the media', *Critical Studies in Mass Communication*, 7: 48–71.

Douglas, Mary (1966) *Purity and danger*, London: Routledge (repr. 1984).

Dubois, Betty Lou (1985) 'Popularisation at the highest level', *International Journal of the Sociology of Language*, 56: 67–84.

——, (1986) 'From New England Journal of Medicine and Journal of the American Medical Association through the Associated Press to a local newspaper: Scientific translations for the laity', in Theo Bungarten (ed.), op. cit.: 243–53.

Dubos, René (1960) *Pasteur and modern science*, New York: Doubleday.

Dudgeon, R.E. (1882) *Hahnemann, the founder of scientific therapeutics*, London: E. Gould.

Durant, John R. *et al.* (1989) 'The public understanding of science', *Nature*, 340, 6628, 6 July: 11–14.

Eco, Umberto (1980) 'Metafora', in *Enciclopedia Einaudi*, Torino: Einaudi: 191–236.

Edge, David (1989) 'Metaphor in science', in William F. Bynum and Roy Porter (eds), *Dictionary of the history of science*, London: Macmillan.

179

Eliot, Henry C. (1974) 'Similarities and differences between science and common sense', in Roy Turner (ed.), *Ethnomethodology*, London: Penguin: 21–6.

Elliott, Paul (1987) 'Vivisection and the emergence of experimental physiology in nineteenth-century France', in Nicolaas Rupke (ed.), *Vivisection in historical perspective*, Beckenham: Croom Helm.

Elston, Mary Ann (1987) 'Women and anti-vivisection in Victorian England, 1870–1900', in Nicolaas Rupke (ed.), op. cit.

Encyclopedia of Philosophy (1967) New York: Macmillan.

Epstein, Steven (1996) *Impure science: AIDS, activism and the politics of knowledge*, Berkeley: University of California Press.

——, (1995) 'The construction of lay expertise: AIDS activism and the forging of credibility in the reform of clinical trials', *Science, Technology and Human Values*, 20, 4: 408–37.

Ezrahi, Yaron (1990) *The descent of Icarus*, Cambridge: Harvard University Press.

Farber, Celia (1988) 'AIDS: words from the front', *Spin* 4, (tr. it. AIDS parole dal fronte, *Rockstar* 7: 51–3).

Farrands, John L. (1993) *Don't panic, panic!*, Melbourne: Text.

Farr, Robert M. (1993) 'Common sense, science and social representations', *Public Understanding of Science*, 2: 189–204.

Ferrari, Gianfranco (1977) *Ricerca scientifica e paradossi*, Trento: Unicoop.

Ferrari, Giuseppe (1987) *Raccontare la scienza*, Parma: Pratiche.

Ford, Jeffrey D. and Backoff, Robert H. (1988) 'Organizational change in and out of dualities and paradox', in Robert E. Quinn and Kim S. Cameron (eds), *Paradox and transformation: Towards a theory of change in organization and management*: Cambridge: Ballinger: 79–96.

Fleck, Ludwik (1979) *Genesis and development of a scientific fact*, Chicago: University of Chicago Press.

Fleischmann, Martin Pons, Stanley and Hawkins, Marvin (1989) 'Electrochemically induced nuclear fusion of deuterium', *Journal of Electroanalytical Chemistry and Interfacial Electrochemistry*, 261: 301–8.

Franks, Felix (1981) *Polywater*, Cambridge: MIT Press.

French, Roger (1975) *Antivisection and medical science in Victorian society*, Princeton: Princeton University Press.

Friedman, Sharon M., Dunwoody, Sharon and Rogers, Carol L. (eds) (1986) *Scientists and journalists. Reporting science as news*, New York: The Free Press.

Freud, Sigmund (1905) *Der Witz und seine Beziehung zum Umbewussten*. Leipzig u. Wien: Deuticke [tr. and ed. by James Strachey, New York and London: Norton & Co.].

Fujimura, Joan H. and Chou, Danny V. (1994) 'Dissent in science: styles of scientific practice and the controversy over the cause of AIDS', *Social Science and Medicine*, 38, 8: 1017–36.

Fye, W. Bruce (1990) 'Vasodilatator therapy for angina pectoris: The intersection of homeopathy and scientific medicine', *Journal of the History of Medicine*, 45: 317–40.

Gallo, Robert (1991) *Virus hunting. Aids, cancer and the human retrovirus: a story of scientific discovery*, New York: Basic Books.

Gamson, William A. (1988) 'The 1987 distinguished lecture: a constructionist approach to mass media and public opinion', *Symbolic Interaction*, 11: 161–74.

Gamson, William A. and Modigliani, Andre (1987) 'The changing culture of affirmative action', *Research in political sociology*, 3: 173–7.

Garfinkel, Howard (1956) 'Conditions of successful degradation ceremonies', *American Journal of Sociology*, 41: 420–4.

——, (1981) 'The work of a discovering science construed with materials from the optically discovered pulsar', *Philosophy of the Social Sciences*, 11: 131–58.

Gastel, Barbara (1983) *Presenting science to the public*, Philadelphia: ISI Press.

Gavroglu, Kostas (1994) 'Physicists and chemists appropriating each other's concepts: A public negotiation at the end of 19th century', paper presented at the Royal Institution Conference on 'Science and its Publics in Britain, 1851–1914', London, 21–23 September.

Geison, Gerald (1990) 'Pasteur, Roux and Rabies: Scientific vs. clinical mentalities', *Journal of the History of Medicine*, 45: 341–65.

——, (1995) *The private science of Louis Pasteur*, Princeton: Princeton University Press.

Gerson, Elihu M. (1983) 'Scientific work and social worlds', *Knowledge*, 4: 357–77.

Gevitz, Norman (1993) 'Unorthodox medical theories', in *Companion Encyclopedia of the History of Medicine*, vol. I. London: Routledge.

Gieryn, Thomas F. (1983) 'Boundary work in professional ideology of scientists', *American Sociological Review*, XLVIII: 781–95.

——, (1992) 'The Ballad of Pons and Fleischmann: Experiment and narrative in the (un)making of cold fusion', in Ernan McMullin (ed.), *The social dimensions of science*, Notre Dame: Notre Dame University Press.

——, (1995) 'Boundaries of science', in Sheila Jasanoff *et al.* (eds), *Handbook of Science and Technology Studies*, Thousand Oaks: Sage.

Gieryn, Thomas F., Bevins, George M. and Zehr, Stephen C. (1985) 'Professionalization of American scientists: Public science in the creation/ evolution trials', *American Sociological Review*, 50: 392–409.

Gieryn, Thomas F. and Figert, Anne (1986) 'Scientists protect their cognitive authority: the status degradation ceremony of Sir Cyril Burt', in Gernot Böhme and Nico Stehr, *The Knowledge Society*, Dordrecht: Reidel.

——, (1990) 'Ingredients for a theory of science in society: O-rings, ice water, c-clamp, Richard Feynman and the press', in Susan E. Cozzens and Thomas F. Gieryn (eds), *Theories of Science in Society*, Bloomington: Indiana University Press.

Gilbert, Nigel G. (1976) 'The transformation of research findings into scientific knowledge', *Social Studies of Science*, 6: 281–306.

Gilbert, Nigel G. and Mulkay, Michael (1984) *Opening Pandora's box: A sociological analysis of scientific discourse*, Cambridge: Cambridge University Press.

Gillispie, Charles C. (1960) *The edge of objectivity. An essay in the history of scientific ideas*, Princeton: Princeton University Press.

Goffman, Erving (1959) *The presentation of self in everyday life*, Garden City: Doubleday.

——, (1974) *Frame analysis*, New York: Harper and Row.

Goldstein, James H. (ed.) (1986) *Reporting science: The case of aggression*, Hillsdale: Erlbaum.

Goodel, Rae (1986) 'How to kill a controversy: the case of recombinant DNA', in Friedman *et al.* (eds), *Scientists and journalists, Reporting science as news*, New York: The Free Press.

——, (1987) 'The role of the mass media in scientific controversies', in H. Tristram Engelhardt Jr and Arthur L. Caplan, *Scientific controversies*, Cambridge: Cambridge University Press.

Goodstein, David L. (1994) 'Pariah Science', *American Scholar*, 63: 527–41, (tr. it. 'Che fine ha fatto la fusione fredda?', *Sapere*, April 1996: 56–64).

Green, Jeremy (1985) 'Media sensationalism and science: The case of the criminal chromosome', in T. Shinn and R. Whitley (eds), *Expository Science*, 139–61, infra.

Greenwood, Major (1886) *A few words on vaccination*, (2nd edn) London: Douglas & Co.

Grmek, Mirko D. (1976) *Psicologia ed epistemologia della ricerca scientifica*, Episteme: Milano.

Gusfield, Joseph R. (1976) 'The literary rhetoric of science: Comedy and pathos in drinking driver research', *American Sociological Review*, 41: 16–34.

——, (1986) 'Science as a form of bureaucratic discourse: rhetoric and style in formal organizations', in Theo Bungarten (ed.), op. cit.

Hansen, Anders (1992a) 'What if there are multiple intentions? Journalistic practices and science coverage in the British press', paper presented in the session 'Communicating scientific knowledge to the public: messages and agendas', The Annual Meeting of the American Association for the Advancement of Science, Chicago, 6–11 February.

——, (1992b) 'Journalistic practices and science reporting in the British press', *Public Understanding of Science*, 3: 111–34.

Hansen, Anders and Dickinson, Roger (1993) 'Science coverage in the British mass media: media output and source input', *Communications*, 17: 365–77.

Hawking, Stephen (1988) *A brief history of time*, New York: Bantam Books.

Hermann, D. (1880) 'Vaccination', *Bibilothèque Homéopathique*, 2: 41.

Hesse, Mary B. (1966) *Models and analogies in science*, Notre Dame: Notre Dame University Press.

Hilgartner, Stephen (1990) 'The dominant view of popularization', *Social Studies of Science*, 20: 519–39.

Hilgartner, Stephen and Bosk, Charles L. (1988) 'The rise and fall of social problems: a public arenas model', *American Journal of Sociology*, 1, 94: 53–78.

Hirsch, Walter (1962) 'The image of the scientist in science-fiction: A content analysis', in Bernard Barber and Walter Hirsch, *The Sociology of Science*, New York: Free Press.

Holmquest, Anne (1990) 'The rhetorical strategy of boundary-work', *Argumentation*, 4: 235–58.

Holton, Gerald (1986) 'Metaphors in science and education', in Holton, *The advancement of science and its burdens*, Cambridge: Cambridge University Press.

Horton, Richard (1996) 'Truth and heresy about AIDS', *The New York Review of Books*, 23 May 1996: 13–24.

Huizenga, John (1992) *Cold Fusion: The scientific fiasco of the century*, Rochester: Rochester University Press.

Hume, Ethel Douglas (1923) *Bechamp or Pasteur? A lost chapter in the history of immunology*, Chicago: Simpson & Co.

Jacobi, Daniel (1985) 'Références iconiques et modéles analogiques dans des discours de vulgarisation scientifique', *Social Science Information*, 24, 4: 847–67.

——, (1986) *Diffusion et vulgarisation: itinéraires du texte scientifique*, Paris: Les Belles Lettres.

——, (1987) *Textes et images de la vulgarisation scientifique*, Berne: Peter Lange.

——, (1993) 'Discours de vulgarisation', in Lucien Sfez (ed.), *Dictionnaire critique de la communication*, Paris: PUF: 1468–74.

Jacobi, Daniel and Schiele, Bernard (eds), (1988) *Vulgariser la science: le procès de l'ignorance*, Paris: Champ Vallon.

——, (1989) 'Scientific imagery and popularized imagery', *Social Studies of Science*, 19: 731–53.

Jaki, Stanley L. (1989) *God and the cosmologists*, Edinburgh: Scottish Academic Press.

Jal, Claude (1873) *Le choléra morbus, traité en Russie par l'homoeopathie*, Paris: P. Barthes et C.te, Libraires.

Jasanoff, Sheila *et al.* (eds) (1995) *Handbook of science and technology studies*, Thousand Oaks: Sage.

Jerome, Fred (1986) 'Media resource services: getting scientists and media together', *Impact*, 144: 373–8.

Jones, Steven E. *et al.* (1989a) 'Observation of cold nuclear fusion in condensed matter', *Nature*, 338: 737–40.

——, (1989b) 'First detection of cold fusion neutrons', paper presented at the Cold Fusion seminar at Erice, 12 April.

Kantrowicz, Arthur (1967) 'Proposal for an institution for scientific judgement', *Science*, 156, 3: 763–4.

Kasperson, Roger and Stallen, Erik (1991) *Communicating risk to the public*, Dordrecht: Kluwer.

Keller, Evelyn Fox (1995) *Refiguring life: Metaphors of twentieth century biology*, New York: Columbia University Press.

Klein, Etienne (1991) *Conversation avec le Sphinx*, Paris: Albin Michel.

Knight, David M. (1993) 'Pictures, diagrams and symbols: visual language in nineteenth century chemistry', in Renato G. Mazzouni (ed.) *Non verbal communication in science prior to 1900*, Firenze: Olschki.

——, (1994) 'A Review of science: William Crookes' Quarterly Journal of Science', paper presented at the Conference 'Science and its Publics in Britain 1851–1914', London.

Knorr-Cetina, Karin (1981) *The manufacture of knowledge*, Oxford: Pergamon.

Kohn, Alexander (1986) *False prophets*, Oxford: Blackwell.

Krieghbaum, Hillier (1967) *Science and the media*, New York: New York University Press.

Krige, John (1993) 'The public image of CERN', in John Durant and Jane Gregory (eds), *Science and culture in Europe*, London: The Science Museum.

Krippendorff, Klaus (1984) 'Paradox and information', in J. Dervin and B. Voigt (eds), *Progress in communication science*, New York: Norwood.

Kuhn, Thomas S. (1962) *The structure of scientific revolutions*, Chicago: Chicago University Press (2nd edn 1969).

——, (1979) 'Metaphor in science', in Andrew Ortony (ed.), *Metaphor and thought*, Cambridge: Cambridge University Press.

La Follette, Marcel C. (1982) 'Science on television', *Daedalus*, 111: 183–97.

——, (1990) *Making science our own: Public images of science*, 1910–1955, Chicago: The University of Chicago Press.

——, (1990) 'Shifting priorities and new communications: faxing about fusion', paper presented at the session on 'The Cold Fusion case: Ethics and the Politics of Science Competition', AAAS annual meeting, New Orleans, 17 February.

Lalouette, Jacqueline (1990) 'Vivisection et antivisection en France au XIXe siécle', *Ethnologie Française*, 2: 156–65.

Latour, Bruno (1983) 'Give me a laboratory and I will raise the world', in Karin Knorr-Cetina and Michael Mulkay (eds), *Science observed*, London: Sage.

——, (1984) *Les Microbes: guerre et paix*, Paris: Metailié.

——, (1986) 'Le théatre de la preuve', in Claire Salomon-Bayet (ed.), *Pasteur et la révolution pastorienne*, Paris: Payot.

——, (1987) *Science in Action*, Cambridge: Harvard University Press.

Latour, Bruno and Woolgar, Steve (1979) *Laboratory Life. The social construction of scientific facts*, Princeton: Princeton University Press.

Larry Laudan (1977) *Progress and its problems: Towards a theory of scientific growth*, London: Routledge.

La Vergata, Antonello (1988) 'Charles Darwin', in Paolo Rossi (ed.), *Storia della Scienza*, Torino: Utet.

Law, John (1987) 'Technology and heterogeneous engineering: The case of Portugese expansion', in Wiebe Bijker, Thomas Hughes and Trevor Pinch (eds) *The social construction of technological systems: New Directions in the sociology and history of technology*. Cambridge: MIT Press.

Lehay, Peter and Mazur, Alan (1980) 'The rise and fall of public opposition in specific social movements', *Social Studies of Science*, 10: 259–84.

Lerner, Eric J. (1991) *The Big Bang never happened*, New York: Simon & Schuster.

Lessl, Thomas M. (1988) 'Heresy, orthodoxy and the politics of science', *Quarterly Journal of Speech*, 74: 18–34.

Lewenstein, Bruce (1991) 'Preserving data about the knowledge creation process: developing an archive on the cold fusion controversy', *Knowledge: Creation, Diffusion, Utilization*, XII, 1: 79–86.

——, (1992a) 'Cold fusion saga: lessons from the science world', *Forum for Applied Research and Public Policy*, 7, 4: 67–77.

——, (1992b) 'The meaning of "public understanding of science" in the United States after World War II', *Public Understanding of Science*, 1: 45–68.

——, (1992c) 'The changing culture of research: processes of knowledge transfer', Report to the U.S. Congress Office of Technology Assessment.

——, (1992d) 'Cold fusion and hot history', *Osiris*, (second series), 7: 135–63.

——, (1995a) 'From fax to facts: Communication in the cold fusion saga', *Social Studies of Science*, 25: 403–36.

——, (1995b) 'Science and the media', in Shiela Jasanoff *et al.* (eds), *Handbook of science and technology studies*, Thousand Oaks: Sage.

——, (1995c) 'Do public electronic bulletin boards help create scientific knowledge? The cold fusion case', *Science, Technology and Human Values*, 20, 2: 123–49.

Lewenstein, Bruce (1991a) 'The funny side of cold fusion', unpublished research paper, Cornell University.

——, (1991b) 'Testing truisms about cold fusion', paper presented to the Association for Education in Journalism and Mass Communication, Boston, 7 August.

Lewenstein, Bruce and Baur, Wolfgang (1991) 'A cold fusion chronology', *Journal of Radioanalytical Chemistry*, 152: 173–98.

Leyens, Jacques Philippe (1988) *Psicologia del senso comune e della personalità*, Milano: Giuffrè.

Lievrouw, Leah L. (1990) 'Communication and the social representation of scientific knowledge', *Critical Studies in Mass Communication*, 7, 1: 1–10.

Luhmann, Niklas (1990) *Die Wissenschaft der Gesellschaft*, Frankfurt: Suhrkamp.

Lupton, Arnold (1914) *Vaccination and the state*, London: National Anti-Vaccination League.

Lynch, Michael (1993) *Scientific practice and ordinary action: Ethnomethodology and social studies of science*, Cambridge: Cambridge University Press.

Maddox, John (1988) 'High dilution experiments: A delusion', *Nature*, 334: 287.

——, (1989a) 'Cold (con)fusion', *Nature*, 338: 361–2.

——, (1989b) 'Down with the Big Bang', *Nature*, 340: 425.

——, (1991) 'Editorial', *Nature*, 353: 13.

——, (1993) 'Has Duesberg a right of reply?', *Nature*, 363: 109.

——, (1995) 'Big Bang not yet dead but in decline', *Nature*, 377: 99.

Majone, Giandomenico (1989) *Evidence and argument in political decision making*, Yale: Yale University Press.

Mallove, Eugene F. (1991) *Fire from ice: Searching for the truth behind the cold fusion furor*, New York: Wiley.

Martin, Brian and Richards, Eveleen (1995) 'Scientific knowledge, controversy, and public decision making', in S. Jasanoff *et al.* (eds), *Handbook of science and technology studies*, Thousand Oaks: Sage.

Mazzolini, Renato G. (1988) *Politisch-Biologische Analogien in Frühwerk Rudolf Virchows*, Marburg: Basilisken.

McAllister, James W. (1992) 'Competition among scientific disciplines in cold fusion research', *Science in Context*, 1, 5: 17–49.

McConnell, Craig (1998) 'The Big Bang – Steady State controversy: cosmology in public and scientific forums', PhD dissertation, Department of History of Science, University of Winsconsin-Madison.

McVail, John C. (1887) *Vaccination vindicated, being an answer to the leading anti-vaccinators*, London: Cassell & Co.

——, (1919) *Half a century of smallpox and vaccination*, Edinburgh: E & S Livingstone.

Merton, Robert K. (1957) 'Priorities in scientific discovery', *American Sociological Review*, 22, 6: 635–59.

——, (1973) *The sociology of science*, Chicago: University of Chicago Press.

Michael, Mike (1992) 'Lay discourses of science: Science-in-general, science-in-particular, and self', *Science Technology and Human Values*, 17, 3: 313–33.

Miller, Neal E. (1986) 'The scientist's responsibility for public information: A guide to effective communication with the media', in S. Friedman *et al.* (eds), op. cit.

Miller, Steven (1994) 'Wrinkles, ripples and fireballs: cosmology on the front page', *Public Understanding of Science*, 3: 445–53.

Milnes, Alfred (1902) *What about vaccination? The vaccination question plainly put and plainly answered, with other contributions*, London: National Antivivisection League.

Morrison, Douglas (1989) *Cold fusion newsletter*, No. 12, 7 May.

Mortureux, Marie François (1985) 'Linguistique et vulgarization scientifique', *Social Science Information*, 24, 4: 825–45.

Moscovici, Serge (1961) *La psychanalyse, son image, son public*, Paris: PUF.

——, (1984) 'The phenomenon of social representations', in Robert M. Farr and Serge Moscovici (eds), *Social representations*, Cambridge: Cambridge University Press.

Moscovici, Serge and Hewstone, Miles (1989) 'Il gioco della scienza e il gioco del senso comune', in Serge Moscovici (ed.), *Psicologia Sociale*, Bologna: Borla: 508–33.

Moulin, Anne Marie (1991) *Le dernier langage de la medicine: de Pasteur au SIDA*, Paris: PUF.

——, (1992) 'La metaphore vaccine', *History and Philosophy of the Life Sciences*, 14: 271–97.

Mulkay, Michael (1974) 'Conceptual displacement and migration in science: A prefatory paper', *Science Studies*, IV: 205–34.

——, (1979) *Science and the sociology of knowledge*, London: Allen & Unwin.

——, (1986) *The word and the world*, London: Allen & Unwin.

——, (1988) *On humour*, Cambridge: Polity Press.

Mulkay, Michael and Gilbert, Nigel (1982) 'Joking apart: Some recommendations concerning the social study of science', *Social Studies of Science*, 12: 585–614.

Namer, Gérard (1982) 'The triple legitimation: A model for the sociology of knowledge', in Nico Stehr and Volker Meja (eds), *Perspectives in the sociology of knowledge*, Dordrecht: Reidel.

Nelkin, Dorothy (1994) 'Promotional metaphors and their popular appeal', *Public Understanding of Science*, 3: 25–31.

Nelkin, Dorothy and Lindee, Susan M. (1995) *The DNA mystique. The gene as a cultural icon*, New York: Freeman.

Nicholls, Phillip A. (1988) *Homoeopathy and the medical profession*, London: Croom Helm.

Ostriker, J.P. and Steinhardt, Paul (1995) 'The observational case for a low-density universe with a non-zero cosmological constant', *Nature*, 377: 600–2.

Pais, Abraham (1982) *Subtle is the Lord . . . : the science and life of Albert Einstein*, New York: Oxford University Press.

Pasteur, Louis (1939) *Oeuvres complètes*, réunies par Louis Pasteur Vallery-Radot, 7 vols, Paris: Masson.

——, (1951) *Corréspondance*, réunie et annotée par Louis Pasteur Vallery-Radot, 4 vols, Paris: Grasset puis Flammarion.

Peebles, James Martin (1913) *Vaccination, a curse and a menace to personal liberty*, Los Angeles: Peebles Pub. Co., 10th edn (first published edn 1905).

Peters, Hans Peter (1994a) 'Wissenschaftliche experten in der oeffentliche kommunikation über Technik, Umwelt und Risiken', *Kölner Zeitschrift für Söziologie und Sozialpsychologie*, Sonderband: Oeffentlichkeit und Soziale Bewegungen, Herbst.

——, (1994b) 'Mass media as an information channel and public arena', *Risk: Health, Safety & Environment*, 5, 241–50.

——, (1995) 'The interaction of journalists and scientific experts: co-operation and conflict between two professional cultures', *Media, Culture and Society*, 17: 31–48.

Petruccioli, Sandro (1988) *Atomi, metafore, paradossi: Niels Bohr e la costruzione della nuova fisica*, Napoli: Theoria.

Phillips, David M. (1991) 'Importance of the lay press in the transmission of medical knowledge to the scientific community', *New England Journal of Medicine*, 11 October: 1180–83.

Pinch, Trevor J. (1992) 'Opening black-boxes: Science, technology and society', *Social Studies of Science*, 22: 487–510.

Pinch, Trevor J. and Collins, Harry M. (1984) 'Private science and public knowledge: The committee for the scientific investigation of the claims of the paranormal', *Social Studies of Science*, 14: 521–46.

Pollner, Melvin (1974) 'Mundane reasoning', *Philosophy of the Social Sciences*, 4: 35–54.

Porter, Dorothy and Roy (1988) 'The politics of prevention: anti-vaccinationism and public health in 19th century England', *Medical History*, 32: 231–52.

Powell, Corey S. (1995) 'Crisis, what crisis?', *Scientific American*, June: 19–22.

Prelli, Lawrence J. (1989) 'The rhetorical construction of scientific ethos', in Herbert Simons (ed.), *Rhetoric in the human sciences*, Beverly Hills: Sage.

Price, Derek De Solla (1963) *Little science, big science*, New York: Columbia University Press.

Van Ormand Quine, Willem (1966) 'The ways of paradox', in *The ways of paradox and other essays*, Cambridge: MIT Press.

Raichvarg, Daniel and Jacques, Jean (1991) *Savants et ignorants. Une histoire de la vulgarisation de sciences*, Seuil: Paris.

Raup, David M. (1991) *Extinction. Bad genes or bad luck?* Chicago: University of Chicago Press.

Regge, Tullio (1981) 'Ultime tendenze in cosmologia', in Paolo Rossi (ed), *La Nuova Ragione. Scienza e cultura nella società contemporanea*, Bologna: Il Mulino.

Richards, Stewart A. (1986) 'Drawing the life-blood of physiology: Vivisection and the physiologists' dilemma, 1870–1900', *Annals of Science*, 43: 27–56.

Rip, Arie (1986) 'Legitimations of science in a changing world', in Theo Bungarten (ed.), op. cit.: 133–48.

Ritvo, Harriet (1987) *The animal estate*, Cambridge: Harvard University Press.

Roberts, Lissa (1991) 'The significance of naming the calorimeter', *Isis*, 3, 92: 199–222.

Rositi, Franco (1982) *I modi dell'argomentazione e l'opinione pubblica*, Roma: ERI.

Rossi, Paolo (1984) 'Le similitudine, le analogie e le articolazioni della natura', *Intersezioni*, IV, 2: 243–70.

——, (1991) 'La scienza e l'oblio', in Rossi, *Il passato, la memoria, l'oblio*. Bologna: Il Mulino.

Rowan, Katherine E. (1988) 'A contemporary theory of explanatory writing', *Written Communication*, 5: 23–56.

——, (1991) 'When simple language fails: presenting difficult science to the public', *Journal of Technical Writing and Communication*, 21: 369–82.

Rowan Robinson, Michael (1993) *Ripples in the cosmos: a view behind the scenes of the new cosmology*, Oxford: W.H. Freeman.

Rudwick, Martin (1975) 'Caricature as a source for the history of science: De la Beche's anti-Lyellan sketches of 1831', *Isis*, 66, 234: 534–60.

Rupke, Nicolaas (ed.) (1987a) *Vivisection in historical perspective*, Beckenham: Croom Helm.

——, (1987b) 'Provivisection in England in the early 1880s: Arguments and motives', in Rupke (ed.), op. cit.

Saks, Mike (1992) 'The paradox of incorporation: acupuncture and the medical profession in modern Britain', in Mike Saks (ed.), *Alternative medicine in Britain*, Oxford: Clarendon Press.

Sainsbury, Richard (1987) *Paradoxes*, Cambridge: Cambridge University Press.

Salomon-Bayet, Claire (1986) 'Penser la révolution pasteurienne', in Claire Salomon-Bayet (ed.), *Pasteur et la révolution pasteurienne*, Paris: Payot.

Scarpelli, Giacomo (1992) ' "Nothing in nature that is not useful", The anti-vaccination crusade and the idea of "harmonia naturae in Alfred Russel Wallace"', Nuncius, VII, 1: 109–30.

Schlanger, Judith E. (1971) *Les metaphores de l'organisme*, Paris: Vrin.

Schiele, Bernard (1985) 'Les enjeux cachés de la vulgarisation', in S. Ait El Hadji and C. Belisle, *Vulgariser: un defi ou un mythe?*, Paris: Cronique Sociale.

Schroeder, Gerald L. (1990) *Genesis and the Big Bang*, New York: Bantam Books.

Schutz, Alfred (1956) *Saggi sociologici*, Torino: UTET.

Shapin, Steven (1974) 'The audience for science in eighteenth century Edinburgh', *History of Science*, 12: 95–121.

——, (1984) 'Pump and circumstances', *Social Studies of Science*, 14: 481–520.

——, (1990) 'Science and the public', in R.C. Olby *et al.*, *Companion to the history of modern science*, London: Routledge.

Sharp, William (1889) *Notes on vaccination*, London: George Bell & Sons.

Shaw, Bernard (1906) *The doctor's dilemma*, Harmondsworth: Penguin (reprinted 1975).

Sheets-Pyenson, Susan (1985) 'Popular science periodicals in Paris and London: The emergence of a low scientific culture, 1820–1875', *Annals of Science*, 42: 549–72.

Shils, Edward (1976) 'Faith, utility and the legitimacy of science', in Holton and Blanpied (eds), *Science and its public: The changing relationship*, Dordrecht: Reidel: 1–16.

Shinn, Terry and Whitley, Richard (eds) (1985) *Expository science: Forms and functions of popularization*, Dordrecht: Reidel.

Shyrock, Richard A. (1930) 'Public relations of the medical profession in Great Britain and in the US: 1600–1870', *Annals of Medical History*, 2: 308–39.

Siljestrom, Per Adam (1883) *A momentous education question*, London: W. Young.

Silverstein, Arthur M. (1989) *A history of immunology*, S.Diego: Academic Press.

Silverstone, Roger (1985) *Framing science: The making of a BBC documentary*, London: British Film Institute.

——, (1992) 'Constructing and reconstructing science in the media', lecture given to the International Symposium for the Public understanding of Science and Technology, Tokyo, 2–5 October.

Smoot, George and Davidson, Keay (1993) *Wrinkles in time*, New York: William Morrow.

Sorensen, Roy (1988) *Blindspots*, Oxford: Clarendon Press.

Star, Susan Leigh and Griesemer, James R. (1989) 'Institutional ecology, "translations" and boundary objects, amateurs and professionals in Berkeley's museum of vertebrate zoology, 1907–1939', *Social Studies of Science*, 19: 387–420.

Starr, Paul (1982) *The social transformation of medicine*, New York, Basic Books.

Stevenson, Lloyd G. (1977) 'Physiology, general education and the antivivisection movement', *Clio Medica*, 12, 1: 17–31.

Sullivan, Dale L. (1994) 'Exclusionary epideictic: NOVA's narrative excommunication of Fleischmann and Pons', *Science, Technology and Human Values*, 3, 19: 283–306.

Swan, Joseph (1936) *The vaccination problem*, London: C.W. Daniel.

Tamaccio, Alice (1990) 'Homeopathy: from Hahnemann to the present', *Medicina nei secoli*, 2: 5–45.

Taubes, Gary (1993) *Bad science: The short life and weird times of Cold Fusion*, New York: Random House.

Taylor, Charles A. (1991) 'Defining the scientific community: a rhetorical perspective on demarcation', *Communication Monographs*, 58: 402–20.

Taylor, Peter Alfred (1881) *Current fallacies about vaccination*, London: E. W. Allen.

Tebb, W. Scott (1899) *A century of vaccination and what it teaches*, London: Swan, 2nd edn.

Toumey, Chris (1996) 'Conjuring science in the case of cold fusion', *Public Understanding of Science*, 5: 121–33.

Tyndall, John (1871) *Fragments*, London: Longmans.

Ullrich, Hartmut (1979) *La classe politica nella crisi di partecipazione dell'Italia Giolittiana*, Roma: Camera dei deputati.

Valentino, Gianfranco (1994) 'Claude Bernard, Louis Pasteur e la nascita della "medicina di laboratorio"', *Intersezioni*, 3, 14: 471–87.

Väliverronen, Esa (1993) 'Science and the media: changing relations', *Science Studies*, 2: 23–34.

Vallery-Radot, René (1900) *La vie de Pasteur*, Paris: Flammarion (30eme edn, 1931, Paris: Hachette).

Verhaegen, Philippe (1990) 'Aspects communicationnels de la transmission des connaissances: le cas de la vulgarisation scientifique', *Recherches Sociologiques*, 21, 3: 323–51.

Verona, Onorato (1972) *Opere di Pasteur*, Torino: UTET.

Vosniadou, Stella and Ortony, Andrew (1989) 'Similarity and analogical reasoning: a synthesis', in S. Vosniadou and A. Ortony (eds), *Similarity and analogical reasoning*, Cambridge: Cambridge University Press.

Westacott, E. (1949) *A century of vivisection and antivivisection*, Ashingdon: C.W. Daniel.

Webster, A. J. (1979) 'Scientific controversy and sociocognitive metonymy: The case of acupuncture', in Roy Wallis (ed.), *On the margins of science*, Sociological Review Monograph, 23: 121–37.

Weinrich, Arnald (1976) *Metafora e menzogna: la serenità dell'arte*, Bologna: Il Mulino.

Whitley, Richard (1984) *The social and intellectual organization of the sciences*, Oxford University Press: Oxford.

——, (1985) 'Knowledge producers and knowledge acquirers', in T. Shinn and R. Whitley (eds), *Expository science*: 3–28, op. cit.

Wible, James R. (1992) 'Fraud in science', *Philosophy of the Social Sciences*, 22, 1: 5–27.

Wilkinson, J.J. Garth (1881) *Pasteur and Jenner, an example and a warning*, London: William Young.

Wofe, Richard J. (1993) *Richard C. Hinckley and the recreation of the first operation under ether*, Boston: Medical Library.

Wolpe, Paul Root (1985) 'The maintenance of professional authority: acupuncture and the American physician', *Social Problems*, 32, 5: 409–24.

Woolgar, Steve (1983) 'Irony in the social study of science', in Karin Knorr-Cetina and Michael Mulkay (eds), *Science observed*, London: Sage.

——, (1988) *Science: the very idea*, London: Ellis.

Wynne, Brian (1987) *Risk management and hazardous wastes: Implementation and the dialectics of credibility*, London: Springer.

——, (1991) 'Knowledges in context', *Science, Technology and Human Values*, 16, 1: 106–121.

——, (1992) 'Misunderstood misunderstandings: social identities and public uptake of science', *Public Understanding of Science*, 1: 281–304.

——, (1993) 'Public uptake of science: a case for institutional reflexivity, *Public Understanding of Science*, 2: 321–37.

——, (1995) 'Public understanding of science', in S. Jasanoff *et al.* (eds), *Handbook of science and technology studies*, Thousand Oaks: Sage.

Yoxen, Edward (1985) 'Speaking out about competition: An essay on "The double helix" as popularisation', in T. Shinn and R. Whitley (eds), *Expository science*: 163–81, op. cit.

INDEX

Abbott, A. 137
AIDS (Acquired Immuno-deficiency Syndrome) 18, 20; as boundary object 132; public negotiation of 132–3; social representations of 6
Alfvén, H. 99
Algarotti, F. 2
Alpher, R. 84
Alvarez, L. 11, 19, 20
Amaldi, U. 50
analogies in science communication 22; in the cold fusion case 80–1
Ansley, D. 43
Appleyard, B. 97
Arp, H. 86
Asimov, I. 99
Atiyah, M. 100

Backoff, R. H. 27
backstage 123–30; exposure of in the cold fusion case 64, 66, 129–30; Goffman's definition of 123; institutionalization of 127; scientific laboratory as backstage 126; specialist discussion as backstage 126; tension between backstages and frontstages 128, 129
Balmer, B. 10
Benveniste, G. 125
Berdoe, E. 116
Bertin, A. 39, 61

Big Bang 82–100; as boundary object 31–2, 98–100, 133; and COBE results 82; criticism of 85–7, 91; label coined in the mass media 19, 83; as paradigm 90–1; public appeal of 87; resonance with religious concepts of 87
Bishop, J. 70
Black, M. 22
Bloch, E. 69
Bloor, D. 142, 144
Blowitz, H. de 103
Bockris, J. 41, 64, 68
Bodereiner, J. 68
Bogle, P. 70
Bohr, N. 25
Bondi, H. 84
Boslough, J. 85–6
Bouley, H. 105
boundary objects 30–2, 132–3; metaphors and paradoxes as 30–2; and scientific paradigms 31; and social representations 31, 133
boundary work 15; around a scientific paradigm 17, 131, 138; between science and non-science 17, 130; between scientific disciplines 17, 131; constitutive boundary work 15–17, 137–8; as related to deviation 15, 130–46
Boyd, R. 23–5
Breeders, The 82

Trapattoni, G. 54
Turner, M. 82
Tyndall, J. 15

vaccination 114–22
Virchow, R. 16, 25, 112
Vitale, A. 39, 61
vivisection 110–11; and
  homeopathy 113–14; Pasteur
  accused of 113
Vogüé, E. M. de 121
Vosniadou, S. 22

Wagoner, R. 92
Webster, A. 15

Weinrich, A. 22, 26
Weldon, F. 96
Westwood, B. 94
Whitehouse, D. 82, 90
Whitley, R. 12
Wilkinson, D. 92
Willner, R. 129
Wilson, R. 84, 92
Wolfendale, A. 98
Wolpert, L. 97

Young, T. 25

Zeno 27–8
Zichichi, A. 45, 50